Reconceptualizing
Critical Victimology

Reconceptualizing Critical Victimology

Interventions and Possibilities

Edited by Dale C. Spencer
and Sandra Walklate

LEXINGTON BOOKS
Lanham • Boulder • New York • London

Published by Lexington Books
An imprint of The Rowman & Littlefield Publishing Group, Inc.
4501 Forbes Boulevard, Suite 200, Lanham, Maryland 20706
www.rowman.com

Unit A, Whitacre Mews, 26-34 Stannary Street, London SE11 4AB

British Library Cataloguing in Publication Information Available

Library of Congress Cataloging-in-Publication Data

The hard back edition of this book was previous catalogued by the Library of Congress as follows:

Names: Spencer, Dale C., editor. | Walklate, Sandra, editor.
Title: Reconceptualizing critical victimology : interventions and possibilities / edited by
    Dale Spencer and Sandra Walklate.
Description: Lanham : Lexington Books, [2016] | Includes bibliographical references and index.
Identifiers: LCCN 2016001272 (print) | LCCN 2016013037 (ebook)
ISBN 9781498510264 (cloth : alk. paper)
ISBN 9781498510288 (pbk: alk. paper)
ISBN 9781498510271 (electronic)
Subjects: LCSH: Victims of crimes.
Classification: LCC HV6250.25 .R43 2016 (print) | LCC HV6250.25 (ebook) | DDC 362.88--dc23
    LC record available at http://lccn.loc.gov/2016001272

∞™ The paper used in this publication meets the minimum requirements of American
National Standard for Information Sciences Permanence of Paper for Printed Library
Materials, ANSI/NISO Z39.48-1992.

Printed in the United States of America

To Nils Christie

Contents

Acknowledgments   ix

Introduction: Themes and Issues in Critical Victimology   xi
Dale C. Spencer and Sandra Walklate

1   Sovereign Bodies, Minds, and Victim Culture   1
Ronnie Lippens

2   Still Worlds Apart?: Habitus, Field, and Masculinities in
Victim and Police Interactions   15
Dale C. Spencer and Jillian Patterson

3   Boys to Offenders: Damaging Masculinity and Traumatic
Victimization   33
Rebecca S. Katz and Hannah M. Willis

4   The Parent as Paradoxical Victim: Adolescent to Parent
Violence and Contested Victimization   45
Rachel Condry

5   Victims of Hate: Thinking Beyond the Tick-Box   63
Neil Chakraborti

6   Punishment or Solidarity: Comparing the U.S. and Swedish
Victim Movements   79
Robert Elias and Carina Gallo

7   Restorative Justice as a Boundary Object: Some Critical
Reflections on the Rise and Influence of Restorative Justice
in England and Wales   95
David Miers

8   Victimhood and Transitional Justice   111
Kieran McEvoy and Kirsten McConnachie

9   A Change for the Better or Same Old Story?: Women, the
State, and Miscarriages of Justice   133
Annette Ballinger

10   Hierarchical Victims of Terrorism and War   155
Ross McGarry

11   Bereaved Family Activism in Contexts of Organized Mass
Violence   173
Jon Shute

Conclusion: Critical Victimology beyond Academe: Engaging
    Publics and Policy   191
    Sandra Walklate and Dale C. Spencer

Bibliography   203

Index   233

About the Contributors   241

Acknowledgments

The editors thank Tracy Galloway, Brighid Stone, and Lexington Press for their sustained support for this project. In addition, the editors appreciate the patience of contributors throughout the production of this volume. Lastly, we are grateful to Carmen Warner for her help bringing this collection to fruition.

Introduction

Themes and Issues in Critical Victimology

Dale C. Spencer and Sandra Walklate

When thinking of the place of critical victimology in the twenty-first century, consider the following victimological phenomenon:

- In the past thirty years more than 1,200 Indigenous women in Canada have been murdered or gone missing (Jiwani and Young 2006; Kuokkanen 2008; Nagy 2013). Despite condemnations from the United Nations as a grave human rights violation, the then prime minister of Canada, Stephen Harper, declares in December 2014, that missing and murdered indigenous women is not "really high on our [government's] radar."
- On April 20, 2010, the Deepwater Horizon rig about fifty miles off the coast of Louisiana exploded and caused the death of eleven workers and tremendous ecological and economic devastation (Spencer and Fitzgerald 2013; Ruggiero and South 2010). Despite such destruction, President Obama lifts the moratorium on offshore drilling just over six months after the spill.
- On January 14, 2015, Zackery Davies shouts "White Power" as he attacks twenty-four-year-old Dr. Sarandev Bhambra with a machete and a claw hammer at a Tesco supermarket in Mold, North Wales (Moore 2015). Despite the apparent intent to inspire fear into Dr. Bhambra and other nonwhite minorities, Davies's assault is not tried, nor reported in the media, as an act of terrorism.

What these three seemingly unrelated circumstances and events hold in common is the politics of recognition in relation to victimhood, the role of powerful actors in committing harms through commission or omission of acts, and the role of the media in depicting and drawing attention to (or not) harms committed by corporations, state agencies, and private citizens. What these circumstances, and others like them, reveal is that harm and the granting of victimhood is contingent on how such harms are articulated and under what social, political and legal conditions they are voiced (cf. Mcgarry and Walklate 2015). Drawing on past work in critical victimology and resources drawn from manifold theoretical backgrounds, *Reconceptualizing Critical Victimology: Interventions and Possibilities* serves as a crucible to demonstrate the complexities of and the multitude of factors that interact to complicate victim status, the vagaries of victim response, and the phenomenology of violence and victimization.

In the early 1990s two texts were published—*Towards a Critical Victimology* (Fattah 1992) and *Critical Victimology* (Mawby and Walklate 1994)—that concretized critical victimology as a paradigm within victimology. Since then, the field has remained conceptually stale and with a few exceptions there has not been a considerable body of works from a critical perspective. Now, more than twenty years later, *Reconceptualizing Critical Victimology* provides a rejoinder to the two aforementioned texts and demonstrates how critical victimology can be reconceptualized, where interventions can be made in this victimological paradigm, and possibilities for future theorizing and research in this provocative field.

STARTING POINTS: VICTIMOLOGY AS A SUB DISCIPLINE

Before delving into the substance of critical victimology, in this section we offer an overview of how victimology came to be a sub discipline of criminology. We offer an overview of the genesis of the focus on victims in the postwar period and the development of victimology as a *positivistic* study of victims and victimization. We then engage with an overview of critical victimology.

Since at least the 1960s, the field of victimology has developed into a variegated discipline with its own theoretical and methodological traditions (O'Connell 2008; Rock 2007). Victimology emerged in the post–World War II era as a response to the atrocities of the Holocaust and as a corrective to criminology. In relation to the former, in the wake of the mass extermination of Jews, homosexuals, disabled persons, and other groups, there became a need among Western states and survivors to make sense of why the Nazis chose the groups they did and to question the genesis of genocide more generally. This questioning began from the standpoint of trying to understand what is it, particularly, about a given victim that makes them more prone to victimization and how such groups or persons contribute to their victimization.

Hans Von Hentig, curiously a *German* criminologist, is considered one of the founding "fathers" of the sub discipline of victimology. He pointed to the fact that the majority of conventional criminal acts involve an offender and a victim that equally animate criminal behavior (Von Hentig 2009). This is a "doer-sufferer" relationship that is fundamentally a close relationship between the criminal and their victim. He argued that victims provide some of the necessary stimuli to the criminal event. This sentiment regarding the criminal and their victim is replicated in the work of Benjamin Mendelsohn (1963), who held that, as members of a "penal couple," victims bore some responsibility for the crime. The focus on the role of victims in precipitating their victimization is and remains a dominant heuristic within positivist victimology.

Concomitantly, as a corrective to criminology, victimology challenged its offender-centrism. That is, victimology confronted criminology's lack of engagement with the victim, who is an integral part of the criminal event. Paul Rock (1994, 11) suggests that this is due to the fact that "criminology is an empirically-driven discipline, it has tended to ignore those things that do not bear the name of crime, criminals, and criminal justice." The greater focus on victims was engendered by the introduction of victim surveys. The introduction of surveys illuminated that far more people were victims of crime than had been revealed in crime rates and, inter alia, people are reluctant to initiate the criminal justice process (Walklate 2007).

Emerging in the wake of work by Hans Von Hentig and Benjamin Mendelsohn and drawing on victim surveys as its primary heuristic, the positivist approach has solidified itself as the dominant "scientific" paradigm in victimology. Positivist criminology tries to account for the causal conditions for criminal behavior. As a paradigm, it is predicated on the assumption that the presence of these conditions makes an offender at variance with law-abiding members of society. A similar approach has been applied in positivist approaches to victimology (Wolhuter, Olley, and Denham 2008). Positivist victimology, then, is focused on the measurement of the amount of victimization, the development of typologies of victimization, explanations of why some people are more prone to victimization than others, and the relationship between criminal and victim, which may indicate the ways in which victims may precipitate crime. This is referred to as victim precipitation and is based upon the notion that the victim contributed to their victimization in some capacity.

ON CRITICAL VICTIMOLOGY

Critical victimology serves as a radical corrective to many of the tendencies of positivist victimological theory, inquiry, and practice. It also builds on and, in some cases, sidesteps some of the tendencies of Marxist criminology and feminist victimology. In relation to the former, while critical victimology pays attention to the role of capitalism in producing human suffering, the responsibility for all the world's ills is not put at the feet of capitalism. Similarly, critical victimology pays attention to the disproportionate representation of women as vulnerable to victimization, but it does not reduce oppression to patriarchy and recognizes the resilience of survivors (Walklate 2011). Here we consider three primary ways that critical victimology challenges conventional, positivist victimology: contestation over the ontological and epistemological basis of victimization; state and corporate victimization, especially in relation to green crimes; and victim blaming, particularly as it pertains to female victims.

Ontological and Epistemological Starting Points

Before the advent of critical victimology, Richard Quinney (1972) asked "Who is the victim?" He argued that the "victim" is a social construction. He contended that we are guided by doxa when perceiving the world and this, in turn, defines who is or who is not a victim in any given circumstance. This opens the question of the victim up to a consideration of how we "see" and narrate who is a victim in society (Walklate 2012a). In addition, this opens the line of thought that victimization is not an "objective" reality, but is integrally a personal, embodied, and relative experience.

This sensitivity to the broader cultural politics of the victim experience and the affixing of the label to some traumatized bodies and not others serves as a guiding pillar of critical victimology (Spencer 2014; Spencer 2015; Mcgarry and Walklate 2015). Due to the nature of the victim label and the overarching politics of victimization, critical victimology is particularly inimical to positivist victimology's quixotic quest for standardized measures in victimization through reliance on legally defined offenses. This is predicated on the notion that the experience of victimization almost never matches with the legal definition of victimization (Spencer 2011a). An additional problem lies in the fact that is not clear what is trying to be measured in victim surveys. Ezzat Fattah (2010, 51; see also E. A. Fattah 1997) has gone so far as to question the point of victim surveys: "Is their objective to measure those criminal victimizations that meet the legal criteria set by the criminal code, or are they meant to measure the subjective victimizations experienced by the respondents? These, needless to say, are two different realities. In other words, are the surveys designed to measure crime or victimization?"

The rejection of positivist victimology leads to an epistemological focus on the experiences and meanings related to victimization. This involves utilization of qualitative and feminist methodologies that serve to document, inter alia, the experiences of interpersonal violence and rape, which are so often not reported to the police or uncovered in crime surveys. This epistemological foundation leads to a privileging of the voices of victims/survivors and an interrogation of the cultural politics of victim status that haunts so many of those whose voices are heard and those whose are not (Mcgarry and Walklate 2015).

The State-Corporate Nexus and Victimization

With modernity criminal justice repositioned the state as the victim of crime. That is, since the modernization of police agencies and the courts and the displacing of the king (and sovereign power) as the prime arbiter of justice, the state has stood in as victim of crime. The victim is no longer a flesh-and-blood human or animal that was once foundational to criminal justice (Spencer and Fitzgerald 2015; Beirne 2011; Derrida 2009), but rather is a state, a nebulous thing that exacts justice on those who transgress laws. While this conception of state as victim has been somewhat troubled and victims are no longer the "forgotten actors" (Zedner 2002) of the criminal justice system, the state as harmful "agent" in its own right remains, in both populist and legal understandings, an underrecognized phenomenon.

In a notable and path-breaking way, in Rob Mawby and Sandra Walklate's (1994) early iteration of critical victimology, they foregrounded the role of the state in contributing to the victims who are seen and heard alongside those victims who are not. It demanded an understanding of the state's responses to victimhood by situating those responses within their socioeconomic and comparative context. In addition they were keen to argue that the concept of victim itself was neither simple nor straightforward and not necessarily given by criminal law. They also challenged traditional approaches to justice for victims, and for more of an appreciation of the victim in the criminal justice system, a focus that remains with critical victimology today.

Since that time there has been some development in appreciating some issues regarding the state's role in defining victimhood, and this is especially reflected in the work of Elias (1985) in relation to the politicization of the victim, Rock (2002) in terms of understanding the nature of "victim identity," and Furedi (2004) in placing a culture of victimhood squarely on the academic agenda. Moreover, research in this area has demonstrated the role of states and state leaders in manufacturing racialized and gendered "enemies" (e.g., Jamieson and McEvoy 2005; Bartov 1998; Pion-Berlin and Lopez 1991). For example, Neil Chakraborti and Irene Zempi (2012) show how state actors and policies produce an "us" versus "them" dichotomy that constructs veiled Muslim women as "other" and creates fear, hostility, and suspicion that makes these women subject to Islamophobic victimization.

Moreover, the interest in the role of the state in defining victimization has also had implications for how critical victimology examines state forms of victimization. For example, John Hagan and Wenona Rymond-Richmond's (2008) work on Darfur has shown how the Sudanese government enlisted Arab Janjaweed militias to destroy black African communities. They demonstrate that the United States, having knowledge of what was transpiring, chose to not intervene in the ongoing genocide. Moreover, they showcase the voices of survivors of this form of state victimization, a hallmark of the epistemological feature of critical victimology (see also Faust and Kauzlarich 2008). Elsewhere, critical victimological work has documented the role of states on an international level in engaging in ordinary crimes on an individual level (e.g., Rothe and Steinmetz 2013) and those of genocide, war crimes, and crimes against humanity (see Letschert et al. 2011; Kauzlarich, Matthews, and Miller 2001; McEvoy and McConnachie 2012; Rafter and Walklate 2012).

Critical victimology has also analyzed the harmful outcomes of state and corporate partnerships. While positivist victimology seemingly overlooks the crimes of the powerful, namely corporations, in victim surveys, critical victimologists have demonstrated how corporations play a prominent role in committing some of the more egregious forms of economic, social, and ecological harms. In relation to the latter, forms of environmental victimization are far from homogenous (Hall 2013b; Hall 2013a); are disproportionally found in economically poorer areas of the Earth, particularly the global South (Nixon 2011); and, most significantly, are committed by powerful, *transnational* corporations (Spencer and Fitzgerald 2013; White 2011; White 2003; White 2013).

Victim Blaming, the Ideal Victim, and Intersectionality

Critical victimologists have rightly pointed out the widespread and uneven depictions of women as victims (Landau 2006). In one of her initial criticisms of victimology, Stanko (1985) comments that women's experiences of sexual and physical violence take on an illusion of ordinariness. The reputed "father" of victimology, Benjamin Mendelsohn (1963), held that "the" victim, presumed to be a woman, possessed certain essentialized notions regarding the victim's identity. Mendelsohn urged for a position of doubt and certain a priori "facts" regarding "the" victim. According to Mendelsohn, women by their "nature" are less believable and their bodies are more "inexpugnable" to rape because their sexual organs are not external but internal to their bodies and are protected by powerful legs. Victimology, here, began from the standpoint that those women who are victims of rape in many cases are "deserving" victims (see Stanko 1985; Rock 2007; Walklate 2003). This underlying connection or conflation of victim with woman remains implicit in most conventional approaches to victims. In many cases, to be a viable victim is to be female (Newburn and Stanko 1995). With the emphasis on predicting various forms of victimization, especially in the context of neoliberal forms of government (O'Malley 2004a), the effect of such an approach repositions women as risky subjects responsible for their own victimization and mythologizes rape and other forms of violence committed against women.

In contradistinction to the positivist approach, critical victimologists utilize the concepts of the ideal victim and intersectionality to challenge the tendency of victim blaming. In relation to the former, the ideal victim is a person or category of individuals who when they are victimized are most readily attributed the complete and legitimate status of being a victim. In the relation to the latter, intersectional analysis understands that individuals experience the complex interplay of numerous systems of oppression working concurrently in the world (Collins 1998; Crenshaw 1991). Critical victimological scholarship has combined these concepts to understand the intersectional components to how some individuals in society, particularly women and racialized populations, are denied victim status. For example, Jennifer Kilty and Sheryl Fabian (2010) demonstrate how after Reena Virk was murdered by a group of teenagers, her racialized identity was rendered invisible and she was denied victim status in media discourse.

BRIEF OVERVIEW OF THE VOLUME

In *Reconceptualizing Critical Victimology*, our contributors remain committed to the ontological and epistemological standpoints described above and move toward pushing the discipline in recognizing manifold forms of victims and victimization. Contributors interrogate the role of the state in defining victims, victimization, and justice and focus on how states contribute to forms of victimization at various scales and locales. The contributions have been divided into three distinct sections. In the first section, the contributors engage with the production of conceptions of victims, critically deconstruct victimhood, and unsettle the division between victims and offenders. While conventional victimology begins with presuppositions regarding dynamics between victim and offenders, contributors upend these conceptions and demonstrate the complexity of attributions of victim status. In the second section, contributors explore responses to victims and victimization from restorative justice, victim services, and transitional forms of justice. In the third, final section, the contributors interrogate the role of the state in responding to and oppressing victims of such harms as miscarriages of justice toward women, terrorism, and mass killing.

ONE

Sovereign Bodies, Minds, and Victim Culture

Ronnie Lippens

The body is not just a lump of living flesh. It is of course that, but it holds and projects around itself, depending on the cultural context in which it moves and is moved, a variety of different, culturally coded images and metaphors, or "body myths," as Cecil Helman (1991), one of the foremost medical anthropologists, calls them. The body, Helman writes, "exists in the domains of narrative and myth" and is thus "the repository of all sorts of metaphors of the human condition" (1991, 4). Different cultures variously use "body myths" (or body metaphors and body images) to think about and come to grips with the world. But the body is itself of course not immune to the images and the metaphors of the cultural world in which it finds itself. The latter have an impact on the body. The way the body exists in the world, how it behaves, and how it moves (or not, as the case may be) is, at least to some extent, the outcome of a never-ending barrage of cultural myths that impact upon it, whether this outcome is culturally desirable or not. This is an insight that has not been lost on sociologists.

In his long and influential essay on the sociology of the body, Arthur Frank (1991) outlined a typology of four sociological bodies, that is, the disciplined body, the mirroring body, the dominating body, and the communicative body. In particular forms of life or at particular historical junctures, one or more of those types may be predominant. Building on Frank's essay I shall, in this contribution, make an attempt to explore how the impact of the experience of the Second World War was such a historical juncture. It unleashed a pervasive process, first in Western de-

1

mocracies, and later more globally, whereby the hitherto culturally dominant disciplined and disciplining body gradually gave way to the mirroring body and to the dominant and dominated body, and whereby the cultural space for anything like a communicative body to emerge at all has shrunk to what, well into the twenty-first century, seem to have become residual proportions. One of the consequences of these postwar cultural developments that I shall be exploring in subsequent sections was—or so I hope to be able to argue—the emergence of a deeply entrenched, almost ineradicable victim culture.

The postwar developments hinted at above relate to the emergence, already during the war, of an attitude, perhaps only a mood at first, which at its very heart harbored quite radical and, to a significant extent, radically new desires. These desires were rooted in the sheer shock of the war experience itself. This experience engendered a sharp and near total distrust in authoritarianism, in authority as such even, and in the foundational codes on which both rest. In turn this distrust unleashed desires for, or perhaps better, a will to absolute personal sovereignty. There is very little coincidence in the fact that in the immediate aftermath of the war, Nietzsche-inspired philosophers such as Georges Bataille (1954, but published posthumously as late as 2012) began to seriously think through the problem (and highly paradoxical problem at that) of radically absolute personal sovereignty. In this contribution, an attempt will be made to make connections between this notion of radical personal sovereignty on the one hand, and Frank's "sociological body" typology on the other. This connection can and should be made, for the desire for, or will to, absolute personal sovereignty—however paradoxical, imaginary, or illusory this desire or will, of course—is a desire, or a will, that not only flows in or through actual, physical bodies, but is one that also generates and simultaneously depends on cultural images of bodily presence and action.

The starting point will be provided by the work of two postwar radical artists, Jackson Pollock and (another Nietzsche scholar) Mark Rothko. Visual artists such as Pollock and Rothko were indeed very quick to pick up, in those postwar years, the desires that began to flow at the heart of what could be called a newly emerging form of life. Philosophers and writers, or indeed philosopher-writers such as Albert Camus (again a Nietzsche-inspired author) for example, were equally preoccupied with, and gave voice to, those desires. Let us say a few words here on Camus's oeuvre, which in more than one way introduces themes that we shall be exploring in some detail later. Meursault, the protagonist in one of Camus's early novels, *L'Etranger* (The Outsider, or The Stranger), published during the war (in 1942), lives his life in "indifference." He is indifferent to the codes of the world he just observes. Any code that comes his way (for example, the code of courtship or marriage, or the code that says "thou shalt be respectful to the dead, especially if the deceased is your mother," and so on) is met with radical indifference. Meursault neither submits to the code nor resists it. This indifference, however, does not prevent him from interacting with the world (for example, in sexual relationships). If and when this happens, it does so on an almost biological level, if not mechanical, and always, however, with indifference. On the one hand, we have Meursault the indifferent observer and contemplator, and, on the other, Meursault the indifferent organism, pure flesh. Ultimately, though, Camus seems to be suggesting that such radical indifference cannot be maintained for long, and if you try, the codes out there will encroach upon you, and possibly even destroy you (in Meursault's case, they took the form and shape of the guillotine). Some level of engagement with the world and some negotiating of the codes in it, Camus implies, are both necessary and desirable. But such engagement should not include the submission to, or adoption of, codes of dominance, especially not the codes that hide under or behind abstract words and concepts such as "justice" (on this, see Camus's play Les Justes, 1950). Nor can it include submission to, or adoption of, codes that spread like wildfire, like the plague, through whole populations, affecting/infecting one fleshy body after another (here Camus's novel La Peste, 1947, is worth reading). Ever since Le Mythe de Sisyphe, Camus's philosophical essay (also published in 1942), Camus made the point that there is no ultimate redemption or salvation, and that all we could hope for is a never-ending Sisyphus-like politics of careful engagement with and negotiation of the world, in the full awareness that all codes are, ultimately, not just destructive, but also self-destructive (Camus's play Caligula, 1947, actually deals with the ultimate destructiveness of all codes). Let us explore these themes and their relevance for what might be called postwar victim culture in some more detail. For reasons that shall become clear, we will start with the work of artists such as Jackson Pollock (†1956) and Mark Rothko (†1970) who both achieved their signature style in the dying years of the Second World War.

POLLOCK AND ROTHKO

Both Pollock and Rothko changed their painting style as a consequence of the experience of the war (on this, and on the import of both painters' artwork for governance studies, and for an overview of and references to scholarship on those themes, see earlier work in Lippens 2010, 2011a, and 2012). Jackson Pollock's signature artworks, that is, those paintings that are the result of his "drip-painting" technique, are well known. At the time of their appearance, some viewers believed that, in his paintings, Pollock attempted to express pure chaos. But the painter himself, who was otherwise notoriously inarticulate, particularly when it came to discussing his own work, always maintained quite vehemently (something that has been picked up by many a commentator) that his work was most definitely *not* about chaos, but about *control*. During the act of painting, and in the painted result as such, Pollock wanted to express and, at the same time, achieve a state of absolute control. Absolute control, in Pollock's work, can only be achieved in constant, permanent flight, that is, the flight from all coded structure and indeed the flight from all law. In Pollock's drip technique, attempts are even made to elude the sheer law of physics and gravity (a point made by Cernuschi and Herczynski 2008). He (he or she of course, henceforth he) who allows himself to be captured by law, code, or structure could never be in control.

There is probably little coincidence in the fact that Pollock was quite inarticulate about his art. Language is a structured code and a coded structure par excellence. It is, so to speak, the vehicle of Law itself. Pollock was uncomfortable with words. Constantly frustrated by them and by their lack of capacity to come to grips with the world, he made constant attempts in his paintings and during painting to dive into a codeless and structure-less primordial zone, a zone before and beyond all law. This is a zone, as Pollock once said, where there can be no accident. There can be no accident in a primordial zone because no codes, no structures, and no laws are present there that could then be "accidentally" broken. In a quite paradoxical way, the primordial zone—a zone where no one and nothing controls, neither by setting a code, nor by smashing it—is a zone of total and utter control. Pollock's dive into the primordial "flesh of the world" (to evoke Merleau-Ponty's [1964] phraseology here), that is, his constant flight from code, structure, and law, is at the same time an attempt to reach a state of total sovereignty. He who is totally, absolutely sovereign, is he who is in total control, and to be in total control, one has to be able to elude law, *all* law.

This attempt to achieve absolute sovereignty is of course a highly paradoxical and annoyingly agonizing one, for indeed, if one is to achieve sovereignty through dissolution into the primordial, one would still need a coded Self to actually decide and make the jump. Once in the primordial zone (if that were at all possible), one would, with the coded structure of the Self, also have lost all capacity for sovereign control. There is a lot of agony in Pollock's drip paintings. With each twist of the arm, the dripping paint escapes from the structures on the canvas, yet, in the process, they produce their own swirls and eddies and those cannot do anything but form the kernel for a new coded structure, which, in turn, will have to be eluded by the next tweak of the arm. The force of Pollock's work resides in the extremism with which it expresses the paradoxical agony in the desire for absolute sovereignty. On the flight from code and law, and during the dive into that which he imagines to be a primordial state of absolute control, the aspiring sovereign becomes hypersensitive. Everything appears to him as a potential cluster of code and law, as a block on the road to ultimate deliverance. The tiniest of eddies and the smallest of specks—real or imagined—become insufferable in the eyes of the aspiring sovereign.

In Pollock's work, absolute sovereignty can only be attained in what Bataille (who, let us remind ourselves, was writing at about the same time Pollock was perfecting his drip technique), in his book *Eroticism* (1957), called "continuous life." Continuous life is life before or beyond the strictures of functionality; it is life before or beyond civilization as such. This is life in a zone where everything is continuous with everything else, and where no code, structure, or law prevails that commands: *this is not compatible with that and should therefore be discontinued, excluded or destroyed.* As is the case in Pollock's work, Bataille's road toward sovereignty in discontinuous life is one of unrelenting transgression. Life here is life at the level of sheer uncoded immanence, or, as the French novelist Michel Houellebecq (2010) has it in his novel about late modern, thoughtless, burnt-out hedonism, the level of elementary particles.

Unlike Pollock, Rothko, a Nietzsche scholar of some renown, was very articulate. He spoke and wrote a lot about his work (see the anthology in Rothko 2006). His signature shapes, rectangular or square, floating as they seem to be doing in the undifferentiated fluid of their surroundings, amid other similarly floating shapes, Rothko stated, actually represent entities that, having freed themselves from their shackles, move about without the need to conform or violate anything that dares to present itself as norm, code, law, structure, or stricture. In a way, the shapes express something of the superhuman indifference of Nietzsche's Zarathustra (see also Camus's *Outsider* or *Stranger*, mentioned above). Unlike Pollock's aspiring sovereigns though, Rothko's are extremely reluctant to dive into the flesh of the world. There is nothing in the flesh of the world that attracts them. They are indifferent to what they perceive to be the undifferentiated mass of the world. Their sovereign aspirations are not so much about dissolving the Self in a bid to elude capture by all kinds of code and structure, as it is about making extreme efforts to control the world by keeping it—undifferentiated mass—at bay, in order to thus preserve the pure uniqueness of the Self. Rothko's sovereigns, in other words, never dive. They ascend. They transcend. They are continuously making efforts to transcend the world. Floating around in a state of indifference, they constantly and "freely" reflect upon the world. They live in a voidlike ethereal zone, seemingly protected by the shield of their reflections that gently propel them through the mass of the world, which should not and could not reach them. Rothko's aspiring sovereigns are not interested in what connects them to the flesh of the world: their body and the desires that flow through it. They *will* be independent from all this. However, like Pollock's aspiring sovereigns, Rothko's will inevitably strand themselves in sheer agonistic paradox. Cutting themselves off from the world, they immediately lose all capacity to intervene in it. All sovereign control then becomes impossible: if you do not intervene in the world, the world will intervene in you, as Camus's Meursault came to realize very well. The tiniest of coincidences could destroy your fragile bubble. Somehow Rothko himself must have been aware of this paradox, for in a number of statements he, ever the Nietzsche scholar, admitted that his paintings also express the fundamentally and inescapably tragic nature of the human condition.

Both Pollock and Rothko were, and remain, icons of postwar culture. What is often overlooked though is that in their work, both painters, each at opposite sides of the spectrum of artistic form, acted as harbingers of a newly emerging form of life. This new form of life, forged in the experience of the authoritarian disaster that we know as the Second World War, was one in which an older default "logic" or life strategy, which once was quite dominant across whole population segments, gradually came to be replaced with a new one. The older logic went as follows: *if all else fails, submit to foundation and the promise of ultimate redemption and accept sacrifice.* The new default logic however that emerged, wavering at first, in the wake of the war, goes like this: *if all else fails, refute all foundation.* This form of life is one produced by and inhabited by aspiring sovereigns in search of absolute control. This aspiration cuts across class, gender, and status. There is no space here to explore, in any depth, the ramifications of this quite pervasive cultural shift (but see Lippens 2011b, 2015a and 2015b). What we need to stress for the purposes of this contribution though is that this shift, it can be argued, generated the transition from (foundational) disciplinary society to what has become known as (antifoundational) control society. Aspiring sovereigns do not want to be disciplined, nor do they want to discipline (why indeed would they want to make themselves dependent on all this, or on the codes that inevitably underpin discipline?). Aspiring sovereigns are content to merely exercise control, and to do this in total, uncoded and codeless, "indifferent" responsiveness (however imaginary, illusory, and paradoxical this aspiration of course).

That said, we now arrive at the core theme in this essay: aspiring sovereigns in search of total, antifoundational responsive control, tend to live agonistic lives. On the road to sovereignty and to responsive control, they encounter ever more hindrances and stumbling blocks. What in earlier forms of life was just taken as part of life, or on the chin, or as something that could and would eventually get fixed, now becomes an object or an issue to "control." The tiniest speck on the road to absolute (albeit imaginary) sovereignty can now, in the new form of life, at least potentially, become the focus of inconsolable irritation and anger and the source of unrelenting bouts of ever-widening control. In agony, the aspiring sovereign feels constantly under attack or under siege. He is, he claims, the eternal *victim* of the world. Before we explore this theme in more detail, we first need to revisit some of the topics that we have introduced above.

SOVEREIGN ASPIRATIONS

If the experience of the Second World War has indeed catalyzed the emergence of a new form of life, one that is fueled by a newly crystallized default "logic" at its very core, the question arises as to the extent of this new form of life and the shape of its manifestations and consequences. Easily posed, the question is not easy to answer. Forms of life are not monolithic. They emerge and disappear in processes of hybridization and what little coherence they carry in them radiates outward only partially and unevenly. And so it should not surprise us if the form of life mentioned above—let us call it antifoundational control society—penetrated and pervaded Western culture only gradually, in fits and starts, and never completely. It did manifest itself though in a number of disparate ways. Again, there is no space here to exhaust this topic, but a few things can be said for our purposes, about the desire for, or will to absolute sovereignty and control (albeit, as said, highly imaginary, illusory and paradoxical sovereignty and control) that formed and continues to form one of its main aspects. As noted above, artists such as Pollock and Rothko were among the first to sense the new mood. In Pollock's expressive artwork, the new desire for absolute sovereignty and control can only be accommodated if the Self dissolves itself in the primordial, undifferentiated flesh of the world. In Rothko's, the Self transforms itself into an indifferent reflection chamber that floats, voidlike, amid the mass of the world. Both seem to agree though that, in the wake of the war, the beginning of the end of what we now, in Foucauldian parlance, tend to call the disciplinary society, became imaginable.

It is possible to make connections here with Arthur Frank's typology of "sociological bodies." In the newly emerging form of life, the default logic ("all else failing" though) hollows out the need for discipline. Aspiring sovereigns no longer feel the need for discipline. If all else fails, they no longer feel the need to discipline themselves. All else failing, they no longer feel the need to discipline others. They are beginning to bluntly refuse all commands that order: "Thou shallt, for thy own sake, accept this sacrifice and submit to that ultimate foundation," and in turn, they are no longer interested in imposing foundations themselves. They are beginning to lose interest in the alignment of bodies and minds under "order words," that is, words that code, order, and structure (see Gilles Deleuze's short paper on "control societies" 1995). To aspiring sovereigns, any such coded alignment constitutes a potential block on the road to absolute, responsive sovereignty and control.

Once shattered, the disciplinary order and the mind-body alignment that supports it make way for new, *sovereign* life strategies and "logics" to emerge. In one of those strategies, the "mind," or the Self, dissolves in the body, and therefore simultaneously, as we have seen, also in "the flesh of the world." In another strategy the "mind" locks itself into what it believes to be a reflecting chamber, perfectly and hermetically insulated from the body and from the world. There is a third strategy imaginable of course, as Camus reminded us, one in which the "mind," or the Self, engages with the body and with the world, not in coded, structured, ordered alignments of discipline, but rather, in ever-renewing attempts to transform, and to keep transforming, all that presents itself as inescapable law or code. In this strategy, the default operative antifoundational "logic" which we described above is shot through not just with an awareness of the paradoxical limitations of both previous strategies (absolute sovereignty is absolutely impossible), but also, and more importantly so, with a sense of the precariousness and fallibility of all attempts to achieve sovereign control. Real sovereignty can only be partial and fallible. Sovereignty can only be achieved in the act of creation, and that, creation, inevitably implies one engages with the world. Here, the aspiring sovereign is aware of the need to explore the matter, or the flesh of the world, to reflect upon it, and to intervene in it in a bid to creatively add to it, indeed to transform it. Only in this act of creation will something like real sovereignty be possible. But this sovereignty, since it is of necessity the result of localized engagements between a limited Self and fragments of the world, could never be more than a Sisyphus stone, which will have to be rolled up the mountain, time and time again. Sovereignty and sovereign control can never be absolute. Aspiring sovereigns in this third, alternative life strategy are fully aware of this.

One could argue that, during the best part of the postwar era, we have been able to witness an often-dizzying variety of combinations of those strategies coagulating into an even wider variety of social and cultural practices. One could, for example, mention the democratization of hedonism; authors such as the French philosopher Michel Onfray (2012) have been building a whole philosophy on this theme (unlike Bataille's philosophy of sovereign transgression and expenditure though Onfray's hints at Spinoza's *Ethics* [1677] to argue for a hedonism that increases the world's bodies' capacities, i.e., their "power to act"). Or one could point to increasing levels of isolation and active retreatism in contemporary culture; or to the explosion of energy with which, since the postwar days, taboos and other social and cultural norms have, the one after the other, been thoroughly deconstructed, reversed, or otherwise transformed in an almost kaleidoscopic spectrum of social and cultural movement. These themes could indeed be linked to Arthur Frank's typology. But before we do that, it is worthwhile to explore the emergence and development of this postwar form of life a little further.

The potential for sovereign aspiration, which became available with the gradual demise of discipline, it could be argued, was eventually captured and overcoded, so to speak, by a parody it had spawned. This parody is the one we now call consumer culture. In this consumer culture (already thoroughly theorized by authors such as Guy Debord in 1967), the aspiring sovereign's desires for absolute sovereignty and absolute control are captured and locked into a surrogate, indeed *parody* of sovereignty. Diving hedonistically in the stream of consumer items and consumer images that take the place of the "flesh of the world," the faux sovereign-consumer accepts the illusion of sovereign control. Reflecting upon lifestyles and lifestyle choices while floating around in this stream of commodity/image, the faux sovereign contemplates his faux mastery of the world and of himself. Constantly selecting and deselecting commodity and image in ever so many attempts to constitute and reconstitute his Self, the faux sovereign believes he is creatively transforming both himself and the world. But this illusion of sovereignty and control is just that: an illusion. The faux consumer sovereign only submits to what has actually become a new overarching code, a new foundational "order word" of sorts: "Consume or perish!" This parody of sovereignty captures and mobilizes some of the pervasive culture of indifference that goes hand in hand with sovereign aspiration. This indifference also fuels an uncoded, unstructured, indeed lawless "economy of precarity," which in turn captures and mobilizes it. This economy forms another backdrop against which faux sovereignty takes shape. In a paper on art in our economy of precarity, for example, Vassilis Tsianos and Dimitris Papadopoulos (2015) argue how this indifferent economy (or this economy of indifference) no longer needs economic actors' (whether they be producers or consumers) focused (that is: disciplined) dedication. It only needs abstract quantities from them, such as time and energy. Beyond this, the actors are "free" to engage in what they then might perceive to be sovereign pursuits.

It probably requires only a little stretch of the imagination to suggest that the forms and shapes of faux sovereignty have been able to mobilize and eventually overcode at least some of the reservoir of sovereign aspiration that was opened up during and immediately after the experience of the war years, and from which faux sovereignty itself, to some extent, originated. As such, to evoke Frank's typology once more, the *mirroring body* of the consumer has become quite dominant in late modern culture. Diving into and wading through the stream of commodity and images, so typical of a thoroughly pervasive consumer culture, and unreflectively allowing himself to be impacted by this unrelenting stream of consumer desires, the faux sovereign merely mirrors the aspirations and gestures of other consumer sovereigns. Even the retreating reflecting sovereign, who has lost the connection with his body, and who has severed all links with the flesh of the world, can only reflect like a mirror. His body, an irrelevance cast adrift, can do little more than float on a stream of impacts. Both the aspiring immanent sovereigns and the aspiring transcendent ones, however, whether in their genuine or in their faux forms, tend to carry a serious potential for irritation and anger within them. This irritation and this anger can be unleashed whenever the aspiring perceives a stumbling block on his road to ultimate redemption. And in the form of life which we have termed antifoundational control society, peopled as it is by aspiring sovereigns who are inclined to refute *all* foundation (all else failing), that can and does happen very often. Indeed, the aspiring sovereign ultimately accepts no code that would order and structure, or rank hindrances in, for example, hierarchies of harm (e.g., "this here is, in view of the code which you have subjected yourself to, not so serious an event, but that one over there is"). He therefore tends to take even the tiniest of bumps on his road very seriously. This in turn often leads him to draw lines in the mass of the world in order to be able to exercise control over it, or dominate it if he thought the situation would require this. Arthur Frank's *dominating body* type always is a distinct possibility in the form of life lived by *responsive* sovereigns.

So, of course, is the *transformative body*. However, to the extent that sovereign aspiration has been overcoded by faux consumer sovereignty, the likelihood of the transformative body becoming the dominant type is quite remote. Genuine transformation requires mind/bodies that genuinely engage with the world with a view to creatively adding to it. But that requires a willingness to communicate and cooperate. Faux consumer sovereigns in particular do not really have such inclinations. Why would the faux sovereign need communication and cooperation? Communicate and cooperate to achieve what exactly? There is nothing worth achieving. The faux sovereigns' mirroring and dominating bodies need neither communication nor cooperation. They exercise control by mirroring and by dominating the mass of the world. These aspiring sovereigns have abandoned all willingness to suffer anything or anyone, and that includes communicating and cooperating with the mass of the world with an eye on what inevitably will be an effort to creatively produce or transform a code, however temporary that new code may be. This form of sovereignty is thoroughly noncommunicative, a point already made by Debord in his *La Société du Spectacle* (1967). The French sociologist Michel Maffesoli (1996) has argued, albeit in a slightly different context, that the best one could hope for, in our consumerist age, is mute and noncommunicative chatter in *neo-tribal* gatherings of mere hedonistic proximity. Michel Houellebecq would probably agree.

CONCLUSION: TOWARD VICTIM CULTURE

The emergence of a new form of life, the outline of which we have made an attempt to sketch above, is likely to have significantly contributed to what could be called "victim culture," that is, a culture in which is becomes habitual to use words such as "victim" or "victimized" to denote the condition of having to go through unwanted experiences. In what follows we hope to be able to supplement—not replace, just supplement—other explanations for the rise of victim culture such as, for example, victim culture being closely linked to dependency cultures, or to the emergence of postwar human rights discourse, or to the decline of the welfare state and the gradual replacement of its regulatory apparatus with a plethora of more responsive regulatory strategies. There is no reason to deny the validity of such explanations. What we are arguing though is that underneath the developments referred to in these explanations, and to some extent underpinning them, one might be able to discern a deeper trend linked to the emergence of a new form of life at the heart of which one is likely to find on operative code, or "logic" that says: "All else failing, refute all foundation." This code or logic is the aspiring sovereign's. We have already touched upon the basic dynamic that, at least in some measure, fuels this new form of life. Aspiring sovereigns, unrelentingly agonizing on the never-ending road to absolute sovereignty, tend to perceive potential blocks and hindrances everywhere. While eluding all law and all code in a bid to exercise sovereign control, they bounce from one issue that needs to be "controlled" to the next. We now need to unpack this analysis in some more detail. We first note a formal similarity between on the one hand the "sovereign" position, and the "victim position" on the other. Both are ultimately positions of separateness, or aloneness.

This is quite obvious in the case of the "transcending" reflective aspiring sovereign. But even in what Bataille termed "continuous" sovereign life, that is, the Self-less and therefore code-less life lived in a primordial "continuous" zone of pure potential and pure expenditure, the aspiring sovereign is—quite paradoxically so of course—separate and alone, or at least he wishes to be separate and alone. Throwing himself—or better, his "mirroring body" (dixit Frank)—into the undifferentiated mass of the world, the aspiring sovereign is caught agonistically in all kinds of attempts to elude all law, all code. In the midst of the mass of the world, in continuity with the mass of the world, the aspiring sovereign nevertheless is separate and alone. He does not really engage with the world. He does not want to transform the world, or his own Self for that matter. He is, then, no longer interested in cooperation and communication. The world is only a mass of elements (i.e., matter, code, and events) that somehow needs to be controlled, responsively, that is, beyond all fixed law or code (which, in turn, implies separateness and aloneness). The aspiring sovereign hopes he will be really sovereign if he is able to act or react totally responsively. Foundational codes in any shape or form only limit his capacity to act and react responsively. He is therefore no longer willing to accept or submit to foundational codes. That this is bound to lead him into contradiction and incoherence in his actions or reactions is not a problem for the aspiring sovereign who imagines he resides in complete separateness from the mass of the world. If, for example, the situation he finds himself in is such that risk is to be explored in order to hone his controlling skills then he will gladly engage in what has become known as "edgework." On other occasions he will be inclined to mobilize his "dominating body" and brutally block off anything that has a whiff of undesired risk about it. In other words: the aspiring sovereign is part of the engine in what has been called the precautionary culture in late modern life. He refuses to engage in democratic debate about risk. With one wave of the hand he rejects cost-benefit calculations. There is nothing to calculate. There is nothing to construct. There is nothing to communicate about. Should his barrage of precautionary measures eventually undermine his sovereign aspirations, as they invariably do, then this contradiction and this incoherence will be dealt with by the aspiring sovereign the only way he knows: by looking at the consequences of his earlier bouts of precaution as so many additional elements in the mass of the world to responsively control.

Although he thinks of himself as someone who is a master of his actions, the aspiring sovereign is actually always reacting to the world. Refusing to engage with the world, he is, not unlike Camus's Meursault, a receiver, rather than a giver. He does not produce the world. He consumes it. There is of course an exception to this. As we have seen, there is a form of sovereignty imaginable that is all about creatively engaging with the world with a view to transform it (with antifoundational awareness, to evoke Camus once more). But this form of sovereignty—a very modest and highly sensitive form—has largely been taken hostage by the faux sovereignty of the consumer-sovereign who, as Debord noticed, lives his nonproductive and noncommunicative life in separation. One produces with others, and with the world. But one consumes alone, in the world. Aspiring sovereigns are of course perfectly capable of cooperation and communication, and for temporarily accepting the codes that underpin productive and constructive projects. And they often do demonstrate this capability, that is, if the situation requires it. Let us remind ourselves that the "logic" at the heart of their form of life is, basically, a logic "by default." It kicks in when "all else fails."

But if the above is the case, then it should come as no surprise that aspiring sovereigns will have no problems with using and mobilizing the "victim" sign to denote their experiences if they believe it will help them to control the mass of the world. The fact that the very word "victim" suggests, or might suggest, powerlessness, or dependency, and so on, is not an issue for those who have learned not just to live with contradiction and incoherence, but to even exploit this responsively. The sign "victim" is a very useful implement in the aspiring sovereign's tool kit. It often allows him to keep law and code at bay, and to control the mass of the world in particular situations. It allows him to remain separate and to keep receiving ("I am a victim. You must therefore give to me"). Living in a world whose mass seems to be encroaching upon him unrelentingly during his never-ending flight from law and code, the aspiring sovereign, in agony and wading through the mass of a *criminally* relentless world, mobilizes the sign as he thinks fit.

In the consumer world of faux sovereigns, this becomes quite acute. Here, having thrown himself in the stream of commodity and image, the sovereign's *mirroring body* is, potentially at least, very extended. It includes all that he has been able to amass. As his body thus stretches out into the far distance, connected as it is to all manner of consumer goods, the consumer-sovereign grows even more sensitive than he already, in all his agony, was. Whoever touches his consumer items actually touches his extended body. Burglary, for example, always an emotionally laden intrusion as such, becomes almost unbearable in an age of consumer-sovereigns (a point well made by Kearon and Leach, 2000). But the non-consumerist aspiring sovereign, who, in his state of indifference, has transcended into a void of pure reflection, will be inclined to mobilize the "victim" sign responsively. His body may have disappeared to the point of becoming an irrelevance; his reflective mind roams and reflects everywhere. He will, on occasion, shout "Victim!" when an element in the mass of the world encroaches upon it.

TWO

Still Worlds Apart?

Habitus, Field, and Masculinities in Victim and Police Interactions

Dale C. Spencer and Jillian Patterson

In 1998 Lori-Ann Ellis filed a missing person's report regarding her daughter Cara Ellis with the Vancouver police in British Columbia. Cara is one of twenty women—sex workers on the Downtown Eastside of Vancouver—that serial killer Robert Pickton was charged[1] with murdering and disposing of their bodies at his infamous pig farm. It was not until 2004, when the members of the Missing Women Task Force visited Lori-Ann Ellis in Calgary, that she found out that the report she had filed had never been "actioned" (i.e., it had never been acted upon). At a 2011 public inquiry regarding the police handling of the Pickton murders, an infuriated Ellis recalled how she phoned the Vancouver police to follow up on her first missing person's report and spoke to a woman that said to her: "If Cara wants to be found, she'll be found. Why don't you leave us alone and let us do our job." The officer then informed Ellis that Cara was "probably on vacation" (Drews 2011, 1). Beyond the limited institutional capacity of police to help vulnerable victims, what the Ellis case reveals is an indifference, if not intolerance, to the plight of certainly potential, but less than "ideal" victims (see Christie 1986; Kilty and Fabian 2010). This chapter interrogates the ostensible divide between victims (both primary and secondary) and the police and demonstrates the gendered and corporeal elements that constitute this relationship.

Due in large part to the pressure of victims' rights movements in Western countries over the last thirty years, victims of crime are certainly no longer the "forgotten actors" in the criminal justice system (Doak 2008; Zedner 2002). Victims' rights movements in Western countries have resulted in reforms to the criminal justice system to improve the treatment of victims of crime, including the response of police to sexual assault and domestic violence. Concomitantly, Jordan (2001, 679) has argued that police and rape victims remain "worlds apart" in their perspectives and needs and as such, "little in the way of substantive improvements appears possible within this historically and cross-cultural fraught area." While Jordan limits her assertion to rape victims and police, portions of the critical victimology literature point to a significant disjuncture between the worlds of criminal justice systems and victims of crime more generally (e.g., Dunn 2001; Belur 2008). Recent academic literature indicates that victim interactions with police and their experiences with many features of the judicial process too often continue to replicate the dynamics of victimization (Regehr et al. 2008; Maier 2008; Temkin and Krahe 2007).

In this chapter, we probe the interactions between victims and police to locate the points of continuity and change of the relationship between police and victims. In addition, we analyze victim service organizations' directors, coordinators, and volunteers' interpretations of police and crime victim interactions in the wake of criminal victimizations. Unpacking the relationships between victims and police is a particularly valuable endeavor, as the character of interpersonal interactions between victims and authorities may have the greatest impact on how victims judge the justice meted out in relation to their victimization (Wemmers 1996, 2010; Bradford et al. 2009; Richardson-Foster et al. 2012).

In this chapter, Pierre Bourdieu's concepts of field and habitus are used to analyze the relationship between victims and police (cf. Chan 1996). The concept of habitus is particularly valuable as it allows for the examination of the corporeal and mental dispositions within police culture that constitute police practices in relation to victims of crime (cf. Wacquant 2011). Field is useful for the present purposes as it provides a differentiated analysis of social context under which the reflexive transformation of identity unfolds (McNay 1999). By drawing connections between field, habitus, and policing culture, I identify policing practices that have both detrimental and beneficial consequences for the interactions between police and victims. In addition, in linking the concept of policing habitus to extant discussions of masculinities (see Connell 2002, 2008; Anderson 2009), I advance understandings of the embodiment of masculinities among police. By connecting the policing and victimology literature with the masculinities literature, I offer a way of understanding both the disjuncture and synergy between the worlds of victims and police and the changes in masculine practices within this occupation. I demonstrate how policing masculinities have been both articulated in familiar ways, but also less familiar ways through inclusive masculinities that are far more oriented to victims' needs.

Drawing on victim service organizations' directors, coordinators, and volunteers' narratives regarding interactions between victims and police, I develop the concepts of stoic and inclusive masculinities embodied by police. In the context of police work, stoic masculinity is characterized by such practices as bodily distance between the victim and the police officer with little to no interaction, an unreflexive carrying out of policing mandates, and an insensitivity toward the safety and feelings of traumatized victims. Inclusive masculinity is based on an ethic of care with an empathetic approach to victims where police officers go beyond the mandates of "law and order" and attend to the needs of victims in the wake of events of victimization (cf. Anderson 2009). It is particularly salient to understand masculinities within policing as a way of moving toward increased public understanding of and improvement in the experiences of crime victims (see Connell 2008).

This chapter is structured in three main sections. In the first section, we draw from the work of Pierre Bourdieu on habitus and field as well as sociological discussions of masculinities as a way of framing the relationship between police and victims. In the second section, we discuss the methods of this study. The third empirical section analyzes narratives from victim service organization personnel to explore the interactions between victims and police and the embodiment of stoic and inclusive masculinities among police officers.

HABITUS, FIELD, AND MASCULINITIES

The work of eminent sociologist Pierre Bourdieu (1977, 1990, 2010) is vast and variegated; therefore, I will limit my discussion to his work on habitus and field, two of his most dynamic and useful concepts. Habitus is a mediating concept that assists in revoking the commonsense duality between the individual and the social by capturing "the internalization of externality and the externalization of internality," that is, the way society becomes inscribed in persons in the form of enduring dispositions, or trained capacities and structured propensities to think, feel, and act in determinate ways, which then guide them in their creative responses to the constraints and solicitations of their extant milieu (Bourdieu 1977; see also Spencer 2009). Keeping with his sociology of practice, Bourdieu's habitus is not acquired through conscious learning or ideological imposition, but is acquired through practice (Lovell 2000). At every moment, the habitus structures new experiences in accordance with the structures produced by past experiences. These experiences are modified by new experiences that are only within the limits "defined by their power of selection," which engenders a unique integration with experiences common to people of the same class or group (Bourdieu 1990, 60). Habitus, then, varies across groups, cultures, and societies, reflecting the accordant membership (see also Durkheim [1913] 1995; Mauss 1973). New information that calls into question accumulated past experience is often rebuffed because of the constancy of the habitus. It is by the exposure to new information accidently or by force that changes in the habitus *may* be produced (Bourdieu 1990). In relation to the present work, the habitus can explain obdurate ways of thinking regarding victims, but also how new information can challenge long-standing dispositions toward victims. On the other hand, it should be noted that habitus is not a uniformly imposed structure or fixed way of being, but rather is a generative structure that is formed in a dynamic relation with certain social fields (McNay 1999). This illuminates how there is a differential distribution of habitus among individual police officers within the policing field.

Fields, for Bourdieu, are the structured contexts that shape and produce processes and practices. Fields are "a series of institutions, rules, rituals, conventions, categories, designations, appointments, and titles which constitute an objective hierarchy and which produce and authorise certain discourses and activities" (Webb et al. 2002, 21). Interactions of the habitus within various fields are a matter of learning the "rules of the game" (Bourdieu and Wacquant 1992). It is this interconnection between fields qua institutions and habitus that enables an identification of a policing habitus. Concomitantly, it is the boundaries between fields where struggles take place (Bourdieu 1990). For the present purposes, boundaries can be understood through the confrontations between the victims' movements (and related victim service organizations) and policing fields. Struggles over how victims should be treated in the wake of victimization and meanings associated with victims form the division between victim advocates and policing fields. The durability and change in practices are revealed in the interactions between police and victims.

Through the initial and continuous training regimes police officers are subjected to and through living out their day-to-day lives in their roles as police officers, they form a *policing habitus* that affords the police a sense ("a vision") of their own place and also a sense of criminalized persons, victims and the "general public" (see Kitchen and Schneider 2005). The policing field provides the "rules of the game," the rituals of the profession, and the hierarchy of the policing institution. The uniform of officers is part and parcel of what separates police from victims, criminalized persons, and the general public and works to signify their masculine identity qua policing habitus. Undergirding the policing habitus are dominant notions regarding gender, specifically the "natural" hierarchy between men and women (Bourdieu 1990, 2001) that is created and sustained in overarching societal gender norms (see Chambers 2005).

Sociologists of gender have long posited the existence of multiple femininities and masculinities (e.g., Connell 1995; Courtenay 2000). Gender is defined here as socially produced distinctions based on sex differences enacted through various practices that (re)work bodies in specific ways in the attempt to signify specific masculinities and femininities (see Connell 1995; 2002; Whitehead 2002; Bourdieu 2001). Masculinities are defined in relation to femininities in-so-far as masculinities are continually signified as antipodal to femininities. With this emphasis on the plurality of genders, Connell (1995, 2002) has constructed the concept of hegemonic masculinities and femininities. Hegemonic masculinity signifies a status of cultural authority and leadership, formed in relation to various subordinate masculinities as well as in relation to women (Connell 1995, 2002). Hegemonic masculinities are said to be associated with such ideals as domination, aggressiveness, competitiveness, sexual and athletic prowess, control, and stoic affect. Within this concept, men are believed to consent to sustaining hegemonic masculinity, but individuals vary in their replication of, and relationships to, the aforementioned ideals (Connell 1995). On the other hand, hegemonic femininity is formed within a class-based structure, with strong interconnections to heterosexual sex and romance. In addition, hegemonic femininity is associated with passivity and aligned with the ideal feminine body as white, thin, and toned (Krane et al. 2004; Kilty and Fabian 2010). Femininities and masculinities are multiple, contested, dynamic, and contradictory, based on different cultures and periods of history that construct gender differently (Connell 1995; Courtenay 2000; O'Brien, Hunt, and Hart 2005).

As noted, gender is not a fixed entity embedded in the body or personality traits of individuals. This moves us toward recognition of the malleability of bodies. Based on this premise, policing masculinities can be understood as embodied in manifold ways that are reflected in, inter alia, characteristic postures, speech, and gait of police officers (see Manning 2007, 68; Loftus 2007, 196). In regards to police organizations, the criteria for good performance at work defines ideal masculine embodiment that is often defined through strong codes of dress, speech, and deportment (see Connell 2008).

As concepts, hegemonic masculinity and hegemonic femininities are often deployed at a far too global level and fail to explain the performance of dominant masculinities within local contexts (Spencer 2009, 2011; Whitehead 2002). It is far more important to understand the *emergence* and *embodiment* of specific masculinities and femininities within local contexts. For example, police officers can embody specific masculinities that emerge from the practices associated with policing. These specific masculinities are often not dissimilar to the policing masculinities that are found across geographically diverse contexts because of the similarity of practices within policing institutions (Paechter 2003, 2006) that constitute the habitus of police officers. As such, attention to practices and the habitus of police officers in local contexts is important to understand the actual performance of masculinities. Here we delve into the embodiment of a stoic masculinity found among police officers and to the emergence of an inclusive masculinity. In the context of police work, stoic masculinity is characterized by such practices as bodily distance between the victim and the police officer with little to no interaction, an unreflexive carrying out of policing mandates, and an insensitivity toward the safety and feelings of traumatized victims. Inclusive masculinity is based on an ethic of care with an empathetic approach to victims where police officers go beyond the mandates of "law and order" and attend to the needs of victims in the wake of events of victimization (see Anderson 2009). In the next section, we describe the methodology of this study.

METHOD

Forty semistructured interviews have been conducted with victim services organizations personnel in Ottawa, Edmonton, and Winnipeg, three census metropolitan areas.[2] These areas were chosen because the Ottawa, Edmonton, and Winnipeg Police Services have dedicated victim crisis units. These units are dedicated to providing crisis intervention and post-trauma counseling to victims of crime and tragic circumstances. Historically, the establishment of police victim service units was predicated on police organizations' response to victims' rights struggles at the local, provincial, and national level to make policing practice more receptive to victims' needs. Based on these organizational orientations toward victims, the interactions between police and victims *should* be more positive than those reported in past studies of police and victims interactions.

The emergence of victim services organizations is due, in part, to the victims' rights movement. Victim service organizations operate to meet the needs of victims that are not met by the criminal justice system. For example, victim service organization personnel and police officers accompany victims of domestic violence to their previous domiciles to acquire their belongings. These organizations are professional and volunteer-based organizations and, in the main, are funded by provincial and federal sources but are not part of their local police organizations. As units of analysis, victim service organization personnel are ideal candidates to elucidate the interactions between police and victims as they regularly consult with victims of sexual assault, domestic violence, and other types of victims at various stages of engagement with the criminal justice system. Their experiences with police transcend individual victims' interactions with police as many have been working with police for over twenty-five years and are able to reflect on the durability and changes in police practices in this time period.

Forty in-depth interviews have been conducted with ten volunteers, eighteen coordinators, and twelve directors in twenty-three different victim service organizations. Interviewees (thirty-four women, six men) ranged in age from twenty-three to sixty-five years of age. Thirty-eight interviewees were born in Canada. Twelve were married, seventeen were in relationships, and eleven were single at the time of the interview. Half of the participants were parents. In terms of education, five participants' highest level of education was high school, twenty-five participants' highest level of education was an undergraduate degree, eleven had completed graduate degrees, and one had completed a PhD. For professional victim service organization personnel, experience in their current positions ranged from six months to thirty-four years. For volunteers, experience ranged from six months to ten years.[3]

Interview subjects were asked a range of questions regarding their roles as victim service organization personnel, including their views of the criminal justice system, conceptions of victims' rights and justice, and their experiences of working with victims of crime. In addition to asking questions regarding their sentiments toward the criminal justice system, I asked for stories of their interactions with police, the courts, and crime victims (their clients). This allowed for an understanding of the texture of the interactions between police and crime victims. An interpretive methodological approach (Denzin 1989) has been used to analyze the narratives from the interviews. Members of organizations have multiple senses of self and offer multiple interpretations of any given event (Czarniawska 2004). In relation to the latter, this is important as different victim service organization members offered different interpretations of victim and police interactions.

HABITUS, GENDER, AND VICTIM-POLICE INTERACTIONS: LESS-THAN-IDEAL FEMININITY

Complicating the relationship between victims and criminal justice agencies is the variability of recognition of victims. While a victim may inhabit the world of victims they may not have the recognition of the broader communicative network (see Strobl 2010) and may not possess the language to be recognized as victims by broader formal criminal justice agencies and publics. What constitutes a victim remains doxa (Bourdieu 1993) and is rarely articulated in contemporary discourse in the media and at a governmental level. Due to this lack of reflection, many forms of victimization, in fact, do not result in an individual being accorded the status of victim. The status of victims is also contingent upon the background characteristic of both the assailant and the potential victim (Kilty and Fabian 2010; Comack and Balfour 2004; Razack 2000). The contingency of the title of victim has led Nils Christie (1986) to put forth the concept of the ideal victim. By ideal victim, he is referring to those who are automatically accorded the complete, legitimate status of the victim after victimization. These are primarily those who are weak (children, the elderly, etc.) and are persons who were, when victimized, engaging in a respectable project, and therefore could not be blamed for being in the wrong place (e.g., the street) at the time of victimization. Lastly, the assailant is most legitimate if s/he was big and bad and unknown to the victim. This conception of the ideal victim maps onto precepts of normative femininity. To be an ideal victim, a woman must be in a heterosexual relationship, preferably married, and engaged in various "normal" activities at the time of victimization; that is, she cannot be transgressing heterosexual norms. She must also meet the mandates of femininity associated with passivity and fragility. The specific femininities qua victim types *are produced in relation to the dominant masculinities* engaged with as a result of criminal justice response and guided by normative gender mandates immanent to broader witnessing publics.

Within the criminal justice system, police officers are the first respondents to victims in wake of an event of criminal victimization. As they enter the lives of victims (the field of victims), those victims are suffering the effects of trauma and an existence that will never be the same. This further evinces the importance of police in responding to victims of crime irrespective of their status as being "less-than-ideal" victims. In addition, the victim services organizations, directors, coordinators, and volunteers we spoke with indicated that their organizations were reliant on the police for referrals and to be made aware of victims in need. Victim service personnel expressed that the police often treated victims, especially in domestic violence and sexual assault cases, with skepticism and misogyny undergirded by victim-blaming myths. This skepticism on the part of police officers can result in forms of victimization not being recognized. The following response from Mary and Suzanne illustrates this circumstance:

> Mary: We just had a crisis call today where there was a recent sexual assault that was questioned by RCMP [Royal Canadian Mounted Police]. This was a younger, less experienced constable. It's not always males, sometimes females, who are buying into the myths around victims and victim blaming. In any other crime, I don't think we approach victims in any other way. We don't start asking questions "Well, did you want to get punched in the face?" The questioning implies some sort of complicity or guilt on the part of the victim only in sexual violence or domestic violence circumstances, which in relation to other forms of victimization, I don't think we have that same form of perspective. This is what happened with this victim [of sexual assault].
>
> Suzanne: I have had so many women that have said that: "if I ever known how this would go, I never would have called the police. I would let him kill me, but I would not call the police. Had I known what is coming." You also have cases where you think: who is the victim? There is a paradox there. I have had a couple of very educated clients, very well spoken, eloquent women, and knowledgeable. The constable comes to her, because domestic violence happens across all

social groups, and the constable may feel inferior and these women were treated so badly by the police and the investigators, because you could not bullshit them. These women have knowledge of the criminal justice system, so I see that kind of discrimination. But that is the exception; usually it is related to income. It is something that is never spoken, obviously never spoken, but if there is high incidence of police calls in certain neighbourhoods and addresses where low-income or subsidized income housing, they don't respond adequately, that is one of the biases I have seen.

Mary explains a particular attitude toward victims by police officers, which is informed by myths regarding female victims of domestic violence and sexual assault: that there is a certain level of complicity in their victimization. Within these myths is the notion that women are given over to the wills of their bodies. In Suzanne's narrative, she notes that the experiences of secondary victimization are so traumatic to some victims that it makes them regret contacting police for intervention. She also evinces the intersection of class and gender in the interactions of police with victims and how such positions impinge on the treatment of victims in the wake of victimization. Due to prevailing myths regarding violence against women, these forms of victimization are not reported and because the cases are not reported, the victims do not receive much needed aid from victim service organizations. While perceptions of women as being complicit in their victimization are prevalent in broader society, the habitus of the police officers reflects this perception in their treatment of victims of crime.

STOIC MASCULINITY

Many scholars have noted that the criminal justice system is still dominated by a white, masculine, and heterosexual ethos (Messerschmidt 1993; Miller et al. 2003; Brown 2007). Former police officer turned academic Thomas Nolan (2009, 251) avers that policing masculinity "endorses deliberate misrepresentation, regardless of the factual truth or falsity of statements or representations" (see also Punch 2003). Furthermore, Nolan (2009) argues that police organizations maintain a militaristic code with a hierarchical chain of command that reinforces allegiance to the organization. This hierarchy within the police field manifests itself in terms of the masculine status attributed to those "who work in drug investigations [and] are perceived as more 'male' than those who work with sexual assault victims (who are largely female)" (223). These two factors—wilful misrepresentation and the hierarchical organization of policing—are characteristic of the police field and contribute to prevailing myths regarding victimization, such as the ones Suzanne and Mary mentioned above. They also contribute to the distinctions between the fields of police and victims, making interactions between police and victims of domestic violence and sexual assault harmful. The actualization of this hierarchy and approach toward victims is manifested in practices related to *stoic masculinity* that are detrimental to the already painful experience of victimization. The following three victim service organization volunteers' narratives reflect this form of masculinity:

> Vivian: A lot of the police officers that we have had come to the police accompaniments for victims of domestic violence, especially female I hate to say it, were really awful. They were not sensitive to the needs of the victims, like I would be struggling with the suitcases of the victims, and the big burly men wouldn't even think to say, "Oh, can I help you with that?" They were very disengaged. Not all of them, but a good majority of them. They would say, "Let's get this over with, this is wasting my time." Like very abrupt to the victim.
>
> Vanessa: Yes, I have had incidents where they were not interactive; they did not want to talk. They just came in and got the information from the victim and that was it.
>
> Samantha: In terms of accompanying the police and I think it has gone as expected. Police officers when they are doing those interviews are pretty cold. Maybe it has to be that way, I don't know. They say that it has to be that way from a legal standpoint, because a defense attorney can argue that someone was being led in an interview. . . . They call it an interview but it is really an interrogation. . . . They don't always have someone for them to talk to after the interview. I don't know; if I had to go through the interview that this woman had to go through and did not have someone to talk to after the fact, it would have been very tough. It is very intense and very cold. This is about very personal and embarrassing information.

Stoic masculinity is marked by absence; its performance is in not acting. Unlike other masculinities, it is a masculinity that does not need to be proven. In relation to the police officers Vivian interacted with, she indicates that there is a marked avoidance of engaging with victims and a verbal affirmation of the belief that police accompaniments of domestic violence victims are not part of "real" police work. Furthermore, this dismissal also involves the underlying cynicism toward domestic violence as a problem that police must address. This serves as an enactment of the distinction between the fields of victims and police.

Vivian, and Mary before, reveal that the assumption of the addition of women police officers will necessarily ameliorate some of the problems of insensitivity toward victim is unfounded (cf. Corsianos 2009; Silvestri 2007; Prokos and Padavic 2002). Rather than challenging the prevailing myths, female masculinity (see Halberstam 1998) is performed in accordance with the stoic masculinity of the overarching policing field (cf. Morash and Haar 2012; Brown and Woolfenden 2011; Rabe-Hemp 2009). Regardless of the sex, the police officer habitus maintains an insensitive disposition toward victims. In relation to the interrogation process, Samantha notes that in the course of accompaniments to sexual assault victim statements there is "coldness" toward victims despite the fact that they are trying to testify about traumatic events. This form of insensitivity is part of the continuous secondary victimization that many victims of sexual assault report when they are going through the "interrogation" process and on to their experience of cross-examination by defense lawyers.

Along with a habitus characterized by cynicism toward victims of violence and an uncaring, insensitive misogynistic approach toward women, this disposition is also marked by an unthinking bureaucratic execution of tasks ostensibly associated with police work. The following two narratives illustrate this aspect of stoic masculinity:

> Sherry: So I will give you an overview of the scenario. We came up to the apartment building; and they were there right away, which never happens. We were lucky that way. But, the two officers showed up and did not introduce themselves to the victim at all. They saw a guy over in the park, which looked a bit out of it or whatever. They immediately walked over there and left us [the two victims organization personnel] with our victim at the door. As people, were nice enough, chatty, but they were just kind of there. They were not interacting with her at all. They were having their own conversation about police work, while we were doing our thing. She was on a lease, but her boyfriend had changed the locks. So she had a right to be in the apartment, so we got into the apartment. The maintenance guy wanted us to hurry, because he did not want any trouble. The officers told me just grab what you can, but the whole thing, they were very distant. There was not relationship building between the victim and the police. Her stuff was all over the apartment building and we had to go pick up some more stuff and they asked us, "Do you really need us?" I am like, "Yes, you have to stay here!"
>
> Suzanne: Sometimes I feel that the police investigation part, in certain units, and certainly not all of them, there is the drive to just do their job, like step 1, 2, 3. It is about them and what they have to do; it is not about the victim. Sometimes they push hard for the victim to disclose and there is no adequate protection for the victim. You have women who were assaulted; who were beaten. There may be drugs involved. They [the police] want them to make a statement so that they can go after big fish, the fact that the big fish can kill her is not that important. I feel that there is not adequate follow up in terms of protection for victims by the system. The victim, and the purpose of the whole job, is somehow lost in the process and the procedures. It is not only the police, it is the justice system, and there are so many gaps, which have not been addressed.

Sherry, who has aspirations to become a police officer, reveals an incident with all the aforementioned practices associated with stoic masculinity.

First, the police officers establish distance between themselves and the victims. Second, the questioning of the need to be at the scene to protect victims from additional victimization further reveals how police officers, more often than not, perceive domestic violence intervention as not part of police work. Sherry's narrative shows the bureaucratic element of stoic masculinity when the police officers left the victim outside her apartment to attend to the "real" police work of establishing law and order—that is, pursuing the man who was "a bit out of it." The police officers only interpret that which is within their policing habitus and as such, consider confronting "criminal" populations more salient than attending to victims. In relation to Suzanne's narrative, she indicates that there is an emphasis among police officers on procedure with no consideration for victims. This bureaucratic element leads to an unreflexive carrying out of practices that places victims outside of consideration, possibly leading to revictimization. The police officers are guided by their police habitus and fulfill the mandates of policing culture. The stoic masculinity of the policing field holds implications for victims and how they experience the trauma associated with domestic violence. Amanda's narrative illustrates the effects of practices associated with stoic masculinity:

> Amanda: Now, I understand that police are busy, but this guy was busy. There seemed to be very little patience for what was happening and what this was emotionally for her [the victim], to go into the apartment. This particular situation she had not been in the apartment for a week and her pets were at the shelter and her husband was not there, but I remember her going in there and her apartment was empty and it was not empty the week before. I felt like the whole incident was rushed; I felt like there was no time to absorb what was going on. He was just like, "Get her stuff, and get out of there." She needed a moment to contemplate, "Where is all my stuff?" So I felt in that situation there was very little patience and consideration.

Here Amanda is involved in a police accompaniment and evinces practices associated with stoic masculinity. The execution of the police accompaniment in an emotionally distanced and expedient fashion leads to an additional level of trauma for the victim. Far from being a benign masculinity, the lack of care and attention associated with stoic masculinity, at a moment where victims most need it, is detrimental to the lives of victims and contributes, to the experience of an unfamiliar world. In addition, trapped within the policing field and performing stoic masculinity, police officers often fail to see the corruption within their own ranks:

> Janet: There is a contingent of police officers that are abusing their positions to have access to marginalized women, to do whatever they want. So you see police officers that will pick women up and start harassing them for their names, what they are doing and why they are out on the street. And then, they will not get to go home unless they give them a blowjob or fuck them. Whatever it is they happen to want

them to do. We have cops that will go to women's houses, because they have the authority to "find drugs" [respondent uses fingers to denote scare quotes]. Women know that they have so much authority, that they know if they do not cooperate with that officer, involving some sexual activity that they are going to be further criminalized. We have officers who are just violent to women, we have officers who seize evidence that never make it into the evidence room; they are dumped out of the cop car. All of the levels of police corruption that you would hear about or suspect in any other police force, you will find here. We have those here as much as anywhere else. Simultaneously, you have some well-meaning officers, who, stuck within police culture, gloss over knowledge of fellow officers that are committing these acts. I have spoken to them about specific officers, given names, and they still don't want to hear it or they just don't see it.

Janet's narrative cites extreme cases of police corruption, where marginalized sex workers are subject to (secondary) sexual victimization and physical violence at the hands of certain police officers. What is particularly revealing about Janet's narrative is that, despite informing other officers (those that do not engage in this type of corruption) of this abuse of authority, they fail to see the behavior. The police habitus makes it difficult for police officers to envisage the bad apples within their ranks, and therefore, contributes to the "rotting of the barrel" (cf. Punch 2003).

INCLUSIVE MASCULINITY: THE BRIDGING FIELDS THROUGH AN ETHIC OF CARE

Another form of masculinity that is often associated with policing is paternalistic masculinity. In contrast to authoritarianism, which is associated with bullying, fear, and coercion in the face of resistance, studies of paternalistic masculinity indicate that it relies on obtaining power in a less overtly coercive way (Collinson and Hearn 1994; Pini 2004). Paternalistic masculinity justifies actions based on being for the putative benefit or protection of those in subordinate positions (see Ackers 2001). Past studies of the paternalistic side of policing have shown it to be infantilizing, insofar as subordinates (often the public and victims) are treated and spoken of as if they need to be "managed" (Deukmedjian 2006; Adlam 2002). With paternalistic masculinity, "family," and "community" are of utmost importance.

While paternalistic masculinity can be seen as preferable in many respects to stoic masculinity, paternalistic masculinity holds many of the same misogynistic assumptions regarding ideal and less-than-ideal femininities. As such, an inclusive masculinity (see Anderson 2009) predicated on empathy and an ethic of care is a more positive alternative. Such an inclusive masculinity is shown in Sarah and Courtney's narratives:

Sarah: One police accompaniment, they always come in twos, the cruisers will come. Often they will get there and it is just a waste of their time. . . . So we were assisting this woman who had a newborn and one of the two officers recently had a newborn, so I think he could internalize what was going on. They were going back to get her things for herself. Usually you can only take your personal things, like you cannot take a computer or a bicycle. In this case, the officer with the newborn was dismantling the crib, even though, and on top of that, he packed both cruisers. He also followed us back to where we were taking her, which is unusual. He followed us to the shelter. They were unbelievable. But I think, given that at the time he had a baby and she had a baby. So there are exceptions. That case I will always remember because we took everything, because he did not want her to go back. He knew that if she got everything out of there, the chances of her returning to him were less likely.

Courtney: The police bring women and children here, and when we have clients who are in house. . . . That's very difficult and I have seen the biggest, you know, pretty tough looking police officers come in here and when there's the kids involved, I can recall of one we had about a year ago where [child services] came in and they had to apprehend the kids and the oldest wrapped his arms around the police officer's leg and said "I promise to be better." And, you know, this big burly guy, you know, was trying to hold back the tears. So no, I have nothing but good things to say about the police, they're so good to us.

Contrary to the customary stoic masculinity, Sarah's narrative reveals an inclusive masculinity founded on an ethic of care. In her story the police officer took on an empathetic stance based on his role as a father and engaged in actions that are beyond the customary response to domestic violence police accompaniments. In Courtney's narrative, the emotional distance that is characteristic of stoic masculinity is not part of the encounter at the women's shelter, but rather an affective commitment is part of the interaction. While taking the aforementioned criticisms of policing into account, here are the beginnings of the bridging of the fields between victims and police. The embodiment of an inclusive masculinity by the police officer reveals the care that is necessary to contest the structures that often keep women in domestic violence circumstances and exacerbate already traumatizing experiences. Accompanying the victim to the shelter, helping her extricate her belongings from her domicile, and positive interactions with police are practices that can reduce the trauma of victimization and renew a sense of justice for victims. Sage, a victim service organization director, reaffirms this assertion:

Sage: I think for me it [justice for victims] involves that first encounter. I think it is that first encounter. I have heard women say that that police officer has made the difference, so that speaks to that right. That police officer got it. Got whatever they needed to get; got how to be a supportive person; understood violence, understood what it looks like. Understood that there is no "typical" [victim], right.

Sage's narrative speaks to the fact that interactions between police have the greatest impact on justice judgments, a finding reaffirmed by the work of Wemmers (1996, 2010). The policing habitus here involves perceptions of victims as singularities, and not generalized categories, with specific needs that have to be met and understandings of victimization that do not involve quotidian myths. The question, then, is how are inclusive masculinities produced? And, what are the organizational practices that lead to such changes? The following three narratives begin to offer some explanation as to how the policing and victims fields begin to be bridged.

> Brandi: They are open to coming and meeting with us and hearing out concerns about the safety in the community, and um, that's definitely been our experience, uh, we've had police officers come out and do presentations and workshops on sexual assault in the past . . . I think it's been a, it's been a positive relationship.
>
> Breanne: For about ten years, we have been training police, and so we did kind of an exchange of training where we offered them training, they did some work on the crisis line to kind of increase their counseling skills and then I worked as a, like a consultant on scene with them when they would have a suicidal person or a domestic situation, so we worked quite closely for those ten years or so doing that.
>
> Alexandra: Our police have a sex crimes unit and it has helped with recognizing and understanding sexual violence, what sexual violence is, um and I think that has been a result of the advocacy of people who have been um victims of that violence. . . . We also have a um a [names city] response team, an interfacilities team that involves [names organization], the health sciences center nurse examiner program, children's hospital, the [names city] police service sex crimes unit, and the victim services. But now we work together to collaborate and coordinate our resources and services so we are ensuring the best possible outcomes for victims of violence.

In Brandi's narrative she reveals that there has been ongoing communication between victims, advocates, and police. This communication between fields serves as a basis to challenge and form the habitus of police officers participating in the workshops. In Breanne's response, she indicates that she has engaged in training of officers for a decade to counsel domestic violence victims. The training received by the officers serves as the basis of reworking the habitus—their perception and relationship to victims—to be more empathetic to victims' plight. In Alexandra's narrative, she evinces that with the establishment of a sex crimes unit there has been an increase in understandings of sexual violence. In addition, she reveals that there is collaboration between manifold organizations, including police and victims' advocacy groups, which work to create less traumatizing experiences for victims of violence. In this instance, the fields of policing and victims are enmeshed, which serves as a basis of changing the habitus of police officers and fostering more inclusive masculinities.

CONCLUSION

This chapter began with a story of Cara Ellis to show that the uncaring approach to victims associated with stoic masculinity is far from benign and can have grave consequences for crime victims. Stoic masculinity effectively divides victims and police. At the heart of this division lie particular conceptions regarding what are ideal or legitimate victims, and what is appropriate police work. Stoic masculinity consists of bodily distance between the victim and police officer with little to no interaction, an unthinking, bureaucratic carrying out of policing practices, and an insensitivity toward the safety and feelings of traumatized victims. The habitus and practices related to stoic masculinity drive the fields of victims and police farther apart, making the experience of victimization far more traumatic.

What this research indicates more than anything else is that both stoic and inclusive masculinities can operate concomitantly and form the basis of struggles between the police and victims fields. If there is going to be an erasure of the divide between police and victims that Jordan (2001) refers to, this chapter shows that there must be a reorientation of the very nature and philosophical underpinnings of police work so that practices of policing are geared toward reducing the trauma associated with victimization and not just the administering of law and order. Furthermore, this chapter demonstrates the points of emergence of inclusive masculinities that are based on an ethic of care, where in cases of domestic violence and sexual assault, police officers recognize that protecting and caring for victims is of utmost importance. On a practical level, it is shown that the dismissal of prevailing myths regarding victims and victim sensitivity training must be part of the ongoing training regimes police officers are subjected to, which will, in turn, reconstitute the policing habitus and lead to inclusive masculinities.

This research was limited to female victims' interactions with police in part by the fact that my interviewees did not discuss their interactions with male victims and also, the reporting by male victims of domestic violence and sexual assault is far more infrequent than that by female victims. Future research could probe the performance of masculinities and femininities within interactions between male victims and police officers. In terms of future qualitative research on habitus within policing cultures, researchers could shadow police officers in their engagement with victims to understand the continuous forging of policing habitus through practices associated with policing culture.

NOTES

1. The charges were stayed by the crown in 2010.
2. A census metropolitan area (CMA) is a grouping of census subdivisions comprising a large urban area and those surrounding urban fringes and fringes with which it is closely integrated. To become a CMA, an area must register an urban core population of at least 100,000 at the previous census. There are thirty-three CMAs in Canada. The data collection of this project in these two areas is ongoing.
3. Pseudonyms were assigned to all participants.

THREE

Boys to Offenders

Damaging Masculinity and Traumatic Victimization

Rebecca S. Katz and Hannah M. Willis

In this chapter we discuss critical victimology and its relevance for examining the life history narratives of twenty-five incarcerated men with significant histories of early boyhood trauma and loss. Critical victimology is an apposite approach because it promulgates an understanding of how victimization is privileged among certain groups and denied among others. This is important research in the context of the growing recognition that incarceration is no panacea to deal with damaged human beings who through their own pain act out, inflicting similar harm on others. Secondly, we review Connell's concept of hegemonic masculinity as well as the broader literature on the performances of masculinity in order to better understand the social, structural, and institutional constraints placed on men and boys that limit their behavioral repertoire in responding to traumatic events. Specifically, we analyze the normative standards of hegemonic masculinity and focus on how those that fail to meet those standards may harm themselves and/or resort to suicide (see Mehrabian 1997; Zimmermann, Mohr, and Spangler 2009). Drawing on the narratives of incarcerated men, we examine how gendered socialization practices and traditional masculine expectations push these men to dominate women and other men physically through sex or violence (cf. Messerschmidt 2000, 2004, 2005, 2010; Websdale 2011).

CRITICAL VICTIMOLOGY AND OFFENDERS

Traditional victimology views victims as those individuals harmed by the traditional street offender. This perspective fails to take into account victims of larger social structural and institutional forces such as poor welfare policies, underfunded schools, limited integration of mental health services, and criminal justice resources. Similarly, conventional victimology fails to account for corporate victimization and abandonment that leave vast swathes of people in American cities and towns jobless and impoverished. In addition, one of the salient points that we attempt to make here is that traditional victimology views victimhood as a kind of banner entitling a punitive stance toward offenders, ignoring research findings that reveal that early victims of child abuse, for example, are significantly more likely to become substance abusers, develop mental illnesses, and become caught up in the criminal justice system (Katz 2000, Stephens and Day 2013).

Critical victimology explores the social, structural, and institutional forces that increase the likelihood of individual victimization, including poverty or economic inequality and overt and covert forms of racism as well as the privileging of some forms of victimization over others (Mawby and Walklate 1994; Landau 2007). There are multiple dimensions of victimization and it is rare that an offender was not also a victim within his or her family. In addition, many of these same offenders are embedded in urban areas characterized by failed social services and mental health services, as well as penal policies that fail to prepare offenders for successful reentry (Light et al. 2013). This perspective argues that any form of human suffering, whether imposed within the family or by the state, creates victims and according to our findings here, victims often become offenders. In this chapter, we probe how early experiences of physical, psychological and sexual victimization contribute to life pathways filled with violence.

MASCULINITIES

In this section we briefly review Raewyn Connell's (1995) concept of hegemonic masculinities and the extant literature on the importance of the culture of masculinities and the social structure of patriarchy in understanding men, boys, and crime. Analysis of masculinities carefully link their formation to economic and cultural settings in which they emerged. The authoritarian, hegemonic type is hypermasculine, particularly involved in the maintenance of patriarchy, marked by hatred for homosexuals and contempt for women, as well as a more general conformity to authority from above, and aggression toward the less powerful (Connell 1995). These traits can be linked to rigid parenting, dominance of the family by the father, sexual repression, and conservative morality (Connell 1995, 18).

Connell (1995) argues that gender is constructed in interaction and both private and public conventions about masculinity are developed through social practice. Connell relies on Messerschmidt's theory on masculinities and crime, positing that among men from all classes, crime is a resource for constructing a particular kind of class-specific masculinity (Connell, 1995, p. 36). Masculinities are also constructed differently based upon race and class settings. Thus men maintain multiple relationships with one another characterized by alliance, dominance, and subordination within the context of their class and race membership (Connell, 1995, p. 37). She explains:

> These relationships are constructed through practices that exclude and include, that intimidate, exploit and so on. There is gender politics within masculinity. . . . In certain schools the masculinity exalted through competitive sport is hegemonic; this means that sporting prowess is a test of masculinity even for boys who detest the locker room. Those who reject the hegemonic pattern have to fight or negotiate their way out. (Connell 1995, 37)

These masculine identities are the result of family of origin dynamics and interpersonal interactions, educational, religious, and other institutional experiences in embodied social interactions (Messerschmidt 2004; Dalley-Trim 2007; Kivel and Johnson 2009; Cohen and Harvey 2006). These identities are performed in accordance with idealized forms of dominant and subordinate forms of masculinities that are socially constructed and reinforced. Failures to successfully negotiate these dominant forms of identity result in what Websdale refers to as a haunting. This experience is characterized as a complete loss of power and the destruction of self, sometimes leading to despair, depression, or a loss of personal agency (Websdale 2010; Hagan, McCarthy, and Foster 2002).

Feelings such as anger and shame become amplified and a diminished self results. Websdale (2010) argues that this diminished self becomes an emotional style of interacting with others that consists of continuities between the visceral (bodily experiences), psychological, social, and historical experiences, which results in being unable to separate emotions from thoughts. He refers to the emotional weight of these identity shifts as "civil reputable hearts" and the "livid coercive hearts." We argue that identities shift away from inclusive forms of masculinity as a result of early victimization, trauma, and interpersonal loss. This results in a downward spiral leading toward crime or hurtful behavior.

METHODOLOGY

Semistructured interview protocols were utilized to interview twenty-five adult incarcerated men in two medium-security prisons over the period of March 2012 through February 2013. The University Institutional Review Board on Human Subjects approved the protocol as well as State Department of Corrections and two prison wardens. The questions included eighty-six open-ended items querying men about their experiences inside and outside their respective institutions, including the following: neighborhoods where they grew up, favorite activities, most pleasant and most painful memories, favorite relatives, the history of involvement in substance abuse as well as delinquency, romantic relationships, prison visitation, prison program participation, educational changes, and new attachment relationships. Other questions included about early family relationships, love relationships and same-sex friendships, work histories, educational histories, history of harmful and helpful behavior, and gang involvement.

This research uses narrative analysis to examine all the men's lives by conducting multiple reviews of the interview notes resulting in unraveling common themes across boyhood, adolescence, and adulthood. These men's lives unfolded in an interview context with an interlocutor who demonstrated empathy and respectful responsiveness. Eight incarcerated men were black, fifteen were white, one was an Asian Pacific Islander, and one was Latino. Two men had been incarcerated for over twenty years and two for over ten years. Seven men committed murders (four were white, and three were black). One white man was incarcerated for assaulting a police officer following a car accident and the discovery of drugs in his automobile. One white man was incarcerated for physically abusing his infant and five men were incarcerated for burglary or robbery. Three other men, one white and two African American, were incarcerated for drug sales, although two reported that they witnessed, shot at and probably killed others, and had been shot or stabbed "on the streets." Only one young African American male was incarcerated for a minor parole violation.

Twenty-four of the interviews were completed, while in one case an individual was transferred after the completion of thirty-six questions. Recording devices were not permitted in either prison. Therefore, extensive field notes were taken in each interview to capture the totality of each man's life as best as is feasible through field notes and quotes when possible. Each man was interviewed over the course of three to five sessions ranging from one hour to an hour and a half. Men ranged in age from twenty-six to sixty-one and most men were heterosexuals; only one man disclosed that he was gay. After each interview, notes were typed into an electronic document file.

FINDINGS

Most of these men's boyhoods were characterized by poor and or neglectful and abusive parenting. Others lived in chaotic and violent neighborhoods with few opportunities for legitimate economic success or the practice and performance of traditional masculinity. Few of these men's fathers demonstrated normative patterns of demonstrating masculinity but rather most of their fathers were either absent or demonstrated a form of masculinity characterized by excessive drug or alcohol use, promiscuity with little regard for maintaining a monogamous relationship with the boys' mothers, violence against the boys and/or the boys' mothers, and other displays of dominant forms of masculinity in interactions with other men. Physicality or the presence of strength, size, and sexual conquest were extremely important to many of these men as demonstrated by youthful involvement in sport as boys and later conjoint gangs as teenagers and young adults. The ability to perform violence and have multiple sexual partners became a necessity and expectation for these men as well. Their childhood relationships, rather than being characterized by love or intimacy, were characterized primarily by neglect, and as young men, they replicated these experiences through the exploitation and sexual conquest of women. It is their ability to conquer and reproduce that reflects their masculinity, not legitimate work, traditional marriage, or fatherhood. Becoming a biological father was more important than being a father. This symbolic fatherhood defines masculinity as much as their ability to commit violence, excessively use drugs and alcohol, and/or sell drugs.

Stories of Chaos and Early Familial and Neighborhood Victimization

Most of the interviewees' childhoods were characterized by psychological and emotional abuse or abandonment at minimum and, in the worse cases, by physical and or sexual abuse. Moreover, their fathers' demonstration of street masculinity and performance of violence was often replicated in their own adult lives. Brian was one such man who participated in a murder when he was nineteen years old and after over fifteen years of incarceration still failed to understand why he committed the murder. However, his family life as a boy was characterized by abuse and neglect, perpetrated by his mother and stepfather. When referring to his mother, he explained:

> Mom didn't have many friends; If they spent too much time with her they would grow to hate her. Mom is a pathological liar. When I was eighteen years old she told me she had cancer and when she came home drunk and throwing up, she claimed it was from the chemotherapy. She never had cancer. She threatened to kill herself with a broken glass when I was twelve or thirteen years old. When I was eighteen

years old she got in her car and was threatening to drive herself into a pole so I jumped onto the hood of the car to try to get her to stop. She finally stopped but she had been going sixty miles an hour. Mom used my Social Security number and ran up credit in my name, spent a lot of money. My Dad paid the bill.

His stepdad and the mother apparently physically abused him after he had a two-hundred-person party with drugs and alcohol at home in their absence. "My Step Dad slapped me twice. My Mom jumped on me and kicked me a few times." While clearly a behavioral infraction, the following beating was clearly abusive. Later, Brian's parents placed him in a number of psychiatric facilities after a suicide attempt as well as other behavioral problems. He was convicted of this murder at the age of nineteen, a little more than a year after leaving home.

Similarly, Sam, a forty-year-old white male, reported frequent physical abuse by his mother and stepfather as a boy following his father's death and his return to her custody. He grew up in the context of his mother's drinking problem. Later as a young man her drinking continued. "I was embarrassed by her . . . she was beautiful and she had become a wreck . . . it took me coming to prison to get her to stop in 2003. My mother beat me to death for not drinking with her." By the age of twelve or thirteen he began drinking with her. "Now she's sorry."

Michael, the only self-professed gay man in the study, was physically abused by his mother until the age of twelve, when he moved into the home of his father. What became Michael's lifelong alcoholism was initiated at the same age. Michael was also harassed verbally and psychologically because he was gay throughout high school by peers whom he had believed were his friends. "It hurt me . . . they were my friends."

One thirty-two-year-old white male incarcerated for selling drugs disclosed that one of his most painful memories was as a child when he saw his father kill another man. Under the influence of alcohol, his father at some sort of clubhouse had an altercation and cut another man's throat. A woman removed Justin from the room as soon as the murder occurred. He knew that his father had killed others. Both of his parents were incarcerated at various periods throughout his life for drug use and sales. With regard to these painful memories, he explained: "I try to block it off to protect myself."

Ken is a fifty-one-year-old white man convicted of alcohol-related offenses including domestic violence, grew up in a home characterized by sexual abuse and physical abuse perpetrated by his father. His father physically abused him as well as his older sister. She was also sexually molested by his father, and she later sexually molested Ken when he was six or seven years old. "He beat the hell of out of me . . . he did hit all of the kids . . . used a belt . . . a broom handle . . . his fists. My sister molested me. It was just once or twice. I've been angry all my life . . . all of it, it's just one big knot." Ken also had been arrested for multiple DUIs, intimate violence, arson, and car theft. He had spent thirty-four of his fifty-one years in prison, most of it associated with drinking-related offenses including violating emergency protective orders (thirteen). With regard to the arson he reported:

> I was renting a house that I set on fire . . . I did it because I was angry with the girl I was living with . . . I had just gotten out of a prison . . . I worked everyday and she was a nasty bitch . . . she wouldn't clean. I was drinking at the time and had been seeing her less than a year.

Sebastien, a forty-six-year-old man incarcerated for murdering his wife, was forced by his father to dress as a girl when he was a boy from about age six to nine. Sebastien's father was consistently verbally abusive to both he and his mother. Both a paternal uncle and subsequently a babysitter sexually abused him as a child. Four years prior to his murder of his estranged spouse during a physical altercation, one of his three adolescent girls committed suicide. This suicide and his history of abuse were devastating losses, propelling his inability to cope with sadness or anger.

Damien, a thirty-three-year-old white man, was incarcerated for murdering his mother. His mother sexually and psychologically abused him throughout his childhood. Following this maltreatment, his early adolescence and young adulthood were characterized by extensive drug abuse. Later, Damien became happily married, fathered two children, and had stopped using drugs until he decided to allow his mother back into his life. Subsequently, she sexually abused his daughter. He relayed that one day after his daughter came home following a visit with his mother:

> She was standing in the door shaking and saying my thingy hurts. I knew something wasn't right. . . . Mom sexually abused her. I took Christy and Angela to her mom's house. . . . I told Christy (his wife) I couldn't handle it . . . and she said I had to. I went to work the third shift. . . . I drank a liter of (alcohol) after work and ½ gram of meth. . . . Mom came to the house and said Christy told me what you said [i.e. that she sexually abused his daughter]. Mom said I'll solve the problem and put you guys in jail and take the kids. . . . I told her I wanted to show her something. I went to the bedroom got the gun came back and shot her four times in the head. I picked her body up and put it in the van and took it to the holler. I told my wife. . . . Christy wanted us all to run. . . . I turned myself in. . . . I couldn't see myself running, not my wife and kids. . . . I wanted to going on living . . . even if it meant not seeing them.

Trevor, a thirty-year-old white male, was incarcerated for shaking his baby as well as for several assaults against his live-in female partner. His first stint being incarcerated was at the age of twelve for assaulting his paternal grandmother. He described his grandmother as abusive to him and his siblings. He described himself at that time as "angry." His mother abandoned him and his siblings when he was approximately five years old. Subsequently, his paternal grandmother began acting as the primary caretaker for he and his siblings while his father traveled for business. Unfortunately, Trevor's father knew about the abuse his mother was inflicting on the children and did nothing to intervene. This neglectful fathering is reflected in Trevor's own abandonment of two children with two different women. Additionally, with regard to parental rights: "I voluntarily gave up my rights. . . . I'm not fit." Trevor relayed that one of his most painful experiences was being sexually abused by a paternal uncle by marriage from the time he was five to seven. It is clear that the source of his anger is rooted in his physical and sexual abuse, as well as his physical and psychological abandonment by his father. By extension several other men also revealed feeling and/or knowing that they were inept fathers and they also reported experiences of abusive fathers as boys. For example, one father of three from two different relationships with women sadly stated: "I was no kind of father."

In a like fashion, a thirty-eight-year-old African American man, Jamie, described his neighborhood economic and educational opportunities as nonexistent. "It was a rough city. In my neighborhood you were either the prey or the predator, you had to pick one . . . of course I didn't want to be the prey. I created a balance between the two by thirteen, kids are harsh. . . . I witnessed the bullies and the victims . . . a few times I had to fight for myself." This binary choice was summed up in his description of his primary male role. "My dad lived a compromised lifestyle . . . he was a gang chief, pimp, and a drug dealer. Everybody was terrified of my dad. I was terrified of my dad." Jamie's father was physically abusive to his mother and, on at least one occasion, physically abused him as well. Jamie has been in and out of prison since he was nineteen years old primarily for drug sales. He also was involved in stealing cars and had multiple sexual relationships with girls, especially after being introduced to sex by his gang-involved father when a female was paid to perform oral sex on him when he was only nine years old. "I found out I was just like him (his dad). . . . I had always said, I never want to be like him. I also hit a woman. I exploited my dad's connections . . . they called my dad "Nap," and he says he became "Little Nap." Everybody had expected more of me, but growing up nobody told me how to succeed." Moreover, Jamie was molested again as an adolescent boy of sixteen by an adult woman who kept him as her sexual toy for a number of years, unbeknownst to his own mother.

A sixty-one-year-old black male, Nicolas, who had been incarcerated for over four decades as the result of multiple rape convictions, grew up in a middle-class military home. He argued that all black men were and remain socialized to sexually exploit women. He connected his sexually violent behavior to the physical abuse perpetrated on him by his father. He knew his father experienced multiple incidents of racism in the military and that may have created his father's rage. Nicolas reported that his father utilized physical punishment on him frequently as a form of discipline and he knew this was physical abuse. "He treated me, the oldest differently [than the other siblings] . . . he was angry." However, Nicolas also experienced physical and mental abuse (racism and violence) as a young basketball star in college, which he also associated with his own rage and sense of sexual entitlement.

Two African American men who were incarcerated by eighteen and nineteen years old for drug sales and murder had both experienced significant losses growing up, one the result of an alcoholic drug-selling and womanizing father as well as profound grief following the shooting death of his favorite uncle by the time he was twelve. The second man, Craig, lost his father to death by the time he was twelve. Craig's own metaphor illustrates the psychic pain caused by parental loss and or abandonment:

> It had an effect on mind . . . my mind was too gone then . . . the streets became my father. . . . I smoked a lot of weed and was with a lot of women. It seemed like the world was ending . . . about the same time I lost an auntie too to cancer and she was my favorite aunt. . . . I played it off like nothing was wrong. . . . I blocked everybody out—even my sister's boyfriend tried to talk to me too. . . . I used sex and drugs to feel better. . . . I didn't have to feel the same pain I was feeling.

Craig's insight about his own early life was mirrored by many of the men who had been incarcerated for over a decade, having had a great deal of time to think through their early constraints and later gained some insight into their own pathways leading to criminal involvement. However, Craig revealed what several other young African American men also alluded to with regard to growing up in poor drug-infested neighborhoods. Many young boys became sexual for the first time with adult women who were "crack whores" in the local crack houses. Craig said that it was common for these boys to go the crack house and exchange crack for sex. No men were there, and often there was a woman pimp there. He believed that this allowed the women to "control the interaction." He understood that this was a type of child molestation but that he and the other boys enjoyed it. However, it is important to note here that physically enjoying the sexual contact does not minimize the traumatic impact of this kind of sexual abuse.

Doing Masculinity: Physicality and Sexuality

The need to be the strongest and to compete to be the strongest—not vulnerable as they had been as boys—became a necessity to overcome the psychic pain of that sexual exploitation and abuse. Their sexual innocence having been spoiled led them to also compete to become the most sexually virile as demonstrated by having multiple children with multiple women. Earning money rapidly also became a focal point of these men's lives as it provided power, just as money does in the legitimate economy. One twenty-nine-year-old African American man's statement sums up each man's primary focus from late adolescence through early adulthood: "Fast money, cars, and women." Each man's early experiences with competition became centered on physicality and legitimate sports involvement, as with many boys, but these men were also concurrently involved in fights in school and on the streets. All of the men were involved in physically competitive activities as boys and adolescents and some had opportunities for legitimate success after high school. This is before their involvement in substance abuse or juvenile delinquency, which after entering the system eliminated those chances. One thirty-eight-year-old white man incarcerated for murder remembered that he was good at sports from about age twelve to sixteen. His dream was to be a world-class soccer player and he was a part of a special state team selection. He was the backup goalie. When he was sixteen he was being recruited by a major university but discovered the religious constraints of the school included far too many rules particularly with regard to prohibitions against sexual activity. As a teen he reported that he saw an ideal male as cool guy, flashy, good with a woman, and intimidating to other guys.

Adrian, a thirty-year-old white male with a long history of selling drugs, had a life characterized by promiscuity and physicality associated with the group of men with whom he sold drugs. His shared athleticism and criminality with these men became a key part of his identity. He viewed these other young men and boys as more like his family than his own dysfunctional family of origin. He stated: "Every Sunday we played neighborhood football, basketball, baseball, street-ball, and softball. Some of the guys even played semipro football. We were very athletic, the older guys in the hood also went to watch sports. A couple of us are still here together. I was young. I hung with older guys and chased girls like they did."

Similarly, Eugene focused on his physicality in his youth as well. One such form was formal boxing, which he engaged in with his father as an adolescent. He also played football in the neighborhood and in league basketball. His favorite activities growing up included boxing, basketball, and football. He was a linebacker in high school football for three years. Like Brian, Eugene was offered an athletic scholarship. He claimed that if not for two injuries, one an athletic injury and the other a gunshot wound to one of his knees, he could have had full scholarships to a state university to play football. Rather than being able to perform athletic masculinity, he began to sell drugs at age thirteen or fourteen because: "I wanted to have my own cash—I didn't want to have to ask my mother and father for anything." Eugene engaged in numerous fights in school and outside of school and modeled his behavior on his father's. "I knew I could win the fights and nobody with mess me. Dad put me on that path." He disclosed that his father used to say: "I'd rather die on my feet than live on my knees." This was his dad's idea of how to live as person who demanded respect. People either respected his father or feared him. Readers should recall he saw his father murder a man in a nightclub when he was a small boy. Similarly, physicality, or being able to intimidate and commit violence was also a part of another thirty-two-year-old white male's lifestyle.

Six men saw themselves of victims of possessive, alcoholic, promiscuous, or resentful women. One denied any family-of-origin victimization while the other's early family background was chaotic and abusive. In these cases, rather than the sexual objectification of women, these men's misogynistic attitudes were cloaked in stories of oppression by women. We argue such narratives reflect "familicidal hearts," a second dimension of masculinity that operates as a "haunting" (see Websdale 2010). These men felt lost when rejected by former or current partners in conjunction with other job- or family-related losses. Timothy, a thirty-five-year-old white male, alluded to having problems with women in his narrative: "the girls didn't want anything to do with me . . . [one] after she got pregnant . . . she was too busy partying. . . . I paid child support until he was eighteen. . . . I saw him once at eight . . . her boyfriend cut my tires." He further claimed that during his first marriage, his wife began seeing a rich man. As a result he later became embroiled in an argument with him and was arrested and subsequently stated: "She filed an EPO on me and I didn't know it." In a second marriage that he characterized as motivated by pity on her and later by jealousy and multiple arguments over respective treatment of each person's son; one particular verbal altercation ended after he kicked a locked door down to their home and: "She came at me with a pistol and shot at me once. . . . I took it from her and I shot her four times . . . and she is paralyzed now . . . two years later she died."

Five other men's narratives were characterized by strained relationships with their wives, who sexually betrayed them or left them feeling betrayed, enraged, and or abandoned. Andrew, who was a successful African American businessman, was fifty-five years old at the time of the interview. His story revolved around the loss of a love object leading to a shooting. "I shot my wife . . . she was having an affair. . . . I was going to go to work for [hamburger chain restaurant] and open two stores. . . . I discovered that she wanted to divorce me on the phone . . . she left a message saying I don't want to be married anymore. . . . I got depressed." Similarly, Garrett, a fifty-three-year-old African American man, was incarcerated for murdering his estranged wife. He explained that she actually died of subarachnoid hemorrhage, but he acknowledged that he "lost it" and beat her up. However, he denied actually striking her in the head. Prior to this, Garrett had discovered that his wife had been prostituting herself. Immediately preceding his attack on her, he found her in a hotel room with one of her clients. Garrett was neglected by his mother as a boy and placed into the custody of his father. He described his mother as much like his wife, a practicing alcoholic who was a "philanderer." These men also worked legitimately throughout most of their adult lives before becoming incarcerated. Given this group of men's legitimate pursuit of normative masculinity, one relationship with one woman at a time, and legitimate jobs if not careers, we argue that the elimination of one of these alone or both, clearly resembles Websdale's (2010) findings with regard to men who are haunted by a significant loss of identity when these traditionally enacted forms of masculinity erode or are perceived to be taken from them.

CONCLUSION

These twenty-five incarcerated men were physically and sexually abused as children, often by their parents or other close family members. Traumatized boys, like traumatized girls, often become sexually promiscuous and substance abusers unable to form healthy pro-social relationships with others. These traumatized boys and their parents before them needed psychological treatment and our social services and mental health facilities failed them all miserably. In the context of a culture of masculinity demanding successful physical and economic performances, such damaged young men have few other choices than to act out their pain and effectively reproduce it to feel as though they have some control over it. We are continuously victimizing these young men in prison settings where they have little opportunity to receive the help they need. Our boys are in trouble, constrained by outdated caveman-like social expectations of stoicism and strength that are only available in their youth. We must improve our ability to salvage our children who, without the breadth and depth of genuine parental love and nurturing, make more interpersonal violence and more children without loving fathers.

FOUR

The Parent as Paradoxical Victim

*Adolescent to Parent Violence and
Contested Victimization*

Rachel Condry

What does it mean to be a victim? Why is this status conferred on some and denied to others? This chapter has a dual purpose: to explore the experiences of parents on the receiving end of violence from their own children, and to consider what their uncertain position in relation to the status of victim and the politics of blame can tell us about the meaning of victimization and its conditional nature. The processes through which we come to assign victim status and come to understand individuals and groups as "victims" are complex and claims to the status of victim are often evolving, contested, and provisional.

The chapter draws upon data from a three-year ESRC-funded study of adolescent to parent violence (APV) in the UK which sought to understand the different ways this complex form of family violence is understood, focusing on the experiences of parents and young people who live with violence and on how reported cases are managed within the criminal justice system. The Oxford APV study found that this form of family violence was a significant problem, though largely unrecognized in the official realm of policy, where parent victims remained invisible. The chapter explores the contested victim status of these parents who clearly suffer harm, but, because of powerful moral, cultural, and legal notions of parental responsibility, struggle with recognition of their plight. The case of adolescent to parent violence illustrates vividly the importance of a critical victimology that questions the construction of the status of victim, the visibility of suffering, the complexity of human interaction, and the need to fully understand the lived realities of those experiencing suffering and the hidden processes that contribute to producing the victims that we see and do not see (Walklate 2007, 48).

THE INTERPRETIVE POWER OF THE STATUS OF "VICTIM"

The social processes through which claims to victim status are mobilized and honored—and the descriptive processes through which victim status is assigned—are the focus of Holstein and Miller's interactional approach, which advocates bracketing the rather simplistic question of who "is" and who "isn't" a victim, and to try instead to grasp the meaning of victimhood to those who claim (and reject) it, the processes through which claims and counterclaims are (and are not) honored, and the consequences of those processes for people's lives (Holstein and Miller 1990, 103). This approach has particular utility in the case of adolescent to parent violence—the status of victim is both claimed and rejected, by both the parents themselves and by those with whom they interact—in that it is contingent, varies across time and place, and has one foot firmly grounded in a moral discourse about the family and parenting and the other foot grounded (though somewhat less firmly) in a normative discourse about domestic violence. The parent is a "paradoxical victim" in cases of adolescent to parent violence and this chapter aims to unpack the processes at work.

The label "victim" has enormous interpretive power and the act of describing someone as a victim or claiming to be a victim oneself signifies important qualities: "Calling someone a victim encourages others to see how the labeled person has been harmed by forces beyond his or her control, simultaneously establishing the 'fact' of injury and locating responsibility for damage outside the 'victim'" (Holstein and Miller 1990, 106). Ascribing the status of victim provides "interpretive instructions" to others about "how they should understand persons, circumstances, and behaviours under consideration" (ibid., 107). As Holstein and Miller explain, the status of "victim" can deflect or remove responsibility from a person; it can assign causes or identify the source of harm by designating its opposite, the victimizer; it can specify responses or remedies, that a person is deserving of help or compensation or that another should be sanctioned or provided restitution; and it can account for personal failings or not living up to expectations which, it is said, might have been otherwise were it not for this victim status, so preserving the personal integrity of the person to whom the status is assigned (ibid.). The term "victim" therefore signifies a number of characteristics, including suffering harm beyond one's own control, deserving help, and a blamelessness for one's own fate which often implies—implicitly or explicitly—concomitant blame assigned to the victimizer.

To Holstein and Miller's interactional approach we can add a more critical perspective which takes account of structural constraints and processes, relationships of power, and situates and understands claims to victim status within certain sociocultural conditions. In the case of APV, the power of the state to obscure or render visible particular forms of suffering and to convey strong normative constructions of family life is particularly striking.

THE PROBLEM OF ADOLESCENT TO PARENT VIOLENCE

Until very recently, adolescent to parent violence was a form of family violence that was widely recognized by those that worked with young people and families "on the ground," but largely absent from academic discourse (particularly in the UK) and from the policy realm. Since 2008, it has slowly begun to garner greater attention with a number of academic publications, the development of a small number of programs working specifically with the problem, and the first recognition of the problem in government policy.

The Oxford APV study is the first large-scale study of APV in the UK. It took as its starting point a broad definition of APV to include "physical violence, threats of violence and criminal damage towards parents/carers by their adolescent children," with a wide age range of thirteen to nineteen years to capture the social range of adolescence rather than limiting focus to that of the youth justice system. Fieldwork for the study was carried out over three years, from 2010 to 2013, and included an analysis of all cases reported to the Metropolitan Police in one year; analysis of one-hundred Police Case Files (fifty from London Metropolitan Borough, fifty from a Home County force); and interviews with 117 people: thirty-seven parents (thirty-two mothers, five fathers); eighteen young people (ten sons, eight daughters); forty-one practitioners (youth justice, parenting, domestic violence, and other experts); and twenty-one police officers (in two forces).

Our analysis of Metropolitan police data was the first analysis of cases of adolescent to parent violence reported to the police in the UK and as far as we are aware, the first published analysis of official data. We found 1,892 cases reported to police and defined as offenses where the perpetrator was thirteen to nineteen years old and the victim was a parent in the London Metropolitan Police area in a one-year period: 2009–2010. This provided some of the first evidence from the UK that this hidden and complex form of family violence exists and, as such, is in need of formal recognition and response. Within these recorded cases, son-to-mother violence was most common: 87 percent of suspects were male and 77 percent of victims were female. However, it was not exclusively so, and these figures might also represent reporting patterns rather than actual patterns of experience. However, our findings do suggest that APV is a gendered problem (see Condry and Miles 2014).

From our interviews with parents, young people, and practitioners, we found that parents experiencing violence from their children find it very difficult to get support. There are only a handful of very small, localized programs that specifically address APV across the UK. Parents in our study described a desperate search for help, often over many years, but many felt that their plight was ignored or misunderstood. Parents find it very hard to speak up about abuse from their own child. They experience stigma and shame and feel as if they are to blame for their child's actions and we suspect that cases reported to the police represent the tip of the iceberg of this form of family violence. Most parents do not report their child to the police, for fear of the consequences for their child. Furthermore, there are few escape routes for parents experiencing APV. Most of the routes available to victims of intimate partner violence are not appropriate in this situation. A parent is very unlikely, for example, to move away from the child into a refuge and break all ties with that child.

Why children are violent toward their parents is complex and needs to be understood in terms of a variety of factors including psychological development, cultural acceptability, and the specifics of individual cases and range of pathways that lead to the problem. There is no one simple explanation for APV. Families we spoke to described a range of other difficulties in which they often sought to locate the source of the violence, including substance abuse, mental health problems, learning difficulties, previous family history of domestic violence, and self-harm. There were some families, however, who could not explain why the violence had happened. They had raised other children who had not displayed any of the same problems and were at a loss to know why this had happened in their family.

APV is a problem that stretches across the social spectrum in society. Some of the families in our study were struggling on benefits and in overcrowded housing, while others had professional jobs and high incomes. This may be even more of a hidden problem for families who can afford to seek private therapeutic interventions. Some ethnic groups were overrepresented in the police statistics, though this may simply reflect general overrepresentation of BME groups in the criminal justice system (see Condry and Miles 2014 for further discussion).

THE PARENT EXPERIENCING ADOLESCENT VIOLENCE

Experiencing violence from an adolescent child can be a lonely and exhausting experience. Many parents we spoke to described feeling "burnt out" and had often been contending with difficulties for years before seeking help. If they did seek help, it was difficult to find organizations or programs with specific expertise, support, and advice. Parents in our study had experienced a wide range of different forms of violence from their adolescent children. Sometimes this violence could be at a serious level and lead to significant injury:

> [He] hits me, kicks me, throws me down, and he's six feet tall now, he's a strong lad. I've had some awful injuries. (Mother, son aged sixteen).
> I was vulnerable [while driving] and then he tried to strangle me then with my seatbelt and I used to have, wear chains around my neck, I don't anymore because he cut my neck open with my chain and [. . .] he'd kick me on the back of the head with his feet. (Mother, son aged fourteen)

In other families, violence tended to be lower-level, but prolonged across time:

> [H]e's destroyed his bedroom. He had a wardrobe and chest of drawers and everything and they got destroyed. Cupboards that got destroyed. Books and toys that got broken. Doors that got holes punched into them. He's ripped my door off its hinges twice in temper. (Mother, son aged sixteen)
> He's lashed out at me, he's broken ornaments, he's broken glass, he's punched a TV out. He's just way out of control when he gets like that. I've just gotta just disappear and let him get on with it and then clear up the mess afterwards. (Mother, son aged thirteen)

Parents described this lower-level violence, including criminal damage and threats of violence, as having a deep impact upon their lives. First, they found it particularly difficult living with the constant threat of violence and not knowing when it might erupt, as this mother explained:

> It could be anything, absolutely anything. You never knew. We were always walking on eggshells, all of us. (Mother, son aged fourteen)

The expression "walking on eggshells" was used often by parents and has appeared in a number of international studies of APV. Parents frequently reported feeling as if they must tread carefully and needing to moderate their own behavior to avoid violence. It could also be hard to predict when or why violence might occur:

> I mean it could be anything. I mean he'd be sitting there quite happy one minute, and then the next minute he'd just flip, and it could be over the slightest little thing. If I've walked across the front of the TV

and he's missed just that second, he'd have a go at that. (Mother, son
aged thirteen)

Secondly, damage to the home and to possessions was particularly significant for parents and remained a constant reminder of the violence. Parents in social housing described how they could not repeatedly report
damage and request repairs from the local authority or housing association. Parents in private housing might also not be able to afford to keep
repairing damage to their property. Even if they could afford to pay, the
embarrassment of explaining constant damage to repair services meant
they sometimes chose to live with broken windows, doors, and damage
to walls. Indeed, in recognition of the impact of this damage on families'
lives, a website dedicated to collating research and practice developments on APV has been named "Holes in the Wall."[1]

The impact of violence upon parents—and other family members, including siblings—can be severe and multifaceted. Following Spalek's
(2006) distinction between types of harm, parents can be said to experience a psychological, emotional, behavioral, physical, and financial impact. Psychological harms include fundamentally altered conceptions of
self and family relationships, removing any sense of safety or security in
the home, loss of a sense of control, self-blame, searching for meaning
and trying to understand why the violence had happened, and struggling
with mixed feelings toward the violent child. The emotional impact described by parents included feelings of fear, helplessness, confusion, anxiety, shame, guilt, and anger. Many parents described symptoms of stress
and physical health problems, depression, and other mental health problems. The behavioral impact included changes in their own behavior and
lifestyle: curtailing one's own behavior to try to avoid violence, changing
how a young person is parented, avoiding friends or family members, or
restricting other visitors to the house. The physical impact in the case of
assault is somewhat obvious, but other physical impacts might also include the worsening of health problems as a result of the stress of living
with violence, or even self-inflicted harm; we heard from some practitioners about mothers experiencing APV who had attempted suicide and
in one case had sadly been successful.

There may be a direct financial impact if a young person steals from a
parent, or makes unrealistic financial demands backed up by the threat of
violence or conflict. Parent-adolescent relationships are often characterized by conflict over money, but in the case of APV, this can take on a
more serious nature and we heard stories of parents taking on considerable debt rather than challenge their child or refuse a demand. A financial
impact can also stem from the damage to property and the home described above. Some parents felt unable to work or said they could not do
so because of health problems leading to a loss or reduction in income. A

young person might also use financial demands to lever control over a parent, as this mother explained:

> He tells me who I can be friends with. Or he tries to. If I say that I'm going out, for a night out, it's almost like I have to ask his permission first. . . . But then I say I'm going out, he then tries to tell me "Well hang on a minute, you can't go out. You told me you had no money to buy me this. So therefore you cannot go out, Mum." . . . He tries to control, control every situation, even down to the fact of, you know, what time he comes in. (Mother aged forty-two, son aged sixteen)

Not all young people sought to exercise control over their parent to such a strong degree, but many did exhibit forms of coercively controlling behavior that had similar features to that seen in adult domestic violence and abuse.

Abuse could also take the form of prolonged verbal attacks and the use of strong and sometimes sexualized language. Parents described this constant barrage as particularly hard to live with as described vividly by this mother:

> She can be very verbally abusive. . . . These are the sort of things that are said to me all the time. . . . "No one likes you. No wonder no one likes you. You're not my mother." At the same time her calling me by my Christian name. And you know that's hurtful because I will say "I'm Mum or Mummy to you." "You're not my mother. Fat bitch. Cow. Loony. Loony, mad bitch. Mad cow. Control freak. Lazy bitch. Lazy cow. Go and die. Only need your money and your lift. Go and sit in your grave. Are you mad? You are completely mad. You can't cook. Cheap shitty food. Effing hate you. Wish you were dead. Poison dwarf . . . because you did nothing with your life. What exams have you got?" I take all Dad's money. "Just do the housework, do your job." You know, she's ashamed of me, ashamed of the house. "As soon as I can I'm going to move out and I never want to see you again." I get called a depressed bitch. I've got special needs. What would I know about sport? I'm a fat bitch. "Effing whore." What have I ever achieved? (Mother of daughter aged seventeen)

A LACK OF RECOGNITION

Clearly, parent victims of adolescent violence experience harm. However, there is a lack of recognition of this harm from their immediate friends and family, from the agencies from which they seek help or intervention, and from government and policy-makers. Parents often felt isolated from friends or other family members and experienced a lack of understanding about the problem of APV in their everyday lives. This may partly be because a parent does not speak out, given the stigma and shame associated with this problem, as this youth justice worker explained:

> So stigmatizing, isn't it, for them? Because. . . . They, if they tell their family or friends, they don't really get it. And it's a bit like, "why are you putting up with that? Why don't you do [this]?" Yeah, so there's no empathy about what they're actually experiencing. (Youth justice worker 12)

Sometimes a parent's own feelings of guilt and shame and an anticipated negative reaction from others served to silence them. This mother described the guilt she felt despite being told it was not her fault:

> Q: What kind of effect has her behavior had on you, would you say?
> A: It's awful, because I feel so guilty.
> Q: Really?
> A: Yeah, I do. It's silly. People keep telling me it's silly, because it's not my fault. But I do blame myself, you know. Where did I go wrong? Could I have done something different? You know, did I bring them up wrong? (Grandmother who has raised and is primary carer for grand-daughter aged fifteen)

Reactions reported by parents from their immediate family and friends were therefore mixed; but, even where a sympathetic response was received, this was rarely followed by useful support.

Parents described numerous attempts to seek help, which were often futile. A few more fortunate families discovered a specialist program in their local area; however, these are few and far between and parents usually had to rely upon other services for intervention. Parents spoke about being reluctant to call the police; for those that did, the response they received was again mixed, with some officers providing an appropriate and helpful response while others demonstrated a lack of understanding of the problem of APV and could even be quite judgmental, not understanding the parents as victims of violence (see Miles and Condry 2015a for further discussion of the police response). As one IDVA[2] explained, parental feelings of guilt or responsibility also interfered with their willingness to call the police:

> Q: What do they tell you about that and the kind of decisions to ring the police or not?
> A: Well they just think, they see that it's their fault that their relationship with the child is broken. And by ringing the police, they feel that they'll damage it even further. So they're just completely against doing that. They do want help and they want support, but it's difficult for them to know what support's out there. (IDVA, Expert 7)

Understanding of the problem of APV is increasing within public services, but it is still a form of family violence that falls "through the cracks" of different services, none of which have parent victims of adolescent violence as their primary focus (Hunter et al. 2010). For example, children's services focus primarily on safeguarding and child protection issues and if a child is the perpetrator of violence but otherwise not at

risk, they often perceive this to be outside of their remit. Parenting services—particularly those within youth justice services—have the primary
aim of teaching improved parenting skills in order to reduce offending
and indeed often construct the parent as responsible for the young person's offending (a point to which I will return).

Furthermore, APV is only just emerging onto the policy agenda as a
"named" problem and recognized by those in the policy realm. Until
very recently, APV was completely absent from youth justice, policing,
education, and health policy. This began to change in 2013 with the introduction of a new, revised definition of domestic violence. Prior to 2013,
violence from children toward their parents was excluded from the cross-
governmental definition of domestic violence, which only applied to perpetrators over the age of eighteen. In 2013, a new definition was introduced which had the effect of lowering the age from eighteen to sixteen
(Home Office 2013). Under this new definition, any incidents of APV
involving children aged sixteen or over fall under the category of domestic violence and should be responded to as such. APV was also acknowledged in a 2014 Her Majesty's Inspectorate of Constabulary (HMIC) report into the police response to domestic violence, which clearly states
that the domestic abuse definition includes "child to parent violence"
(HMIC 2014, 29).

An important development for the official recognition of APV was its
inclusion in 2014 in the government-led "Violence Against Women and
Girls" (VAWG) strategy, which focuses on reducing domestic violence
and abuse. It also includes APV in its latest action plan with an objective
to improve local services for domestic violence and abuse victims
through developing and disseminating "information for practitioners
working with children and families on how to identify and address the
risks posed by adolescent to parent violence" (Home Office 2014, 27). In
March 2015, the Home Office published an information guide (produced
in collaboration with academics and expert practitioners) for practitioners across a range of public services on how to respond to adolescent to
parent violence and abuse, which draws upon the findings of the Oxford
study (Home Office 2015). APV can therefore now be said to have made it
onto the public policy agenda and to have caught the attention of government. However, this is at a very early stage and it is not yet clear whether
it will continue to be addressed or what form this might take; there are,
for example, no additional funds as yet allocated to addressing the problem of APV.

THE PARENT AS PARADOXICAL VICTIM

Parents experiencing violence do elicit sympathy on occasions and there
were examples in our study of kindness and supportive actions from

friends and family. However, the odd examples of sympathy were often drowned out—or at the very least muffled—by blame, whether real or perceived. In contemporary society parents are made accountable, both morally and legally, for their children's deviant behavior. In the case of adolescent to parent violence, parents are in the curious position of being held accountable for behavior of which they are also the victims. They are therefore "paradoxical victims," condemned for their failures while simultaneously suffering often quite significant harm.

Holding parents responsible or making them accountable takes a number of forms. Ideas about poor parenting being the root cause of numerous societal ills have proliferated in recent decades. Parents are seen as wholly responsible for who young people become with a growth in "intensive parenting" (Hays 1996) in response to demands that parents train, educate, and surveil their children in ever increasing ways. Furedi (2008) has described the degree of responsibility leveled at parents as "the myth of parental determinism," which permeates all spheres of social life and has become a key focus of government policy in recent decades. The image of the feckless or failing parent has huge cultural power and is regularly exploited in political discourse.

Understanding how patterns of familial shame and blame are attributed when serious crime occurs is also illuminating in this context. When a violent crime occurs, relatives of the offender are caught up in a "web of shame" based on notions of "kin contamination and kin culpability" (Condry 2007), which takes particular forms in the case of parents. First, they are subject to "kin contamination" constructed around their familial association with their child, sharing a household and being seen—in a looser sense—as somehow the same, and by their genetic connection to the child, which can provoke primitive notions of bad blood. A child is seen as forever part of their parent, particularly a mother who has given birth to them and raised them throughout their life. "Kin culpability" is based upon blame for omission (something that they ought to have done—for example, that they should have been able to do something to stop the violence); commission (something they did do—in this case, raise their child to be violent, or provoke it in the moment); and continuation (that they are somehow to blame for their plight for continuing to support their child or allowing him or her to live at home) (Condry 2007). Blaming the victim—in this case the parent—has echoes of ideas about victim precipitation (Wolfgang 1958) and indeed parents may be blamed for their role in an individual incident of violence. However, the blame leveled at parents runs deeper and is often more fundamentally based upon their responsibility for who their child has become.

Parents experiencing APV might also provoke strong reactions and a lack of public understanding because their plight holds up a mirror to our own fears and anxieties around the family and around adolescence in particular. As Nussbaum has argued, stigmatizing others makes us feel better about our own weaknesses: "in shaming people as deviant, the shamers set themselves up as a 'normal' class above the shamed, and thus divide society into ranks and hierarchies" (2004, 231–232). It is by judging and shaming others that we address our own uncertainties and anxieties; this is particularly strong in relation to the family:

> The family is also an area of great anxiety and lack of control. Families often contain our most intimate relationships, through which we search for the meaning of life. And yet there is much hostility, ambivalence, and anxiety involved in many, if not most, family relationships. Thus shame once again enters the picture: the roles we assign ourselves in the family, as "the good father," "the good mother," are cherished and comforting norms, and precious aspects of people's attempts to define themselves as normal, precisely because there is so much at stake when control is lost and something unexpected happens. People are typically aware of deficiency in their family roles, and thus they need all the more anxiously to shore up their purity. (Nussbaum 2004, 262)

We might surmise that people's attempts to define themselves as good and "normal" parents are even more anxiety-ridden when it comes to parenting through adolescence, a time that usually involves some parent-child conflict. Hearing about cases of APV might provoke our own fears about wayward teens, family conflict, and parental determinism. One middle-class professional mother who had not experienced APV recounted an incident to us that occurred with her adolescent son. In an argument, they had ended up standing very close together, or "nose to nose" as she described it, and for a second she imagined that their situation could so easily tip into physical conflict. It did not—but it was a moment that had stayed vividly in her memory and had come to mind when she had heard about our study. She retold this story to suggest the normality of this type of conflict and how she felt fortunate that in her case, the conflict had defused—"there but for the grace of God go I." We can reflect on what might have stopped this tipping over; an underlying respect? A lack of previous experience of violence in the family? Self-control? But, ultimately, APV is a complex phenomenon with myriad causes and we cannot be certain why her son teetered on the brink of violence but steadied before the fall.

The power of the state to normatively construct the family and to intervene into the lives of those deemed outside of this construction is particularly important here. Parental responsibility has been enshrined in a number of laws and social policies that explicitly make parents accountable for their children's behavior. Reforms under the New Labour government centered on the individual responsibility of young people and their families, along with the birth of a new form of parenting expertise in the shape of parenting practitioners working within youth justice. Over the coming years, a new body of knowledge about parenting developed which constructed parents of young offenders and parent-child relationships in very particular ways. The focus was firmly on "problem families" and a "parenting deficit" as a cause of youth offending. Parents who could not or would not face their responsibilities and control their children would be made to do so, which, as Muncie has argued, ultimately resulted in criminalizing "inadequate parenting" (Muncie 1999) and failed to take account of the effects of structural inequalities and other influences on young people.

The Parenting Order specifically holds parents directly responsible for crimes committed by their children and was introduced in the Crime and Disorder Act of 1998 and further widened in its use in the Anti-Social Behaviour Act of 2003. The Parenting Order is a civil order, though a parent who does not comply without reasonable excuse commits a criminal offense. The continuing assumption underlying parental responsibility laws is that parents of young offenders can be forced to accept responsibility with court orders and financial penalties (Arthur 2005). These measures also make assumptions about the degree to which parents can control their children's behavior: "the attribution of blame to parents for their children's behaviour up to the age of 16 underestimates children's independence and overestimates the ability of parents to control the behavior of young people as they grow older" (Henricson and Bainham 2005, 103).

The picture is further muddied by a dual and contradictory state of holding *both* parents and children accountable for offenses. There are competing conceptualizations of responsibility and blame within youth justice as parents have been made increasingly accountable while, concurrently, the criminal age of responsibility has effectively been lowered to ten with the abolition of *doli incapax* in the Crime and Disorder Act of 1998. Child offenders have therefore been made responsible at a younger age, while at the same time, their parents have been held ultimately responsible for their offenses (Condry and Miles 2012). Furthermore, this is something that is gendered—parenting orders are usually given to mothers.

Measures that hold parents directly accountable for their children's offending seem particularly inappropriate when that parent is the primary victim, yet many parents are subject to these measures and all parents are aware that they exist as a possibility. There is no data available on the characteristics of parents who are given parenting orders and their family histories, or the degree to which they are issued varies between different local authorities. Youth justice services will try hard to work with parents in a voluntary capacity if possible (though their consent is within the context of the possibility of the punitive measure hanging over them). A few parents in our study had been subject to parenting orders or other parental accountability measures while others expressed concern that this might be on the horizon.

Making parents accountable for their children's truanting is a measure that has increased in recent years. Ministry of Justice figures, obtained by the Press Association after a Freedom of Information request, revealed that in 2014, 16,430 people were prosecuted for failing to ensure their children went to school in England, an increase of more than 3,000—or 25 percent—on 2013. More than three-quarters of these parents (12,479) were found guilty of truancy offenses; the courts issued 9,214 fines, averaging £172. Eighteen jail sentences were given for truancy in 2014—compared with just seven in 2013. Ten of those jailed and more than half (58 percent) of those fined for a child missing school were women (BBC Education 2015). This is therefore a relatively common measure and one that parents in our study feared. The problem was recognized by a clinical psychologist that we interviewed:

> But this kind of takes you right back to where we started, with [the problem of] people being able to conceptualize this difficulty [of APV]. Because I've actually come across cases where a mum who's being violently assaulted by her teenage son, who's then been prosecuted because the son won't go to school. And there is no way she can actually make him. And of course anyone saying "well she can't do that," that's deemed as a failure on her part, you know. So . . . the services are not set up to actually take these sort of issues into account at all, you know. (Clinical Psychologist in Youth Offending Service, Expert 12)

This illuminates both the misunderstanding of the circumstances of parents experiencing APV and the pervasive and often misplaced assumption about the ability of parents to exercise control over their adolescent children.

Becoming a victim can be seen as a process, firmly rooted in how others define us and in how we define ourselves (Rock 2002), and involving processes of identification, labeling, and recognition (Mythen 2007). As we saw in the introduction, this interpretive process signifies suffering harm beyond one's own control, being deserving of help, and blamelessness for one's own fate. Parents experiencing APV can be seen to experience harm, but it is not usually seen to be beyond their control or something for which they are wholly blameless.

The process of becoming a victim is also closely linked with vulnerability (Walklate 2011). It is notable that parents experiencing APV are not ordinarily deemed to have a preexisting "inherent vulnerability" (Walklate 2011), which could for example be based on age, frailty, or mental capacity. Parents are constructed as more powerful than their children, physically stronger, and better resourced. A useful comparison can be made in this respect to the problem of elder abuse, where the victim is deemed to have an inherent vulnerability because of their age and their victim status is therefore not paradoxical. Elder abuse is a much more clearly recognized problem both in the public consciousness and within the academic and policy realm. This might also be understood as a "politics of pity" (Aradau 2004, in Walklate 2011) wherein government strategies legitimate or delegitimate the suffering of others as worthy of policy action. Victims need to be seen as deserving and worthy of attention and, until very recently, parents experiencing APV have not been deemed as such.

It is interesting to note that space has opened up for the parent victim of APV to emerge onto the public agenda through "piggybacking" the government's Violence against Women and Girls (VAWG) agenda (Miles and Condry 2015). Although as has been noted, APV is a gendered problem—23 percent of victims in the cases reported to the Metropolitan Police were male and 13 percent of perpetrators were female (Condry and Miles 2014)—so it is not exclusively a male-to-female phenomenon. The VAWG agenda has a very specific gendered discourse of adult perpetrated domestic violence with clear demarcations of female victim and male offender status. It may be that a structural route to impute inherent vulnerability and clear victim status is through the discourse of women's patriarchal victimization by men. This might have utility for recognizing the harm of this form of familial violence, but is less useful for recognizing the youth of the perpetrator and the specific status of the parent-child relationship.

BLAME IS NOT A ZERO-SUM GAME

In considering blame and culpability in the context of APV, the age of the adolescent and their kin relationship—as the child of the victim—needs to be held in focus. First, although we have an age of criminal responsibility in England and Wales of ten years old, this is widely criticized and a strong case made for the need for it to be raised on a number of grounds including capacity, human rights, incompatibility with other countries in Europe and elsewhere, social harm, and the need to ensure best outcomes for children in conflict with the law and the wider community (Goldson 2013). There is not space to pursue these grounds in any depth in this chapter, but we might at least state that children who commit crimes of familial violence should not be held accountable in the same way as adult perpetrators of familial violence. Their circumstances are different: their histories and the explanations for why they have become violent, their adolescent developing brains and level of maturity, and the more positive prospect that they might actually grow out of violence as they mature into adulthood—all the more likely with support and appropriate intervention.

A child in the family being violent toward a parent will have shared a history with that parent going back to birth. At one point, the child will have been completely dependent upon the parent for their very existence, needing the parent to provide care in order to survive. Gradually some independence will have developed as the child slowly begins to separate from the parent—the source of much conflict in adolescence as this process accelerates—and will be in the midst of this process when APV is occurring. In "normal" or nonviolent circumstances the adolescent child will remain dependent on the parent, though to a decreasing degree, and the parent will retain control of finances, important decisions, and so on; and this might be pictured as a continuous negotiation across the years until the child finally becomes an independent adult. In the case of APV, something might be awry with this process and the balance of power can look quite different.

Furthermore, we should note that there are numerous pathways to the problem of APV, and families experiencing it may have complex histories. In some families there may be a history of previous violence. A child might have witnessed domestic violence and seen their parent (often the mother) as a victim in the past. This is a fairly common phenomenon and in the course of research one director of a support organization in the United States explained how they call APV "domestic violence by proxy" to describe this particular family history (again, interesting because the space opening up to understand the parent as a victim is in allying their victimization in APV to their victimization in earlier adult-perpetrated domestic violence and situating the blame for APV with the perpetrator of the earlier domestic violence). However, this is far from the only explanation or pathway. Children might themselves have experienced violence either from the parent who is now the victim, or from another adult in the family, or might have experienced sexual abuse, or neglect. Children might be violent toward a parent in defense, or to protect a nonviolent parent. The violence might also be explained by other factors, such as emerging mental health problems, learning difficulties, substance abuse, and so on. Yet, other parents we interviewed described being at a loss to find a reason, having raised other children who had not been violent.

Patterns of blame and culpability in APV are therefore complex and there are many gray areas, in contrast to the black-and-white constructions of parenthood and childhood in common discourse. In these constructions, children are vulnerable and innocent, intrinsically blameless, while parents are the more powerful and more likely to perpetrate harm upon a child. We are used to the more common notion of child victims and adult perpetrators and the problem of child abuse has high public visibility.

There is more of a fluidity between innocence and culpability in reality, rather than fixed categories, yet as McAlinden has argued in relation to the problem of child sexual abuse, the victim/offender dyad is constructed in terms of a bifurcation of "innocent" and "blameworthy" and hierarchical understandings of what constitutes a legitimate victim or offender status in official and popular discourse (McAlinden 2014).

O'Malley (2004) describes relationships between offenders and victims in actuarial justice as managed in zero-sum terms with victims and offenders set against each other in an all-or-nothing binary. Just as this is the case for the risk that offenders represent to victims, so it is also true for representations of blame and innocence (McAlinden 2014), and has particular salience with the complexities of APV. What Rock (1998b) describes as "strong, antagonistic archetypes of victim and offender" do not capture this complexity.

If we are to avoid zero-sum notions of blame, then we make space for interventions that can recognize the harm caused by violence and the suffering of a victim of violence without resorting to either notions of wholly innocent and passive victims or wholly culpable offenders (who of course may also be suffering—or have suffered—in a number of ways). Therefore, the recognition of the parent victim's status in APV should not imply a piling on of culpability to the other side of the victim-offender dyad and need not lead to a quid pro quo punitiveness for the young person. We must be able to hold on to this tension and to the complexities of real family lives for interventions and support for families experiencing APV to be effective—and not paralyzed by the paradoxical status of the parent victim.

In conclusion, the case of adolescent to parent violence illuminates some of the complexities of the construction of victimization and the need for a critical victimology that interrogates the processes underlying these constructions. Holstein and Miller drew our attention to the interpretive power of the label "victim" and the need to question the meaning of victimhood to those who claim and reject it, the processes through which claims and counterclaims are honored or rejected, and the consequences of these processes for people's lives (Holstein and Miller 1990, 103). As we have seen, the parent victim of adolescent violence has a paradoxical status, suffering harm (though not always visible) but not seen as wholly blameless for their fate. The blame leveled at parents is partly grounded in an everyday discourse of parental determinism, but also entrenched in policies of parental accountability and state intervention into family life. Parent victims of adolescent violence are disempowered and find it difficult to resist the interpretive processes through which they are defined. The case of adolescent to parent violence demonstrates the need to explore the ways in which some forms of suffering are rendered visible or invisible and the power to define what is deemed a problem in need of response and to bestow (or deny) the status of "victim." As McGarry and Walklate have argued:

> critical victimology strives to conceive of the victim as a product of the interaction between the cultural and ideological in particular socioeconomic circumstances. The agenda implied by a critical victimology takes the power of the state seriously as a self-interested arbiter of the

victims (and suffering) that we see and do not see, but whose interests may vary across time and space. (2015, 14)

The case of adolescent to parent violence shows the importance of creating a space in which hidden and complex forms of victimization and suffering can come to the fore and be fully understood as products of their cultural, ideological, and socio-structural contexts.

NOTES

1. See http://holesinthewall.co.uk/.
2. Independent Domestic Violence Advocate. See www.safelives.org.uk.

FIVE

Victims of Hate

Thinking Beyond the Tick-Box

Neil Chakraborti

Hate crime has become an increasingly familiar term within the domains of scholarship, policy, and activism as the harm associated with bigotry and prejudice continues to pose complex challenges for societies across the world. In many respects, the prioritization of hate crime has led to an enhanced level of recognition for victims of hate and improved practical and emotional support to address their needs. At the same time, however, this progress has been undermined by a tendency among hate crime professionals and researchers to overlook particular types of victims, particular strands of victimization, and particular features of the victimization experience.

Drawing from an emerging body of interdisciplinary scholarship, including the author's own body of research and policy engagement, this chapter calls for a more nuanced approach to thinking about hate crime victimization. It suggests that the uncritical, face-value assumptions often made about hate crime victims have overshadowed a range of significant issues, including the experiences of "marginal" groups of victims, the diverse forms and impacts of targeted hate and prejudice, and the ways in which identity characteristics intersect with one other and with other situational factors and context, to exacerbate victims' perceived vulnerability. In so doing, this chapter makes the case for improved recognition, improved research, and improved responses in order to address the lived realities of hate crime victimization.

With problems of prejudice and targeted violence continuing to pose complex challenges for societies across the world, "hate crime" has become a politically and socially significant term that cuts across disciplines, across communities, and across borders. As an internationally used term, it has the capacity to promote collective action among a range of different actors, including law-makers, law-enforcers, non-governmental organizations, scholars, students, activists, and "ordinary" citizens, which is designed to support victims of extreme and "everyday" acts of hate. The demand for such action is clear in the context of a now considerable body of evidence, which shows that hate crimes spawn a particular set of harms that distinguish them from other types of crime (Walters 2011; Iganski 2001; Perry 2001). The multiple layers of damage which accrue from hate crimes are described by the Office for Democratic Institutions and Human Rights (2009) in terms of their violation of human rights and equality between members of society; the greater psychological injury and increased feelings of vulnerability inflicted upon the individual victim; the sense of fear and intimidation transmitted to the wider community to which the victim "belongs"; and the security and public order problems that ensue from the widening of potentially explosive social tensions.

To some extent these problems have been acknowledged through a greater prioritization and improved understanding of issues at an academic and policy level. For instance, to avoid becoming sidetracked by the now familiar conceptual ambiguities of hate crime (see, inter alia, Jacobs and Potter 1999), Iganski (2008) refers to the merits of thinking of hate crime as both a policy and a scholarly domain: the first domain where elements of the political and criminal justice systems have converged through a succession of progressive social movements and campaigns to combat bigotry in its various guises and the second where scholars—ostensibly from diverse fields of study but united in their focus upon the synergies and intersections between different forms of discriminatory violence—apply their empirical knowledge to inform effective interventions. Progress within both of these domains has been accompanied by legislative recognition. Within the United Kingdom alone we have seen a series of laws introduced by successive governments covering different forms of hate crime as well as a wealth of criminal justice policy and guidance and relentless campaign group activism relating to various spheres of targeted victimization. These developments have been mirrored across the world, with the United States, Canada, Australia, and many states across Western and Eastern Europe deploying their own sets of laws, which treat hate crime as a substantive offense or offer the option of enhanced penalties for convicted hate crime perpetrators.

Equally, the volume of theoretical and empirical developments in the hate crime field over recent years has helped to create a significantly more nuanced picture of these multilayered and complex offenses. Put simply, we now know more about hate crime than ever before: more about people who suffer hate crime and who perpetrate hate crime; more about the nature, extent, and impact of victimization; and more about the effectiveness, or otherwise, of different interventions. These developments have shaped thinking across a number of academic disciplines, including criminology, psychology, sociology, history, political science, and legal studies; within statutory, voluntary, and private sectors; and among senior figures in political and criminal justice spheres "down" to activists, campaigners, and community volunteers working at a grass-roots level (Chakraborti and Garland 2014).

Despite this progress, there is much about hate crime victimization that remains peripheral to scholars and practitioners. This has implications for the "real-life" value of empirical work and policy formation, and is contingent on how the parameters of hate crime are framed. This becomes clear through reference to the official hate crime figures that are presented by different countries within the Organization for Security and Co-Operation in Europe (OSCE) region. Figures collated by the Office for Democratic Institutions and Human Rights show considerable variations between OSCE member states. For instance, the number of hate crimes recorded by police in England and Wales in 2013 — 47,986 — contrasts markedly with the corresponding numbers for countries such as Germany (4,647), Spain (1,168), Italy (472), and Greece (108) (ODIHR 2014). Evidently, these figures are not an accurate measure by which to gauge the true scale of hate crime in each respective country; they are more a reflection of how hate crimes are defined, recorded, reported, and statistically collated by different states than of any genuine disparity in levels of hate crime. However, while this set of police-recorded figures from England and Wales paints a much more realistic picture than that offered by most other states, it does not begin to paint anything like a full picture. Recent sweeps of the Crime Survey for England and Wales, which accounts for experiences of victimization not necessarily reported to the police, indicate that approximately 278,000 hate crimes are committed each year (Home Office 2013); a figure nearly six times the "official" number cited above. Moreover, and as discussed in due course, the "real" figure of hate crimes taking place is likely to be higher still, as many cases of hate crime are simply not recognized as such by criminal justice agencies, nongovernmental organizations, or by victims themselves.

This point is important because it suggests that our understanding of hate crime victimization is reliant upon the way in which we choose to frame the boundaries of hate crime. This chapter calls for a more critical reevaluation of this process of boundary-framing and challenges the way in which narrow constructions of identity and community have led to the exclusion of a range of significant issues, including the experiences of "marginal" groups of victims; the diverse forms and impacts of targeted hostility; and the ways in which identity characteristics intersect with one another and with other situational factors and context, to exacerbate victims' perceived vulnerability as targets of hate offenses. Before examining those issues in greater depth, this chapter first considers the key features that have shaped conventional approaches to hate crime theorizing and policy formation.

CONVENTIONAL HATE CRIME FRAMEWORKS

Hate crime is a social construct that has been subjected to a myriad of interpretations. There is no universally accepted definition of what a hate crime is and whom it affects, although some laudable attempts to develop a common understanding that can generate workable responses to hate crime have emerged in recent years. One such attempt has come from The Office for Democratic Institutions and Human Rights (ODIHR) whose guidance for OSCE states describes hate crimes as "criminal acts committed with a bias motive" (2009, 16).[1] For ODIHR, this bias does not have to manifest itself as "hate" for the offense to be thought of as a hate crime, nor does "hate" have to be the primary motive. Rather, bias in this sense refers to acts wherein the victim is targeted deliberately because of a "protected characteristic . . . shared by a group, such as 'race,' language, religion, ethnicity, nationality, or any other similar common factor" (2009, 16). Importantly, ODIHR's guidance does not seek to specify which protected characteristics should form the basis of a member state's hate crime policy, aside from making reference to aspects of identity that are "fundamental to a person's sense of self" and to the relevance of "current social problems as well as potential historical oppression and discrimination" (2009, 38).

This broad, pan-national framework for understanding hate crime was developed in response to an increased awareness of hate crime and its associated problems and the pressing need for states, statutory and nongovernmental organizations across Europe, to acknowledge the problem. However—as illustrated by the divergence in hate crime figures collated by different countries referred to above—there is little evidence of a shared understanding of the concept across nations. As such, there remain vastly differing interpretations of what a hate crime is, who the potential victims are, and what type of legislative response is most appropriate (Garland and Chakraborti 2012). To some extent, such inconsistency is inevitable given the way in which different countries' histories have shaped their prioritization of different forms of hate crime. In countries such as Germany, Austria, and Italy, for example, the association of the term "hate crime" with right-wing extremism and anti-Semitism is a legacy of tragic events in the twentieth century, while at the other end of the spectrum, left-wing extremism is also a significant area of concern in some states (European Union Agency for Fundamental Rights 2013a).

Equally, an emphasis on challenging racism in the UK is attributable to the mass migrations from the Caribbean and south Asia to the UK from the late 1940s and well-documented problems of hostility experienced by minority ethnic communities (Bowling 1999). Although a universal consensus on the implementation and prioritization of hate crime policy may be unfeasible, ODIHR's guidance encourages law-makers and law-enforcers to think broadly when formulating responses to hate crime victimization.

Until recently, the key source of UK policy guidance on hate crime came from the Association of Chief Police Officers (ACPO), whose operational definition was enshrined within their guidelines for domestic police forces (ACPO 2000; 2005). These guidelines contained a number of significant features which have shaped contemporary responses to hate crime, including a requirement for all hate incidents to be recorded by the police even if they lack the requisite elements to be classified as a notifiable offense later in the criminal justice process. At the recording stage, any hate incident, whether a prima facie "crime" or not, is to be recorded if it is perceived by the victim or any other person (such as a witness, a family member, or a carer) as being motivated by hostility or prejudice. ACPO guidelines have since been updated by operational guidance issued in May 2014 by the College of Policing: the professional body responsible for setting standards in professional development across English and Welsh police forces. Their guidance provides more detail on a range of issues directly relevant to the recording, investigation, and supervision of hate offenses, and follows a similar set of principles to those outlined in previous ACPO guidelines, not least by referring to terms such as "targeted hostility" and "prejudice" (and not simply 'hate') as motivating factors in the new guidance (2014, 3).

The College of Policing guidance also follows the stance taken previously by English and Welsh police forces—and reinforced in the 2012 Coalition Government Action Plan (HM Government 2012)—by making reference to five monitored strands of disability, gender-identity, race, religion, and sexual orientation. The police are obliged to record and investigate acts of hostility directed toward these strands of identity as hate crimes although the College of Policing guidance also notes that the five monitored strands "are the minimum categories that police officers and staff are expected to record" and makes clear that forces are free to record other forms of targeted hostility as hate crimes in addition to those protected characteristics (2014, 7). This wider framework has been developed as a result of tragic cases and an emerging body of research highlighting the targeting of "other" identities and groups who have not routinely been considered as hate crime victims, as discussed shortly.

In an academic context, Barbara Perry's (2001) conceptual framework has left an indelible imprint upon contemporary hate crime discourse throughout the world (see, inter alia, Hall 2013; Garland 2012; Chakraborti 2010; Iganski 2008) while offering theoretical substance to the more policy-driven frameworks described above. For Perry, hate crimes are acts of violence and intimidation directed toward marginalized communities, and therefore synonymous with the power dynamics present within modern societies that reinforce the "othering" of those who are seen as different. The process of "doing difference" is a central theme of Perry's framework, which sees hate as rooted in the ideological structures of societal oppression that govern normative conceptions of identity. Within such a process, hate crime emerges as a response to the threats posed by "others" when they attempt to step out of their "proper" subordinate position within the structural order. It is, in other words, a mechanism through which violence is used to sustain both the hegemonic identity of the perpetrator and to reinforce the boundaries between dominant and subordinate groups, reminding the victim that they are "different" and that they "don't belong."

Perry's framework has been of considerable value, not least because it locates hate crime within the broader psychological and sociopolitical contexts that condition hostile reactions to the "other" and recognizes that hate crimes are part of a process of repeated or systematic victimization shaped by context, structure, and agency (Kelly 1987; Bowling 1993). But notwithstanding the significant advances made as a result of this framework and the operational guidance described above, there remains further scope to maximize the "real-life" value of hate crime theorizing to hate crime policy formation, and most importantly, to hate crime victims themselves. There remains much about hate crime that remains un- or underexplored. This is a result of the way in which conventional constructions have been used to shape the parameters of what is categorized as hate crime without giving due regard to whether this satisfactorily accounts for the experiences and motivations connected to expressions of hate. As a result, certain realities of hate crime victimization have remained peripheral to empirical and policy interventions and, in turn, have diluted the perceived and actual value of such interventions to many hate crime victims. The chapter now turns to consider these problems in more depth.

THINKING BEYOND CONVENTIONAL FRAMEWORKS

It is often said that hate crime policy creates and reinforces hierarchies of identity; some victims are deemed worthy of inclusion within hate crime frameworks whereas others invariably miss out. This is a now-familiar criticism of conventional hate crime policy (Mason-Bish 2010; Jacobs and Potter 1998), but one that has not been adequately resolved. At one level, it is an unavoidable outcome of having policy that makes a qualitative distinction between "hate-fueled" victimization and "ordinary" victimization, wherein the needs and experiences of certain groups are prioritized over those of others. However, even if we accept that as a necessary, if uncomfortable, reality of hate crime policy formation, the process of deciding upon this "hierarchy" is perhaps less palatable. As Mason-Bish (2010, 62) notes:

> hate crime policy has been formed through the work of lobbying and advisory groups who have had quite narrow remits, often focusing exclusively on one area of victimisation. This has contributed to a hierarchy within hate crime policy itself, whereby some identity groups seem to receive preferential treatment in criminal justice responses to hate crime.

While the role of activists and campaigners in pushing hate crime to the forefront of political and social agendas has been pivotal to its emergence as an issue of international significance, there is a downside to this process too: namely, that the support offered to victims through hate crime policy and legislation is often contingent upon the capacity of campaign groups to lobby for their recognition under the hate crime "umbrella." Whether through access to greater resources, more public support for their cause, or a more established history of stigma and discrimination, campaigners working to support certain strands of hate crime victims will invariably be able to lobby policy-makers harder than other potential claim-makers. It is that capacity to "shout louder" that can sometimes influence who receives protection from hate crime laws and who does not, meaning that some victims of hate crime may not receive the recognition they expect or deserve.

Moreover, some groups of victims may be altogether denied the benefit of having any campaign or advocacy groups lobbying on their behalf. This is especially true for certain "others" who can find themselves marginal to, or excluded from, hate crime policy and scholarship, despite being targeted because of characteristics fundamental to perceptions of their sense of self. Wachholz (2009), for instance, questions the failure to recognize the all-too-common acts of hostility directed toward the homeless within the United States as hate crime, while a growing body of research in the UK has questioned the lack of support for a range of victims who are regular targets of violent and intimidatory behavior; including Gypsy and Traveler communities (James 2014); members of alternative subcultures (Garland and Hodkinson 2014); sex workers (Campbell 2014); those with mental health issues or drug and alcohol dependency (Chakraborti, Garland and Hardy 2014); and foreign nationals, refugees, asylum seekers, and migrant workers (Burnett 2013; Fekete and Webber 2010).

These groups have much in common with the more familiar groups of hate crime victims in that they too are often singled out as targets of hate, hostility, or prejudice specifically because of their "difference." However, lacking either the support of lobby groups or political representation, and typically seen as "undesirables," criminogenic, or less worthy than other more "legitimate" or historically oppressed victim groups, they are commonly excluded from conventional hate crime frameworks. For these marginalized victims, the process of inclusion and exclusion is much more than simply a thorny conceptual challenge; it is a fundamental human rights and equality issue which has life-changing consequences in the context of experiences of targeted violence that go unnoticed and unchallenged in the absence of policy recognition. Instead, by marginalizing the marginalized within conventional constructions of hate crime, scholars, policy-makers, and practitioners often overlook the victimization directed toward these less visible targets who are typically unable to draw from the power of class or language, the privilege of advocacy groups and support networks, or the bargaining clout of political, economic, or social mobility.

At present, these experiences of hostility tend to fall into the cracks between existing conceptual and policy frameworks, as does another dynamic pivotal to the process of hate crime victimization: the intersectionality of identity characteristics that can be targeted by perpetrators of hate crime. Conceiving of hate crimes simply as offenses directed toward individual strands of a person's identity fails to give adequate recognition to the interplay of identities with one another and with other personal, social, and situational characteristics. Thinking beyond conventional singular constructions of identity has two key advantages. First, it acknowledges the differences within, and intersections between, a range of identity characteristics, including sexual orientation, ethnicity, faith, disability, and gender identity, thereby exposing what Moran and Sharpe (2004) describe as "the differences, the heterogeneity, within what are assumed to be homogeneous identity categories and groups" (400). In reality, these are not homogeneous categories and groups consisting of people with uniform characteristics, experiences, and expectations (see also Garland 2012). Just as none of us should be defined exclusively by any one single identity characteristic (by being an ethnic minority, by having a disability, or by being gay, for instance), nor should hate crime scholars and policy-makers automatically assume that perpetrators target their victims exclusively because of a single identity characteristic.

Second, recognizing that hate crime can be the outcome of prejudice based upon multiple distinct yet connected lines is important in the context of recognizing the interplay between hate crime victimization and socioeconomic status. Many especially harrowing cases of hate crime take place in areas on the economic margins—in areas that many of us reading this chapter can conveniently avoid or ignore—and yet the relevance of class and economic marginalization to the commission of hate crime has rarely been a central line of inquiry to scholars and policy-makers. To use one well-known UK-based example, the years of disablist harassment directed toward Fiona Pilkington and her family, which tragically led to her taking her own life and that of her daughter Francecca in 2007,[2] has since been referred to as a watershed for the prioritization of disablist hate crime. However, although the case serves as a powerful reminder of the nature and impact of prejudice directed toward disabled people, the relevance of related factors such as the family's social isolation and their economically deprived locality should not be discounted. Hate crimes can often be triggered and exacerbated by socioeconomic conditions and some potential targets of hate crime will invariably be better placed than others to avoid persecution by virtue of living at a greater distance from prejudiced neighbors or in less overtly hostile environments (Chakraborti, Garland and Hardy 2014; Walters and Hoyle 2012). Again, there is scope for these lived realities of victim selection to feature much more prominently within scholarship and policy formation.

A related shortcoming of conventional policy frameworks has been a failure to recognize the "ordinariness" of much hate crime: ordinary not in relation to its impact upon the victim but in the sense of how it is conceived of by the perpetrator, and sometimes by the victim too, as discussed shortly (McDevitt et al. 2010; McGhee 2007). Although much political, media, and scholarly discourse is governed by a tendency to conflate hate crimes with the ideology of organized hate groups, supremacists, or far-right extremists, there is compelling evidence to suggest that most hate crimes tend to be committed by relatively "ordinary" people in the context of their "ordinary" day-to-day lives (Iganski 2008; Ray, Smith and Wastell 2004). These offenses may sometimes have little to do with entrenched hate on the part of the perpetrator, but may instead arise through an inability to control language or behavior in moments of stress, anger, or inebriation; or from a sense of weakness or inadequacy that can stem from a range of subconscious emotional and psychological processes; or as a result of a more banal set of motivations such as boredom, jealousy, or unfamiliarity with "difference" (Chakraborti and Garland 2012; Dixon and Gadd 2006; Gadd 2009).

This has practical implications for the way in which responses to victims are constructed and delivered. At one level, it reminds us that hate crimes are not committed exclusively by obvious "haters" whom one might immediately associate with the commission of highly prejudiced offenses. Instead, we must look beyond the realms of convention and recognize the "everyday" acts of targeted hostility that blight victims' lives. But perhaps more significantly, the "ordinariness" of hate crime in this context has important implications for how victims themselves classify acts of hate crime. As recent research has illustrated, much of the repeat violence, harassment, and intimidation directed toward victims of hate crime forms an entrenched, routine part of their day-to-day lives to the extent that it becomes a normalized feature of being "different," and not something that they would recognize or report as "hate crime"

(Chakraborti, Garland and Hardy 2015; Williams and Tredidga 2013). As noted earlier, there will invariably be high numbers of victims who are unfamiliar with the term "hate crime" and who also may be reluctant to share their experiences because they do not believe that such experiences will be treated—or because they themselves do not recognize those experiences—as anything "out of the ordinary." In the absence of inclusive, victim-led policy frameworks, more experiences of hate crime will continue to slip under our radars.

ADDRESSING THE NEEDS OF HATE CRIME VICTIMS

The previous section has outlined the rationale for thinking beyond the conventional parameters of conventional theoretical and policy frameworks in order to capture the realities of hate crime victimization. However, maximizing the "real-life" value of these frameworks for victims of hate crime remains an equally important challenge. Despite an upsurge of political and media attention, a flurry of policy interventions, and a rise in academic interest, many hate crime victims face an uphill struggle to elicit meaningful support. Many find themselves based on the margins of "mainstream" society, where knowledge of hate crime policy and associated publicity campaigns and reporting structures is invariably lower; where people are likely to feel less comfortable about sharing their experiences through official channels; and where the sense of bitterness, alienation, and resentment that often fuels acts of hate crime is likely to be felt all the more as a result of prevailing economic conditions. Moreover— and irrespective of any improvements made to reporting and recording structures or to the quality of criminal agency responses—in reality, many victims are still denied access to support, either by virtue of not knowing what a hate crime is or how to access support, or because they are not "obvious" hate crime victims immediately recognizable to frontline practitioners. As such, they remain disconnected from, and often peripheral to, the activism, policy making, and theorizing going on around them.

Disconnects between the assumed and actual value of policy interventions as perceived by victims can also undermine the credibility of hate crime work. Many readers will be familiar with critiques directed toward hate crime interventions by those more skeptical voices within academic, professional, and political domains, who see the field of hate crime as resembling little more than an "industry" wherein the term is used tokenistically, politically, or cynically, as a buzzword de jour or as a box to tick. In reality, these claims should have little substance in a world where the collective endeavors of practitioners, researchers, activists, and other campaigners are as necessary now as they ever have been in the fight against hate and prejudice. These endeavors, however, do not always translate to meaningful action for victims. For instance, the improved understanding of disability hate crime that has emerged as a result of recent studies has not fully translated to the policy domain where problems of flawed multiagency working, lip service among statutory organizations, and failures to protect victims of disablist violence are still evident (Roulstone and Mason-Bish 2013; Equality and Human Rights Commission 2011; Quarmby 2011). Similar contentions could be made with regard to many other strands of hate crime, and particularly that suffered by some of the more marginalized members of society, such as trans men and women, Gypsies, Travelers and the Roma, and asylum seekers and refugees, to name just a few (James 2014; Blair Woods and Herman 2014; Burnett 2012). These failings can lead to charges of tokenism and can quickly undo any sense of progress, but so too can our inability to fully consider the value of our theorizing or policy making to victims. Most hate crime scholars will have been heartened by the increasing numbers of regional, national, and international hate crime meetings and events held over recent years but will invariably recall too many instances where the term "hate crime" has been interpreted far too narrowly or literally, or where such meetings and events have been used as "talking shops" by practitioners or academics rather than as springboards for more meaningful dialogue and action within and between both domains. This can create a damaging impression of separatism—or worse still of bandwagon-jumping—within the field of hate crime and does little to address the needs and expectations of victims.

Equally, victims can be shortchanged through a lack of clear thinking, a perceived shortage of time, or a desire to find "quick-fix" solutions, as illustrated by Chakraborti, Garland and Hardy (2014) in their study of hate crime victimization in Leicester. As a city with a proud reputation for celebrating its rich diversity,[3] Leicester was found to have what at face value seems like a robust set of processes in place to challenge hate crime via an extensive range of multiagency partnerships, hate crime awareness campaigns, third-party reporting centers, and community engagement strategies. However, within this study, hundreds of hate crime victims expressed grave reservations about these processes. Most were completely unaware of the term "hate crime" despite the growth of local and national awareness campaigns, barely any knew that they could report online or at venues like their local library or community center, and the majority were highly critical of the mechanisms in place to support victims and reduce levels of prejudice (for a more detailed discussion see Chakraborti, Garland and Hardy 2014). Moreover, whether through their continued reliance upon self-appointed community leaders who are commonly out of touch with the breadth of concerns within their communities, or through an inability to see beyond reported cases of hate crime, many of the practitioners entrusted with delivering services to these victims were oblivious to the extent, nature, and wider consequences of problems on their doorstep. These are significant problems which can sustain the perverse situation wherein victims may be unaware of available services; where service providers may be unaware of victims and their problems; and yet, where existing structures to combat hate crime may, prima facie, appear measured and meaningful.

This sense of disconnection can create a disjuncture between what hate crime victims want and what policy-makers and practitioners *think* they want. This point becomes clear when we consider the way in which expressions of hate have been criminalized through the introduction of various legislative provisions. Although their scope and implementation can vary from state to state, hate crime laws—and specifically the enhanced sentencing framework that accompanies these laws—have significant value in terms of their capacity to express collective condemnation of prejudice; to send a declaratory message to offenders; to convey a message of support to victims and stigmatized communities; to build confidence in the criminal justice system within some of the more disaffected and vulnerable members of society; and to acknowledge the additional harm caused by hate offenses (Chakraborti and Garland 2015; Walters 2014a; ODIHR 2009). Within this context, effective legislation and enforcement is important, both for individual freedoms and security and for cohesive communities. But at the same time, the needs of hate crime victims are not always addressed through the conventional punitive approach. Williams and Tregidga (2013) describe the gap between victim-centered reporting mechanisms and evidence-driven criminal justice prosecution processes which can leave victims—and in particular vulnerable victims of persistent "low-level" hate incidents—frustrated and additionally traumatized by the absence of stringent evidential proof required for prosecution.

Similarly, Chakraborti, Garland and Hardy's (2014) research has challenged prevailing assumptions about hate crime victims' inclinations for enhanced prison sentences by revealing an overwhelming preference—shared by victims of different types of violent and nonviolent hate crime and from different communities, ages, and backgrounds—for the use of community education programs and restorative interventions as a more effective route to challenging underlying prejudices and preventing future offending. Indeed, the benefits of restorative approaches to hate crime have become increasingly relevant as scholars have begun to highlight the shortcomings of exclusively punitive responses. As Hall (2013) notes, prisons have limited deterrent value, offer limited opportunity for rehabilitative programs and can be "hotbeds" for prejudice, intolerance, and hate group activity and recruitment (see also Blazak, 2009). Walters (2014b) too has shown that the punishment and labeling of offenders as "hate offenders" does little to challenge hate-motivated behaviors or to support the healing of hate victims, whereas restorative approaches offer a form of dialogue that can help to break down the fears, stereotypes, and prejudices which give rise to hate crimes. With mounting evidence to suggest that victims themselves—and not "merely" academics or practitioners—are calling for alternative interventions, the policy drift toward punitive-oriented "solutions" in isolation becomes all the more questionable. While there are promising signs of change in the way in which responses to hate crime are becoming less prescriptive (Iganski 2014; Perry and Ryan Dyck 2014), the preceding discussion underlines just how important it is to frame policy interventions in line with victims' expectations of justice.

CONCLUSION

Recent years have seen the emergence of new knowledge, new ideas, and new policies in the context of hate crime. This has facilitated some degree of change in political and cultural attitudes toward the hostility suffered by a range of minority groups. A number of themes remain un- or under-explored and they highlight some of the limitations evident within our efforts to capture the lived realities of targeted violence and harassment experienced by those falling within and outside the strands of recognized hate crime victim groups. As we have seen, research and policy frameworks can sideline acts of hate directed toward certain groups of "others" who are not associated with recognized hate crime victim groups. This ties in with the broader arguments of Asquith and Bartkowiak-Théron (2012) who use the terms "vulnerable" and "at risk" to describe people who are left out of the social development of the criminal justice system (young people, the elderly, the mentally ill, and people with addictive behaviors, to use some of their examples) because they are not invited to participate and/or not capable of participating.

With reference to hate crime, this has reinforced the marginalization of less visible victims who fall into the cracks between scholarship and policy frameworks. Such victims may not always "belong" to a fixed identity group in the orthodox sense of hate crime victim identification, but may still be at a heightened risk of victimization because of their "difference" or perceived vulnerability. Those notions are also highly relevant to our understanding of the intersections and interactions at play *within* recognized hate crime strands. Although an identity-based approach to hate crime theorizing and policy formation has done much to challenge those respective strands of hate, this approach can sometimes mask our *multiple* identities and the way in which these identity characteristics intersect with one another and with other situational factors and context. Ultimately, it is this process of intersectionality that can increase our perceived "difference," our perceived vulnerability, and our chances of being victims of hate crime.

These themes offer further support for the central message of this chapter: namely, that thinking more broadly about hate crime enables us to recognize important realities about hate crime victimization that would otherwise remain peripheral, at best, to the process of theory and policy formation. As we have seen, international and domestic policy guidance gives us scope to think broadly about which prejudices, which groups of victims, and which types of experiences we might choose to classify as hate crime. However, in a collective sense, we, as scholars, policy-makers, practitioners, and campaigners, tend to limit the parameters of our hate crime frameworks without accounting for the "real-life" value of these frameworks to those who are victims of hate crime. Whether in terms of the disconnect between hate crime interventions and hate crime experiences, the implementation gaps between different spheres of work, or problems of perceived or actual tokenism, these are challenges which demand further reflection.

Above all else, the key driver for scrutinizing the "real-life" value of academic work and policy interventions should be our collective failure to address levels of hate crime and the needs of hate crime victims. Most reliable measures suggest that these levels remain disturbingly high. As noted in the introduction to this chapter, recent sweeps of the Crime Survey for England and Wales indicate that approximately 278,000 hate incidents are committed every year, a figure nearly six times higher than corresponding police-recorded figures (Home Office 2013). Similarly, contemporary studies of hate crime victimization across the world give little room for optimism when it comes to believing that the volume of hate crime, or its impact, is any less significant than at any time in the recent past (see, inter alia, Asquith 2014; Corb 2014; Chakraborti, Garland and Hardy 2014; Williams and Trediga 2013; European Union Agency for Fundamental Rights 2013b). Ultimately then, and despite the progress that has come through improved knowledge and policy developments, the fact remains that hundreds of thousands of victims continue to suffer hate offenses every year, often in silence and often on a recurring basis. While this grim reality does not invalidate the value of existing work, it is a poignant reminder of the need to do better.

NOTES

1. The Organization for Security and Cooperation in Europe (OSCE) comprises fifty-seven participating states in Europe, North America and Asia. All fifty-seven states enjoy equal status, and decisions are taken by consensus on a politically, but not legally binding basis.

2. Fiona, a thirty-eight-year-old mother of Franceсca, an eighteen-year-old girl with learning difficulties, was driven to kill herself and her daughter in October 2007 by setting fire to her car, with them both inside, near their home in Leicestershire, England, following years of disablist abuse from local youths directed at her family.

3. Leicester is located at the heart of the East Midlands of England and has a population of approximately 330,000 according to most recent Census data (Office for National Statistics, 2011). Leicester residents hail from more than fifty countries from across the globe, making the city one of the most ethnically and culturally diverse places in the UK, and somewhere that is commonly depicted as a successful model of multiculturalism both nationally and internationally.

SIX

Punishment or Solidarity

Comparing the U.S. and Swedish Victim Movements

Robert Elias and Carina Gallo

While early Western criminal law incorporated victims of crime rather directly and intimately in the process, their role became increasingly marginalized more than two centuries ago. Crime became viewed more as a violation of the society rather than of individual victims and prosecutions proceeded on behalf of the state, not individual citizens. This set up a contest between the accused and the state where victims were largely left out. This began to slowly change in the 1960s with the advent of victim restitution and victim compensation programs in the United States. Rather than resorting to punishment for crimes, restitution offered the possibility of offenders assessing their harms and repaying their victims directly. Compensation programs repaid some victims from state resources. While the restitution option quickly faded, compensation programs were expanded in the 1970s and supplemented by other women victim services. This said, the real explosion in victim rights and participation began in the early 1980s. At this time, emerging get-tough, law-and-order policies strongly defined the U.S. victim movement and portrayed victims and offenders as distinct and in stark opposition to each other. Accordingly, victims could therefore best be served by cracking down on offenders: eroding their rights as suspects and defendants and enhancing their punishments.

A different model, however, seems to characterize another nation, Sweden, where the victim movement has followed a welfare model that emphasizes support, information, and treatment, rather than harsher punishment for offenders (Sandeberg and Ljungwald 2012; Ljungwald 2011; Persson 2004). These characteristics suggest an alternative approach to assisting victims, that is, a critical victimology, in practice.

This chapter examines the contrasting approaches to crime victims taken in the United States as compared to Sweden. It will focus on the state of California specifically, since it has long been in the forefront of the U.S. crime victim movement. The United States and Sweden are worthy of comparative study because they often represent polar opposites in terms of criminal and welfare policies. A residual welfare model with punitive criminal justice policies and high incarceration rates characterizes the United States, while Sweden has been regarded as the archetype of a universal welfare model with a strong belief in social solidarity, crime prevention, and rehabilitation. We want to distinguish not only the different policies pursued for victims, but also the contrasting politics and ideologies that lay behind them. What do the different perspectives reveal about these two societies, and what difference does it make for crime victims?

THE U.S. CRIME VICTIM MOVEMENT

The first inklings of concern for crime victims emerged in President Nixon's focus on law and order and the launching of the "war on crime and drugs" in the late 1960s. Already, a backlash was occurring against U.S. Supreme (Warren) Court decisions that sought for the first time to provide protection for the rights of the criminally accused. Rather than defending rights, this was portrayed as protecting criminals, and thus the plight of victims was emphasized by comparison. Since the 1960s, California has spearheaded the U.S. crime victim movement. The state of California established the first crime victim compensation program in the nation in 1965. In 1974, the Alameda County's District Attorney's Office created the first prosecutor-based victim assistance and advocacy program, which served as a model for the rest of the nation. California State University–Fresno has also taken steps toward professionalizing victim assistance by offering the first victims services certificate program in the United States in the 1980s, and the first victimology major in the 1990s. Fresno County introduced the first victim impact statement in 1976, which gave victims a voice in the court's sentencing phase.

By 1979, there were twenty-eight state compensation programs in the United States (Young and Stein 2004). Although these programs suggested a real interest in victims, they left us our first hint that the concern was more apparent than real. Studies evaluating these programs revealed that while they were launched with great fanfare in legislatures and the media, the eligibility requirements and meager funding meant that almost no victims could really recover their losses (Elias 1993, 1996). Despite the overlap of offending and victimization, where many victims are offenders and vice versa, the California Victim Compensation Program still today does not provide compensation to victims who are on felony probation, on parole, or in county jail or prison. One cannot be a victim and offender at the same time. To be eligible for compensation, the victim must also report the crime promptly and cooperate with police and prosecutors to get the offender convicted. As political scientists like to say, these victim compensation programs are good examples of symbolic politics instead of tangible results.

RONALD REAGAN LAUNCHES THE "DECADE OF THE CRIME VICTIM"

During the 1970s, different victim services were added in the United States. Some of this was prompted by the reemerging women's movement of this era, which sought initiatives for female victims in particular. As Burgess (2004) points out, the first rape crisis centers and women's shelters became role models, not only for battered women and their children, but also for other crime victims. The rise of the human rights movement during this time also raised consciousness about victimization.

The women's movement and human rights movement both held out hope for a real improvement in the situation for victims. This promise was largely dashed, however, with the election of Ronald Reagan in 1980. By this time, the victim movement started growing rapidly. In 1983, nearly one thousand victim service programs had been established in the United States and by 1990 this number had grown to five thousand (Fattah 2000). One of Reagan's first new initiatives was to launch the "decade of the crime victim" by establishing a Presidential Task Force on the Victims of Crime. Unfortunately, the Task Force was heavily politicized, and its report painted a highly distorted picture of the criminal process. While it correctly noted the shortfall in victims' participation in the justice system, it exaggerated the abuses victims faced. More importantly, it portrayed the experience for those accused of crime as a kind of paradise of soft treatment and excessive rights protections.

Beginning with the Task Force's recommendations, it soon became clear that the main agenda was not a concern for victims, but rather an interest in rolling back rights for the accused, intensifying punishments and incarceration, and enhancing official power. It was the basis for the Reagan administration's re-launching the war on crime and drugs during the 1980s. This time, however, the war was specifically initiated on behalf of victims. If we really cared about the plight of the victim, it was argued, then it was necessary to unleash law enforcement, sacrifice constitutional protections, and get tough with criminal sanctions. In turn, victims would be granted an enhanced status and role. A flurry of new victim policies emerged in the United States on both the state and federal levels, in legislation such as the 1982 Victim and Witness Protection Act. Funding was increased in a variety of justice and law enforcement agencies to provide for victims. Victim-witness projects were set up in police departments and prosecutor's offices. In 1984, Ronald Reagan signed into law the Victim of Crime Act (VOCA). The Crime Victim Fund was VOCA's centerpiece, which secured a steady stream of funding to the states to create and maintain assistance programs for crime victims. The fund became financed by fines and penalties paid by convicted offenders, not taxes. From 1985 to 2012, the yearly deposits to the fund increased dramatically from approximately $68 million to $2.8 billion (Office for Victims of Crime 2015).

Federal government agencies for victims were also established, which provoked the creation of a series of subordinate nongovernmental organizations. Certain "special" victims, such as children and the elderly, were singled out for particular legislation. Victims were trained in self-defense. Television programs such as *America's Most Wanted* reminded the public that they too could become victims of crime.

During the same period, victims were granted statutory rights in the criminal process. In 1982, the state of California passed the so-called "Victim's Bill of Rights," which enhanced the rights of the victim at the expense of the defendant. These rights were designed to redress what was described as an "imbalance" in the criminal law in favor of offenders and the accused. As a result, victims were given the right to information and to participation in the process—including testifying at trial and providing feedback in victim-impact statements as to the appropriate punishment for the convicted.

Policy-makers also adopted the practice of naming new "get-tough-on-crime" laws after victims of crime. The laws were often named after young white girls and women who had been victims of particularly heinous crimes. For example, Megan and Jessica's laws were enacted to monitor and penalize sex offenders. The laws were named after Megan Kanka and Jessica Lunsford, who were both abducted, raped, and murdered. The state of California adopted Megan's Law in 1996, which allows the public to access photos and descriptions of registered sex offenders. Ten years later, in 2006, the state of California enacted Jessica's Law, which mandates a minimum sentence of twenty-five years for first-time child sex offenders and prohibits sex offenders to live within two-thousand feet of parks and schools. The 2008 amendments to the California Bill of Rights were also named in memory of a victim of crime, twenty-one-year-old Marsy Nicholas, who was stalked and murdered by her ex-boyfriend. Marsy's brother, who donated almost five million dollars to the campaign to place the bill on the ballot, mainly sponsored the bill. Marcy's law further expanded victim rights in California, for instance, by placing limitations on the possibility of parole. Naming these laws after young girls and women who were perceived by the public as pure and innocent, and not unlike their own mothers, daughters, and sisters, made it difficult for opponents to argue against the law or propose amendments to the law once it had been enacted.

Law enforcement and punishment policies were beefed up in the 1980s and 1990s with the imposition of mandatory minimum sentencing, criminal-fine enhancement, and an escalation of the death penalty. In 1994, California enacted the famous "three strikes and you're out" policy, which mandated a prison term of at least twenty-five years to life for an individual's third felony offense. Subsequently, between 1980 and 2008, the U.S. prison population soared, rising from 220 to 755 per 100,000; the highest incarceration rate in the world (ICPS 2015a). The number of executions in the United States also rose from zero in 1980 to ninety-eight in 1999 (DPIC 2015).

Meanwhile, the U.S. Supreme Court and other courts continued to water down, if not overturn, Warren Court due-process protections for the accused and a crusade against drugs was made an integral part of the nation's law-and-order initiatives. In 1994, President Clinton signed the largest crime bill in U.S. history: the Violent Crime Control and Law Enforcement Act (VCCLEA). Apart from expanding the federal death penalty and increasing penalties for immigration-related crimes, the reform included extensive crime victim legislation, including the provisions of the Violence Against Women Act (VAWA). While increasing assistance to crime victims, the VCCLEA reduced services to incarcerated persons, for instance, by overturning a section of the Higher Education Act of 1965 that permitted prisoners to receive Pell Grants for postsecondary education while incarcerated. Concurrently, Clinton (1996) "ended welfare as we know it" with the Personal Responsibility and Work Opportunity Responsibility Act (PRWORA), which placed work requirements on welfare recipients and a stringent time limit on welfare assistance. The bill also blocked many immigrants from receiving welfare assistance. Welfare has never been a right in the United States, but now it was even less than a privilege.

The guiding assumption behind these policies has been that protecting the rights of suspects is diametrically opposed to the best interests of victims—a kind of zero-sum game. Thus, although the due-process safeguards in the Victim Bill of Rights were penned by America's conservative Founding Fathers, somehow their actual protection has been viewed as a radical conspiracy designed to undermine victims and society. Of course, due-process rights were designed not to protect criminals, but rather the accused. Victim policy of the 1980s and 1990s promoted the notion that victims had rights in the criminal process and that they could be secured only by sacrificing the rights we all have against being falsely accused. Yet, Dr. Marlene Young, the founding Director of the National Organization for Victim Assistance (NOVA), the oldest nongovernmental victim assistance organization in the United States, has described President Reagan's 1982 punitive Task Force report as the victim movement's "biggest turning point" and "greatest accomplishment" (University of Akron 2002).

The U.S. victim movement has also made some questionable assumptions about what victims want, and about what is the appropriate victim role in an adversarial criminal process. To begin with, when victims discover what it really means to participate in the criminal process, many of them do not want to exercise that right. For those who do, rather than welcoming them into the process, criminal-justice officials often regard them as an impediment (to striking plea bargain deals, for example) and they seek to "cool out" victims or discourage their participation. The approach also assumed that victims want revenge. Yet, despite the environment of revenge that victim policies have created over the last three decades, it's remarkable how many victims are less concerned with harsh punishment and more interested in simply being heard and acknowledged as people who have been harmed and who need to heal. Besides whether victims *want* to pursue impact statements in order to influence sentencing, there is the question of whether such involvement undermines the integrity of the process. While victims deserve recognition in the criminal process, and certainly assistance, there was nevertheless a good reason why they were marginalized from a direct role in convicting and punishing suspects. Such bias compromises an already challenged, adversarial process in a democratic society.

Crime in the United States began declining before the "get-tough" federal and state crime policies were implemented. Debate continues about what prompted the decline, however it is not correlated with the massive expansion of U.S. prisons (Roeder, Eisen, and Bowling 2015). Some debates point to temporary demographic factors, but in any case, crime—and especially violent crime—has begun to rise again. While some have questioned the wars on crime and drugs, often from a cost perspective, the underlying law-and-order ideology remains. As recently as a few years ago, another attempt was made to amend the U.S. Constitution with the "Victims' Rights Amendment." As Markus Dubber (2006) has convincingly demonstrated in his book *Victims in the War on Crime*, this only further perpetuates policies that are largely empty for real victim interests, but instead grounded in state power and a punishment mentality.

EMERGING IMAGES OF VICTIM AND OFFENDERS IN THE U.S. PENAL SYSTEM

In recent years, the California criminal justice system has undergone some significant changes that may indicate a shifting view of victims and offenders and the appropriate responses to them. In 2005, the California Department of Corrections added the word "Rehabilitation" to its heading. A few years later, in 2011, California passed the historic "Prison Realignment" bill, aiming to reduce the number of inmates in the state's prisons. The U.S. prison population rate has decreased slightly from 755 in 2008, to 707 in 2012 per 100,000 of national population (ICPS 2015a). In 2012, California legislators amended its three-strikes policy by eliminating life sentencing for nonviolent crimes. Just recently, in March 2015, the California Supreme Court declared the residency restrictions for sex offenders established under Jessica's Law unconstitutional. The law had forced many sex offenders to live on the street since it is almost impossible for them to find housing. In 2010, only four years after the law was enacted, the number of homeless sex offender parolees had increased twenty-four times, from 88 to 2,100 (CDCR 2010). There have also been some notable changes in victim policies. In 2013, sex workers became eligible for victim compensation if they were raped or assaulted while working. A recent California Senate bill (2015) proposes that minors be eligible for victim compensation even if they fail to cooperate with law enforcement in the apprehension and conviction of the offender. In addition, the bill suggests that all victims should be able to get compensation for mental health counseling regardless of their felony probation status.

Nevertheless, still today, some victim organizations clearly focus on intensifying punishments and incarceration. For example, the National Organization of Parents of Murdered Children (POMC) runs the so-called Parole Block Program, which is designed to prevent the early release/parole of those convicted of murder or homicide. On their website, POMC asks the public for "help to keep convicted murderers behind bars" by signing petitions and sending them to the Parole Board in question. According to POMC (2015), the program has "protested the early release/parole of more than 1,000 murderers since the inception of the program in 1990." The Justice for Victims of Trafficking Act of 2015 is another recent example of how victims are used to justify an expansion of the criminal justice system. The bill established a Domestic Trafficking Victims' Fund, which will be financed by a $5,000 penalty on anyone convicted of trafficking or sexual abuse. The funds can be used to establish victim assistance programs or to increase law enforcement's resources to target sex traffickers.

THE SWEDISH CRIME VICTIM MOVEMENT

In Sweden, the conceptual identity of the crime victim is relatively new. In fact, the phrase "crime victim" (*brottsoffer*) was not used in the Swedish language until 1970 (Österberg 2002). The spirit of solidarity, equality, and universalism that had guided Swedish welfare reform since the beginning of the twentieth century also characterized penal policy. Crime and punishment were on the whole not considered political questions until the mid-1960s (Tham 2001a). In the postwar period, Sweden had been nearly a textbook example of what the British criminologist David Garland (2001) calls a penal welfarist state, with a solid commitment to crime prevention and rehabilitative ideals. According to Pratt (2008), this "penal exceptionalism" emerged from the Swedish welfare state's institutionalized solidarity and egalitarianism. Throughout the 1970s, Swedish activists, scholars, and political leaders also questioned the legitimacy of prison as an institution. In the mid-1970s, the Minister of Justice, Lennart Geijer, argued that prison was so destructive to society that it should be replaced by other measures to combat crime. Geijer's goal was to reduce the Swedish prison population from four-thousand to seven-hundred. Incarcerated people also started to organize themselves; for example, in 1970, inmates formed a labor union called Sweden's Prison Worker Union (SAAF) (Edling 2004).

In the beginning of the 1970s, the first victim compensation schemes started to take form. Up until the mid-1980s, however, these schemes were marginal and there was little public interest in crime victims. In 1982, the Red Cross opened a victim support center in collaboration with the social services and the police, but the center shut down within a year due to lack of demand.

THE RISE OF MEN'S VIOLENCE AGAINST WOMEN AS A SOCIETAL PROBLEM

Minister of Justice Lennart Geijer's radical vision of the Swedish correctional system was never implemented and the Sweden's Prison Workers Union closed down within a year (Edling 2004). In the 1980s, crime victims started to emerge as an interest group along with an expansion of penal legislation. Some may argue that the rapidly growing interest in victims was a backlash against the progressive criminal justice movements of the 1960s and 1970s, which had been driven too far. To understand the roots of the Swedish crime victim movement we must first recognize the influence of the women's movement.

The "crime victim" was put in the public spotlight in the mid-1970s through a governmental inquiry, which had been launched by Minister of Justice Lennart Geijer to review sexual crimes in the penal code (Tham 2001b). The inquiry's final report (SOU 1976:9) included several controversial proposals, such as that incest between consenting adults and gross procuring of prostitution should be decriminalized and that the penalty for rape should be reduced. The report was met with widespread criticism from the women's movement for "blaming the victim." As a result, none of the report's proposals were implemented and, a year later, a new inquiry was appointed. Around the same time, in the late 1970s, the first women's shelters opened. Many women argued that the compassion and solidarity of the Swedish welfare state was a deception since it failed to address issues related to gender, violence, and sexuality (Elman and Eduards 1991; Elman 2001). Feminist scholars have also criticized Esping-Andersen's (1990) renowned typology of welfare regimes for neglecting gender issues. In more recent work, Esping-Andersen et al. (2002) have provided more gendered typologies, but they have not profoundly changed his original work.

The women's movement lost a bit of momentum in the 1980s, only to be revitalized in the early 1990s, when all political parties from left to right declared themselves feminist. At this point, the women's movement and the crime victim movement became increasingly intertwined. In 1993, the Ministry of Labor appointed the Commission on Violence Against Women to do an overview of questions about violence against women. The Commission on Violence Against Women had close ties to the Crime Victim Commission, which the Ministry of Justice appointed a couple of years later to evaluate measures taken for crime victims in the previous ten years. Women have also had a unique position in victimological research. Almost a third of the 167 research projects that were financed by the Crime Victim Fund between 1993 and 2013 focused on women (The Swedish Crime Victim Compensation and Support Authority 2014).

In 2001, Lundgren et al. (2001) conducted the first prevalent study of men's violence against women, *Captured Queen: Men's Violence against Women in 'Equal' Sweden*. The study claimed that almost half of Swedish women have been exposed to violence sometime after their fifteenth birthday, a quite striking result considering Sweden is considered to have one of the highest levels of gender equality in the world. The study also argued that domestic violence occurred regardless of class, ethnicity, occupation, or level of education. The study made an immense impact among both scholars and practitioners in the crime victim field. It was even a source of inspiration for crime novelist Stieg Larsson; some of the facts in his widespread Millennium trilogy (Larsson 2005, 2006, 2007) are based on the "Captured Queen" study. The study also received heavy criticism for using a very broad definition of violence. The conclusion that domestic violence occurs regardless of income and education is—as Estrada and Nilsson (2004) point out—somewhat remarkable, given that so many other research studies and victim surveys indicate the contrary: that weaker socioeconomic groups present the highest levels of victimization. Men's violence against women could, however, not be put on the political agenda until it was seen as something affecting everyone rather than merely a minority (Peter 2005). Since the early 2000s, the political focus on women has expanded to include other groups of crime victims, such as children who have witnessed violence and victims of trafficking and honor-related crimes.

INDIVIDUALISM AND THE MIGRATION OF AMERICAN IDEALS

The origins of the Swedish crime victim movement cannot be solely explained by an increased focus on violence against women. The formation and expansion of the Swedish victim movement has also coincided with an increased focus on self-reliance and market forces in the Swedish political discourse. An analysis focusing on factors internal to Sweden would also be incomplete. Some would argue that the Swedish victim discourse has been generated from an American rhetoric and that the increased focus on crime victims is part of an individualization trend, where concepts such as solidarity are being undermined (Wacquant 2009).

In the early 1990s Sweden went through an economic crisis that tested the rationale of the Swedish welfare state and the unemployment rate skyrocketed from approximately 2 to 8 percent. At this time, some political parties explicitly started to question Sweden's welfarist penal policies, as well as polarizing victims and offenders. In 1991, the center-right coalition won the Swedish election and the conservative Moderate Party became the second largest party in government with slogans such as "Criminals should be in prison. You should dare to be out." During their time in power (1991–1994), the center-right parties introduced several cuts in the Swedish welfare state. They also invested in nongovernmental organizations to mark that the state could not "solve all our problems."

Concurrently, the crime victim movement grew dramatically. In the Swedish budget proposal of 1992–1993, the "crime victim" was portrayed as legitimizing the whole existence of the penal system (Andersson 2002). Between 1988 and 1995, more than one hundred nongovernmental victim support centers were formed. In 1994, one of the most noteworthy reforms for crime victims occurred with the establishment of the Crime Victim Compensation and Support Authority and the Crime Victim Fund. The Fund provides economic support for research, education, and information concerning crime victims. Unlike the Swedish victim-compensation program, the fund did not become financed through taxes, but rather through a fee of approximately 800 SEK ($95) imposed on everyone convicted of a crime punishable by imprisonment. The fund generates around 30 million SEK ($3.6 million) per year.

Demker and Duus-Otterström (2009) suggest that it was the loss of a collectivist conception of society in Sweden that fed into a situation where crime no longer was seen as an offense against society, but rather as an aggression of one individual against another. Given this perspective, policies become more focused on individual "crime victims." According to Demker and Duus-Otterström, the conservative Moderate Party led the transformation to a more victim-centered criminal policy. The women's movement's efforts to look beyond poverty, education level, and unemployment as key causes of domestic violence also allied some feminists with right-wing forces. Identifying women as victims of "crime" disconnected violence against women from being a class problem for marginalized groups.

Swedish victim programs have also had European influences. In the late 1980s, Swedish victim advocates and organizations entered a number of collaborations with other European countries. In 1988, Sweden ratified the Council of Europe's Convention on the Compensation of Victims of Violent Crime. The same year, Sweden's largest victim support and advocacy organization, Victim Support Sweden, was formed. One of the first initiatives of Björn Lagerbäck, one of Victim Support Sweden's main founders, was to establish the "International Crime Victim Day" in 1989. Several European countries observe the day every year on February 21. One year later, in 1989, a network of national European national victim organizations established the European Forum for Victim Services (now Victim Support Europe) during a meeting in Sweden. The following years, representatives from Victim Support Sweden did several international visits, for example, to Victim Support in England.

VICTIM SUPPORT AND HUMAN RIGHTS

By the 1980s, the Swedish progressive criminal justice thought and reforms of the prior decades gave way to new ideologies that promoted more punitive ideals. Swedish crime policy has to some degree become focused on "individual" offenders and longer sentences. Most would agree, however, that Sweden has *not* gone through a penal crisis. The support for a comprehensive welfare state and humane criminal justice system remains strong, along with a desire to not incarcerate. The Swedish prison population rate has stayed around 60, reaching its peak in 2006 with 79 incarcerated people per 100,000 of the nation's population (ICPS 2015b). This is low, even from a European perspective, where the average prison population rate is estimated around 127. The direct translation of the name of Sweden's national correctional agency is "Criminal Care" (Kriminalvården),[1] which, to this day, emphasizes that imprisonment is harmful and should be avoided. Sweden has also increasingly used electronic monitoring of offenders as an alternative to imprisonment. A recent study on attitudes toward punishment in Scandinavia (Balvig et al. 2015), showed that when asked a simple question, the public wants harsher penalties, yet when presented with more information, the public becomes less punitive and on average demands lower sentences than judges.

Political reforms to support crime victims have, similar to the general development in Swedish crime policy, focused on criminalization to some degree. The inclination to see victims and offenders as distinct and opposing groups has also become more common during recent years (Tham, Rönneling, and Rytterbro 2011). A recent study of crime-policy bills from 2005 to 2010 showed that crime victims are described as good, innocent, and needing help, whereas the offender is seen as a bad, ruthless scoundrel who needs to be punished severely (Heber 2014).

Nevertheless, most would agree that law-and-order policies have not overtaken the Swedish victim movement. Scholars have also challenged the claim that the victim movement is part of punitive ideals, law-and-order policies, and an individualization process. Wergens (2014) argues that victim initiatives may have been launched via a retributive outlook and can perhaps dichotomize victims and perpetrators. Yet her study, which examines how the protection of child victims is expressed in Swedish legislation and policies, actually shows that most measures taken for victims have been directed at victims as a group.

Milestone governmental victim reports and bills, such as the Crime Victim Commission's 1998 final report (SOU 1998:40) and the 2001 "Support to Crime Victims" bill (2001/01, 79) that followed, have also clearly stressed support and treatment for crime victims. Aside from a few exceptions, such as in the section about mediation, offenders are almost completely absent in the above-mentioned bill. Treatment and support of victims is likewise evident in Swedish victimological research. About half of the research projects (48 percent) financed by the Crime Victim Fund between 1993 and 2013 have focused on support and treatment of victims (The Swedish Crime Victim Compensation and Support Authority 2014).

According to Wergens (2014), the Swedish victim movement's emphasis on care and treatment can be seen as a commitment to human rights, such as individuals' equal worth and dignity and the right to a fair trial. This is similar to other European countries, such as the United Kingdom, where human rights have been a driving force behind victim reform (Rock 2004; Hall 2010). The Swedish state has also provided victims with far-reaching possibilities to obtain material compensation. Since 1988, victims of a number of criminal acts have a right to compensation for violation of personal integrity (*kränkingsersättning*). Wergens points out that this compensation, which is provided independent of other injuries and which aims to restore the dignity harmed by crime, complies with human rights standards. Sweden's strong focus on support for vulnerable groups also goes hand in hand with the objectives of human rights law. As a matter of fact, Swedish authorities and organizations have explicitly framed victim support, protection, and compensation as human rights issues. The Swedish Crime Victim and Support Authority (2013), which administers the Swedish crime victim compensation program, has a whole section on their website named "Crime Victims and Human

Rights," where they state that "the very basis for victim rights is the same as in the fundamental human rights conventions, that is, human dignity and equal worth of each individual." Human rights have also influenced the government's work with violence against women. Human rights formed the very basis for the government's 2007 national action plan for violence against women (Enander, Holmberg and Lindgren 2013; Government Communication 2007/08, 39).

Victim Support Sweden has also promoted human rights as one of its primary purposes. Human rights were the key question for Hans Klette, Victim Support Sweden's former chair of the national board. During his thirteen-year term (1995–2008), Klette worked to put Swedish crime victim policy and legislation in an international human rights perspective. Klette has written two book chapters on human rights, one in 2001 in the book *Crime Victims: From Theory to Practice*, and the other in 2004, in the book *Exposed and Vulnerable Crime Victims*. The 2008 Victim Support Sweden's (2008) member journal, *The Crime Victim Magazine*, devoted a special issue to human rights. Similar to the Swedish Crime Victim Compensation and Support Authority, Victim Support Sweden (2015) also has a separate section on human rights on their website, where they state that "it is a human right not to be exposed to violence and abuse, and to receive protection and support if you are exposed."

CONCLUSION

The first victim support centers were established in the United States in the 1970s along with some other west European countries such as the United Kingdom, Germany, and the Netherlands. Roughly a decade later, in the mid-1980s, the first Swedish victim support centers were formed. Other Scandinavian countries developed victim-service programs even later (Victim Support Denmark was not founded until 1998). In Norway, victim services were run as local pilot projects until 2006, when the Criminal Injuries Compensation Authority took over the operation of the local offices (Norwegian Criminal Injuries Compensation Authority 2015).

The women's movement of the 1960s and 1970s was a catalyst for the Swedish and U.S. crime victim movements. Since then, the two victim movements have taken different institutional, political, and ideological paths. On the one hand, the Swedish victim movement has clearly been guided by what van Dijk (1988) has called a "care ideology," which is based on welfare state principles. This ideology advocates that the community should absorb the burden that individual citizens suffer. Most crime victim reform measures have aimed to improve the support and treatment of victims, rather than infringing on the rights of offenders. Independence from law enforcement and other governmental agencies has been key for Swedish victim support organizations and women's shelters. Victim Support Sweden was founded on the idea that volunteers can offer victims a different kind of support than government officials because they, for example, do not have any obligation to document the victim's problem and situation. Still today, some local victim support centers oppose being housed in police buildings out of concern that too-close collaboration with the police will undermine the victim's will. Some victims may not want to report the crime to the police or participate in the criminal justice system. On the other hand, the U.S. victim movement has been guided by what van Dijk (1988) called a "retributive ideology," by focusing on the punishment of the offender and giving victims a strong voice in decisions about prosecution and sentencing. Human rights standards have nothing to offer crime victims in the United States. Quite the opposite, taking away the other's rights, particularly the offender's rights, is viewed as best promoting victim rights (Elias 1986). U.S. victim services are often part of the district attorney's office and victims are required to collaborate with prosecutors to obtain services and compensation.

Differences in policy responses to victims in Sweden and the United States can be attributed to underlying cultural, political, and social factors. One of them is how each society is built. Simply put, victim policies spring from individualistic versus collectivist ideologies of a nation's basic legal and welfare systems, and more broadly, from each country's sociocultural identities. The individualistic orientation in the United States converts every transgression into a fault, which is the philosophical principle for apportioning liability (Ewald 2002). Taking on the "crime victim" identity is thus important, since, by this logic, the appropriate response is to provide compensation only to innocent victims and leave losses to those at fault (Simon 2003). In other words, if there is no one to blame for your problems, you do not have a right to anything (Ewald 2002). Subsequently, victim suffering is blamed on the individual offender, who should be punished. More collectively oriented societies, such as Sweden, are not primarily based on cause and fault, but rather on distribution and risk (Ewald 2002). From a solidarity perspective, as Ewald (2002) points out, the society is a totality and the good and bad of each individual depends on everyone else. By this logic, you do not need to take on the identity of an innocent victim to get access to different resources. Instead, authorities representing the state, essentially the police and courts, are seen as at fault for victims' losses and improving the "treatment" and "support" by these authorities is, as we have seen in this chapter, hence constructed as the solution to victims' problems.

Nevertheless, approaches taken (or not taken) for victims in the two countries have had several consequences. In the United States, victim policies have promoted a false trade-off between victim rights and suspect rights. It has also operated, in practice, far more to enhance official authority and power than to improve the situation for victims. In addition, this policy served to co-opt much of the victim movement into law-and-order perspectives, which diverted it from its roots in human rights. It thus allowed the promotion of an additional political agenda, arguably unrelated to the interests of victims: a vast overcriminalization and the massive incarceration of millions of Americans. U.S. criminal justice policies and practices, however, are, as we have discussed in this chapter, at a crossroads in their treatment of both victims and offenders. The ideology of harsh punishment and rights denials (as a resolution) may be shifting toward a different strategy.

Swedish victim policies have taken a more human rights approach, not only by focusing on care and treatment, but also by largely resisting reforms that limit the rights of offenders. Nevertheless, the political discourse on inequality, class, poverty, and unemployment obscured issues related to violence in Sweden, despite the belief that bodily safety and integrity is an important aspect of human rights and welfare (e.g., Elman and Eduards 1991; Elman 2001). Wergens (2014) has pointed out that human rights practices still do not fully inform Swedish victim policies, particularly in providing protection and solving crime.

FINAL REMARKS

Most of the empirical research on victim support organizations has been centered on Anglo-Saxon countries. This chapter has begun to explore the origins of the Swedish victim movement, and the form it has taken, as compared to the United States. We have shown that the U.S. victim rights policy has been linked to get-tough, retributive crime policy, while in Sweden, victim policies are instead linked to human rights, treatment, and support. More historical and comparative work is needed to better understand why and how specific measures and policies for victims have come to light in different countries. Cross-national studies are, however, challenging since they require a sound knowledge of contextual and cultural variations. Adapting policies and practices from one country to another is also complicated, since they will materialize the same way in a different setting and culture. Scandinavia is sometimes set up as an "idyllic" case for U.S. reform. It may be, but the differences in the two societies must also be taken into account.

Nevertheless, comparative studies can increase our understanding of how different societies have approached issues related to crime and victims, as well as what realistically could be implemented from one country to another. Cross-national research can also force us to challenge predominant assumptions about how victims are best served, the very mission and framework of critical victimology.

NOTES

1. The official English name is "the Swedish Prison and Probation Service."

SEVEN

Restorative Justice as a Boundary Object

Some Critical Reflections on the Rise and Influence of
Restorative Justice in England and Wales

David Miers[1]

What we now understand as restorative justice's core modalities—victim-offender reconciliation and mediation, offender reparation of the victim's loss or injury—were, during the 1970s and 1980s, typically localized diversion and sentencing disposals to be found in a wide variety of community and criminal justice contexts. The history of restorative justice is to be set against the background of major changes to the criminal justice agenda in the 1990s. This revealed the state's continuing frustration with the inability of existing sentencing options to reduce offending or to rehabilitate offenders, and linked that frustration with calls to rebalance that agenda in favor of the victim's interests. Restorative justice came to be seen as offering possibilities to meet two objectives: better outcomes for both victims and offenders. But these possibilities generated theoretical and operational tensions, reflected in an outpouring of academic work that sought to place what was now heralded as a new criminal justice paradigm as an alternative to existing rehabilitative and retributive structures. This work was accompanied by extensive supranational and national resource engagement in promoting and empirically testing restorative justice interventions. Operational questions centered on when, for what offenses, and subject to what governance arrangements should restorative justice be available? The theoretical issues remain less tractable.

These primarily center on the divergent values implicit in the public as distinct from the private resolution of offensive behaviors. This chapter offers a critical analysis of the ways in which these tensions have shaped the development of the restorative justice agenda, in particular in England and Wales. It does so by reference to the concept of the "boundary object," a construct that seeks to capture disparate ideas, theories, and activities pursued by a range of communities of practice and of interest, in order to enhance their value and application.

BOUNDARY OBJECTS: COMMUNITIES OF PRACTICE AND OF INTEREST

The concept of the "boundary object" was first developed by Star and Griesemer (1989) as a means of explaining how the heterogeneity of scientific inquiry can reach common understandings of and reliability across its particular domains. In his review of their social meanings, Fox (2010, 72) summarizes work by Carlile (2002, 451–452), which suggests that boundary objects

> establish "a shared syntax or language" within which individuals in different communities can represent their knowledge; provide a means for these individuals to communicate across boundaries their concerns or questions about a practice or idea; and empower members of different communities to transform their own knowledge in the light of the innovation or idea. These aspects of boundary objects effectively enable communities of practice or knowledge that are normally separated by their perspectives to establish a working relationship around a particular issue, idea or innovative practice.

Boundary objects are those objects that inhabit several "communities of practice"; they are plastic enough to adapt to each community's needs and constraints but are also robust enough to maintain a common identity across a "community of interest" that embraces a number of communities of practice (Star and Griesemer 1989). A boundary object can literally be a physical object, for example, products of medical technology (Fox 2010) or the specimens, field notes, and maps of particular territories held for the purpose of standardization in the development of the Berkeley Museum of Vertebrate Zoology (Star and Griesemer 1989). But a boundary object can also be a process, for example, care gateways in the NHS (Allen 2009), an organization such as a government department (Guston 1999), or an idea or a value, such as restorative justice.

A community of practice is a group of people who undertake a certain type of work, talk to each other about it, and derive some measure of their identity from that work (Wenger 1999; Brown and Duguid 2002). Each of those religious groups and organizations, charities, self-help groups, NGOs, community associations, and the like who, in seeking to address the consequences of aggression in educational settings or the workplace, juvenile and adult offending, housing and family disputes, cultural and religious divisions within local neighborhoods, or multi-ethnic division in a postconflict society, constitutes a community of practice. In placing value on bringing those affected together in order that they may reach mutual and empathetic understanding of each other's standpoint, and where harm was caused to make amends, they share an identity as restorative justice practitioners. As a boundary object "restorative justice" allows each of these communities to practice its own or other practitioners' constructions of restorative justice interventions, although not all practitioners practice all of this work all of the time. But they meet at national and international conferences where, as a community of interest linked by a "shared syntax or language," they swap notes on their respective practices, establishing working relationships around particular issues such as mediation protocols, process governance for victims and offenders, and outcome measures, in an effort to improve upon them. Bound by a common identification, they also seek to disseminate to outsiders and the unconverted what they judge to be its compelling values as a moral, humanist, or even spiritual engagement. Indeed, this is what a number of its early manifestations were predicated.[2]

BOUNDARY OBJECTS: PURPOSES, CONSENSUS, AND COOPERATION

Boundaries exist within communities of practice and of interest for many reasons. Within communities of practice these include quality control and standard setting; for example, what protocols should a mediator follow when engaging with the participants, whether, in the case of criminal conduct, the offender is permitted legal representation, and what should be the impact on any subsequent sentencing decision of a successfully concluded restorative justice meeting? Secondly, boundaries exist and are policed by their practitioners in order to maintain their material, territorial and reputational interests; for example, by defining the elements or the scope of their chosen restorative interventions as models to be protected and emulated. For some communities of restorative practice these definitions may also "assert or imply that their use of the concept is the only proper one" (Johnstone and van Ness 2007, 6). Notwithstanding that these assertions might assume "the tone of a weird inter-faith squabble in an obscure religious sect" (Bazemore and Schiff 2004, 51), the validation of a particular practice as being properly "restorative" goes to these communities' internal and external credibility (Roche 2001, 343).

Within a community of interest boundary objects define and promote particular values that are shared by the communities of practice that it comprises. In the case of restorative justice, prime among these values are

notions of healing, truth and reconciliation, forgiveness, apology, acceptance of responsibility for harmful actions, a moral rebalancing as between a wrongdoer and a victim, or a restoration of the state of equilib-
rium that existed between them prior to the harmful action. That equilib-
rium may be conceived in neo-Kantian terms as the parties' recognition
of each other's moral and personal autonomy (Mackay, 1998), or, in
Braithwaite and Pettit's (1990; see also Braithwaite 2003) "republican"
theory of justice, the restoration of the victims' "dominion" over their
personal liberty that they enjoyed prior to the victimizing event. These
deontological arguments may seem remote from the mundane incidents
of a written letter of apology, a repainted or repaired fence, a sum of
money by way of compensation or other manifestations of a restorative
outcome, but they aim to provide intellectual and moral coherence to an
otherwise disparate set of practices.

For both communities of practice and of interest boundary objects
therefore perform important functions, and, having "the potential to both
analyze and facilitate adoption of an innovative idea, product or technique" (Fox 2011, 72), are purposeful. The question is: will they do their
boundary work successfully? Effective boundary objects must both (a)
bring the diverse stakeholders within a community of interest, that is, the
communities of restorative practice, to a shared diagnosis of their problems of common concerns, and (b) keep them there until an "acceptable"
resolution or common understanding of how those concerns are to be
addressed is reached. Many analysts have noted that boundary objects
can both facilitate these requirements and, as the early disagreements
over what might constitute "true" or "proper" restorative justice practice
illustrate,[3] inhibit them (Fox 2011, 73–74).

In their original paper Star and Griesemer (1989) identified three components to boundary objects of which the third, the dynamic between
their ill-structured and their more tailored uses, is especially relevant to
the development of restorative justice. They explored the question
whether consensus between communities of practice was a necessary
condition of a conceptual understanding of the object and of cooperation
between them. They concluded that while consensus was rarely reached
and was fragile when it was, cooperation nevertheless continued. While a
boundary object resides between communities of practice, where it is ill-
structured, as a set of work arrangements that are at once material and
processual, it is worked on by these communities, who maintain its va-
guer identity as a common object while making it more specific and more
tailored to their use. Their analysis of communities of practice that cooperate without consensus but "tack back-and-forth between both forms
of the object" (Star 2010, 604–605) well describes the restorative justice
dynamic within England and Wales both in the 1980s and 1990s (Miers et
al., 2001) and in the following decade (Shapland et al., 2011, 41–42). But at
the same time the movement between the two forms meant that these

communities' aims and processes had begun, in Star's terms "to move and change into infrastructure [and] into standards (particularly method-ological standards)" (2010, 605). Pranis (2007, 59) commented "restorative justice as a field flows back and forth between practice that informs poli-cy and philosophy that informs practice." For practitioners and their communities of interest there was a felt need to delineate and to establish restorative justice's credentials as an intellectually coherent, humane and effective response to unwanted conflicts.

RESTORATIVE JUSTICE AS A BOUNDARY OBJECT

Star and Griesemer (1989, 410–11) analyzed boundary objects as falling within one or more of four categories. These relate to the ways in which the object's defining features may be classified, what might constitute its "ideal type," how an object whose boundaries are shared by different communities may contain different content, and what performance stan-dards may be met by practitioners who share the object's values and ambitions. Although they are not exhaustive, each category has analytical potential for an understanding of the competing claims made by commu-nities of practice and of interest for restorative justice's definition, proper-ties, scope, and standards.

Classification: Repositories of Knowledge or Practice

The analytical potential of Star and Griesemer's four categories de-pends, first, on how far the different communities of practice and of interest that the objects inhabit have themselves developed a "shared syntax or language" by which they can communicate their concerns or ideas about their practice. One of the ways in which this communication may be impacted by means of "repositories indexed in a standard fash-ion, enabling access by people from differing communities of knowledge or practice (for example, a library catalogue)" (Star and Griesemer 1989, 410; Bowker and Star 2000). Exemplified by analyses of continental Euro-pean restorative justice programmers (Miers 2001; Miers and Willemsens 2004), the need for such repositories arises because communities of prac-tice are diverse, as is their language. As Peters (2000, 15) has commented, "the greatest danger is the illusion of a common language." This diversity is also seen in Canada and New Zealand, where, echoing the indigenous and faith-based initiatives introduced in the United States, Aboriginal practices provided models for family group conferencing and criminal justice services, often operating outside the formal criminal justice sys-tem.

Sullivan and Tifft's collection (2006) well illustrates the definitional challenge that its practitioners face in seeking to identify the common identity of restorative justice's many modalities. The index gives thirteen references under the entry "definition," which includes Marshall's near-universal formulation, firmly set within a criminal justice context.[4] But within that context "restorative justice" assumes many forms: informal mediation, victim-offender mediation, victim-offender conferencing, victim-offender groups, family group conferencing, restorative conferencing, restorative cautioning, community conferencing, sentencing circles, tribal or village moots, community panels or courts, healing circles, and other communitarian associations.[5] The evangelical turn to their introduction, which presents these and other possibilities as being linked by the notion of "making things right" (Sullivan and Tifft 2006, 1), simply masks the question of whether restorative justice has any clear definitional identity (Miers 2006). As Roche (2001, 342) concluded, characterized in terms such as these, "restorative justice" can "mean all things to all people" (see also Weitekamp 2002, 322). The problem, for example in the case of criminal justice, is whether as a boundary object restorative justice is sufficiently robust to persuade others who have the power to advance its practitioners' cause, such as government departments, policy makers, legislators, and judges, to share their conception of the good.

The felt need for a shared language is evidenced in the national and international efforts to create a "repository" of restorative justice practices. The many compendia, overviews, program handbooks, and mapping exercises are attempts to catalog the forms it can assume. Their aim, and only very little of the massive literature can be cited here,[6] is to generate a taxonomy by which restorative justice and its many modalities may be usefully organized for such purposes as their introduction, implementation, and evaluation. Some comprise academic initiatives designed to capture restorative justice's underpinning principles and values (Strang and Braithwaite 2000; Johnstone 2011), some its intellectual and theoretical position compared with other forms of social justice and, in particular, with criminal justice (Fattah and Parmentier 2001; Weitekamp and Kerner 2002; von Hirsch et al. 2003; Hoyle 2009), and some to document its salience and impact in a range of jurisdictions (Weitekamp and Kerner 2003; Aertsen et al. 2006; Gavrielides 2007; Vanfraechem et al. 2010), in particular concerning young offenders (Morris and Maxwell 2001; Mestitz and Ghetti 2005; Crawford and Newburn 2013). Supranational efforts to establish a shared language can be seen in the United Nations' *Handbook on Restorative Justice Programs* (2006) and within the European Union in a sequence of European Commission funded projects. These, such as COST Action A21, *Restorative Justice Developments in Europe (2002-2006)*,[7] have compared restorative justice provision across a number of European jurisdictions. They are aligned with normative initiatives taken by the Council of Europe (1999) and the European Union (2012) that require their member states to make restorative justice services available to victims of crime, initiatives that are inevitably constrained by the continuing variation in that shared language (Pelikan 2004; Miers and Aertsen 2012, 511–546).

It would be laborious to remark on the many definitional variations that can be found in other communities of restorative justice practice and interest.[8] Indeed, for a leading NGO, the European Forum for Restorative Justice (EFRJ), "there is no single definition of restorative justice."[9] In an echo of Peters's (2000, 14) comment over a decade ago, that it presented "a diversified landscape of competing visions," a recent European overview concluded that the literature "on both theory and practice shows a scattered image with regard to the position of the victim in restorative justice" (Vanfraechem and Bolivar 2015, 67). That its key contributors cannot agree on its defining elements means that as a boundary object restorative justice is limited in its capacity to present a scientifically sound and universal basis on which the outcomes of its many communities of practice can usefully be compared (von Hirsch et al. 2003, 22–23; Schiff 2003, 325–331; Dignan 2007, 309; Walgrave 2008, 2).[10] What works for victims or for offenders will depend on each community's practice, which may or may not be scalable to others.

AN IDEAL TYPE

One of the functions that restorative justice as a boundary object could perform is to meet the "minimal demands" of each community of practice, that what they are practicing does indeed reflect some shared understanding of what legitimates their practice as "restorative." This does not imply a static vision; rather, that the object incorporates properties—restorative properties—that the community can "mould to its purposes," or that communities could "extract," "configure," "abstract," or "simplify" for local needs (Star and Griesemer 1989, 404; Fox 2011, 74). "Restorative justice" stands for a set of beliefs and values held or pursued by different communities of practice but which, as an interface between them, has the potential to speak to all of them, offering opportunities for knowledge transfer and for innovation; as might, for example, follow the educational and training events held by its national and international organizations.

A key issue in the development of restorative justice has centered on what its "restorative" properties might be—what makes a practice restorative. Reflecting their variety, there is no "ideal type" in the sense of a single conception shared by all of its communities of practice (Daly 2003). Rather, there is a variety of analyses of the degree to which any one practice might be considered restorative. McCold and Wachtel (2003) allocated particular modalities along a continuum of "restorativeness," for example, family group conferencing and offender compensation of the victim as being respectively "fully" and "partly" restorative. Van Ness (2003a) proposed that restorative justice programs might be evaluated according to their adherence to four value dimensions: encounter, amends, reintegration, and inclusion. Here, too there is a continuum, from a greater to a lesser degree of adherence to that value. These efforts to isolate a practice's restorative properties can be conceived as potential ideal types, which in turn permit one community of practice to determine whether its interventions are optimally restorative and other communities to "extract," "configure," "abstract," or "simplify" according to their conception of "restorativeness." But none is definitive.

A second issue centers on the distinction between deontological and consequentialist conceptions of the good. In a criminal justice context "restorative justice holds the promise of restoring victims' material and emotional loss, safety, damaged relationships, dignity and self-respect" (Hoyle 2002, 101). As a process for achieving better (more inclusive, better accepted and more robust) outcomes for unwanted conflicts, restorative justice practice can be seen as a "better" response to criminal conflicts because it is intrinsically good: it treats victims and offenders as valuable in themselves and apart from any system or community benefits that may accrue. Alternatively (and sometimes, in addition), it is a "better" response to criminal conflicts because it is instrumentally good. It requires the identification and delivery to the victim (or possibly a proxy such as the community) of a tangible product, something of material value that enables the victim to regain or be recompensed for that which was taken or harmed in the conflict. In the case of offenders, it encourages attitudinal and behavioral changes that benefit them directly and the system and the community indirectly.

Deontological and consequentialist justifications assumes political significance where governments seek to co-opt restorative justice practices to improve criminal justice and sentencing outcomes for victims and offenders. The two key research aims the Home Office set for the 2001 study were to identify which elements in restorative justice schemes are most effective in reducing crime and at what cost, and to provide recommendations on their content and best practice. But the study's ambition to generate, in Star and Griesemer's terms, "a representation or abstraction that is "good enough" to serve different communities" (Miers et al. 2001, vi), was inevitably compromised by the fact that the seven schemes varied in their understanding of what restorative justice might mean. The Home Office's subsequent research project was similarly aimed at an evaluation of what works for victims and offenders so that the lessons learned by the funded schemes could be mainstreamed. Here too a consequentialist justification—"to reduce offending"—was to the fore in the first of its two research aims. By contrast, the second was of a deontological nature: to retain a significant focus on the needs and rights of victims. These two aims, the researchers noted, "were originally considered as equal in priority ... [but] as criminal justice priorities changed in England and Wales over the period 2001–2008, so the first aim of reducing offending . . . became more dominant for the government" (Shapland et al. 2011, 16). Nevertheless, and unlike its predecessor, the schemes studied here did yield a number of useful lessons. They also illustrated that while it was possible for its practitioners to cooperate with the criminal justice system, there was less consensus on how communities of restorative justice could both accommodate that system's ideological and normative preferences and retain its defining features (Shapland et al. 2011, 191–192).

AN OBJECT WHOSE BOUNDARIES ARE THE SAME

Major changes in criminal justice over the past two decades have seen both the introduction of new victim services and a continuing state frustration with the inability of existing custodial and noncustodial options to reduce offending or to rehabilitate offenders. The perceived discrepancies between the criminal justice system's treatment of offenders and of their victims was and continues to be a powerful and persistent strand in the politics of criminal justice reform, reflected in a rhetoric which demands that it be "rebalanced" in favor of the victim (Hall 2010, 16–43; Tonry 2010).

Against this background restorative justice's various modalities (even if they were only localized, incomplete, and shakily funded) came to be seen as offering possibilities to achieve better outcomes (Green 2007). Restorative justice practice gives victims of crime an opportunity to tell the offender about the impact of the offending on them and their families and to improve their experiences of the criminal justice system. It treats them as parties in the criminal justice process (as is the case in civil justice), not just as third parties whose participation is confined to being an evidential element in the prosecution case. For their part, restorative justice encourages offenders to accept responsibility for the harm they caused and to make amends. It offers opportunities for their rehabilitation in contrast to a dysfunctional diet of retributive penal measures (Zehr 1997). More radically, restorative justice practice was presented as a means whereby the victim's and offender's conflict could be wrested from a proprietorial and obtuse criminal justice system so that as the parties to that conflict, they themselves enjoyed the power to resolve it (Zehr 1990, 2015; Christie 1977; Bottoms 2003).

As the communities of restorative practice and of interest sought to respond to these new possibilities, some serious theoretical and operational tensions quickly became apparent. These were reflected in a massive outpouring of academic work, some of which was cited earlier, seeking to place the claimed new paradigm within the existing rehabilitative and retributive criminal justice structures. The theoretical tensions centered on the divergent values implicit in the public as distinct from the private resolution of offensive behaviors. The civil law paradigm typically implies compromise between offender and victim, the negotiation of a private wrong to the individual victim's satisfaction, settlement, and the payment of damages typically backed by insurance. The public interest here lies in the vindication of the state's provision of a justice system whereby individual victims can obtain redress against their wrongdoers. But civil justice also involves the formal recognition of the liability of a culpable defendant, and may do so for the public purpose of encouraging others to take care. The criminal justice paradigm traditionally seeks to establish and to stigmatize an offender's blameworthiness, and by their punishment to denounce a public wrong to the state's satisfaction. The public interest here lies precisely in the public shaming of the wrongdoer, the victim's private interests being subordinated to this objective. But in its sentencing practices, criminal justice can order restitution or compensation to victims. In the latter case, in part, or as in England and Wales where a compensation order may be the only sentence,[11] this is wholly settling a public wrong by placing a private cost upon it.

The issue was therefore where to establish restorative justice's boundaries as between the civil and the criminal justice paradigms, given that while they share elements of these values (Walgrave 2008, 44–67), they serve different fundamental purposes. For some, and as a counterpoint to what was for a time heralded as the "rediscovery" or the "rebirth" of the victim (Mawby and Walklate 1994, 69–94; Doak 2008, 7–11), restorative justice could be seen not simply as an alternative to the received criminal justice wisdom (Morris and Young 2000), but as "a new criminal justice paradigm" or a "victim-centered paradigm" (Toews and Zehr 2003). One interpretation of this new thinking was Braithwaite's (1989) development of the notion of reintegrative shaming (see also Strang 2002, 63–87). For others restorative justice constituted its own distinct paradigm, lying between these older, and in the case of criminal justice discredited, conceptions of what ought to be the state's responses to wrongdoing (Galaway and Hudson, 1996). What was greeted as a "paradigm shift" in victim thinking, in turn, inspired those who saw restorative justice as transformative, not only of what had traditionally been dealt with in criminal justice contexts but also in postconflict and transitional justice contexts (McEvoy and Eriksson 2006; Doak and O'Mahony 2011; Clamp 2013; Weinstein 2014).

For its critics, the confrontational analysis between retributive and restorative justice was essentially too simple (Daly 2000; Duff 2005; Matthews 2006), as was "the usefulness of presenting a dichotomous model of restorative justice in opposition to traditional justice" (Goodey 2005, 208). But the essential theoretical objection to these simple depictions was that they dismissed or misrepresented the criminal justice system's core features and purposes. In short, it is not its purpose to remedy the private injury or loss that the victim suffers: that is for civil justice. It is of course true that offenders are seldom wealthy enough to compensate their victims in a civil action, [12] and that victims' experience of criminal justice can be unpleasant, though there are continuing state efforts to improve that experience. For example, in England and Wales' *Code of Practice for Victims of Crime* (Ministry of Justice, 2013a). These are unwanted consequences, but they do not challenge in principle the purpose of criminal proceedings: to address the public wrong individuated in the victim's private injury or loss. This must be accomplished by state institutions governed by the kind of fair trial principles that are established, for example, in Article 6 of the European Convention on Human Rights and by sentencing principles of proportionality, and where appropriate, consistency with regard both to the offense and to the offender. The very fact of the victim's private and active participation in the determination of the state's response to the offender's wrongdoing challenges the fundamental values of transparency, independence, and impartiality.

It is not possible to deal in detail with these objections, which have been powerfully voiced by Ashworth (2002, 2003), Shapland (2003), and van Ness (2003b). One response has been to acknowledge the tension, but seek a balance in which the restorative justice agenda is "not a choice between civil society and state justice, but as requiring us to seek the most productive synergies between the two" (Strang and Braithwaite 2001, 13; see also Pavlich 2005, 14–23). By combining restorative with traditional justice outcomes, the state could respond both to its own and to the victim's interests (Dignan 2003; Walgrave 2003). This pragmatism was to the fore when the Home Office funded its evaluations of restorative justice schemes in 1999 (Miers et al. 2001) and 2001 (Shapland et al. 2011). Since then successive governments have advanced the restorative justice agenda in England and Wales (Home Office 2005; Ministry of Justice 2012a), commencing in 2012 a sequence of annual restorative justice action plans for the criminal justice system. The objective is that restorative justice "can help put the power back in the victims' hands, rehabilitate those that offend, and bring down reoffending" (Ministry of Justice 2012c, 1).

At the operational level restorative justice now occupies a clear place within the criminal justice system's range of responses to offending behavior. It figures first, in informal and statutory diversionary options, of which "conditional cautioning," introduced for adults in 2003 (Home Office, 2003) and extended to young offenders in 2009 is significant. [13] This is to be used where, while the public interest requires a prosecution, the interests of the victim, community, or offender are better served by cautioning an offender who consents to conditions that include reparation and rehabilitation (Crown Prosecution Service 2013, para. 15.1.1). It figures, secondly, as a sentencing option. Sentences may be deferred for up to six months so that court can have regard to the offender's conduct, which may include making reparation to the victim or undertakings to participate in restorative justice activities. [14] Reparation has for some time been a sentencing option for both young and adult offenders as a stand-alone sentence, including the making of orders to compensate the victim for any injury, loss or damage. [15] It now figures in youth referral and youth rehabilitation orders (Ministry of Justice 2015; Youth Justice Board 2010), [16] and in respect to adults, as a "rehabilitation activity requirement" of a community order, which can include activities whose purpose is reparative, such as restorative justice activities. These are defined as activities in which "the participants consist of, or include, the offender and one or more of the victims, whose purpose is to maximize the offender's awareness of the impact of the offending concerned on the victims, and which give them an opportunity to talk about, or by other means express experience of, the offending and its impact." [17]

In contrast to direct engagement with or reparation of the victim, indirect reparation may also figure as a condition of noncustodial adult sentences. "Community Payback," the reparative element of a "community order," consists of unpaid work such as removing graffiti, clearing wasteland, or decorating public places and buildings. [18] These orders are specifically intended to let local people, including victims of crime, see, by virtue of the high visibility vests they wear, that offenders are making amends for their crimes (Home Office 2006, para. 3.17; Ministry of Justice 2010, para. 31). As "punishment and payback" the "restorative activities" that are contemplated by this allocation of the offender's time and labor are some way removed from accepted notions of restorative justice as a boundary object. But they also show that while there may be agreement on its broad aspirations, its content and purpose may well differ between different restorative justice communities.

A STANDARDIZED FORM ACROSS DIFFERING KNOWLEDGE COMMUNITIES

There may be some standardization between the many forms that restorative justice can assume, and there are many published accounts that aim to do so, for example, in the European Union, [19] Canada, [20] the United States, [21] and Australasia, [22] but it is impossible here to detail even some examples of the many statements of practice, of standards of delivery, or the protocols for engagement with victims and offenders that they contain.

Within the criminal justice system of England and Wales, restorative justice comprises, as we have seen, a range of administrative and statutory pre- and post-trial measures having a variety of purposes and managed directly by the government, statutory bodies and the voluntary sector. For example, the obligation to consult the victim before deciding what conditions to attach to an adult or a youth conditional caution, and the definition of "victim" for these purposes, are both matters of primary legislation.[23] Provisions concerning the victim's and the offender's consent to these cautions and to sentences having a restorative element are to be found in administrative guidance issued by statutory bodies (the Youth Justice Board 2010; Crown Prosecution Service 2013), the government (Ministry of Justice 2013b; 2013c), and the voluntary sector, where the Restorative Justice Council (RJC) has published engagement protocols and delivery standards when dealing with adult offenders.[24] Responsible for the use of restorative justice with convicted young offenders, one of the Youth Justice Board's principal documents (2008) contains guidance on delivery, operational management, and strategic management and partnership working,[25] supplemented by a wide range of materials that are also accessible from the Ministry of Justice website. For example, guidance on how a young offender can set about writing a letter of apology to the victim.[26]

These variations in its purpose, formal authority, and institutional basis illustrate the "patchy provision of restorative justice across the justice sector" that the Ministry of Justice identified in its analysis of what would need to be done to meet the victims' Directive to be transposed in November 2015 (European Union 2012; Ministry of Justice 2012b; Shapland 2014, 115–117). The government's vision is to build "good quality, victim-focused restorative justice to be available at all stages of the criminal justice system in the United Kingdom" (Ministry of Justice 2014, 2), supported by the kinds of standards and modes of accreditation for practitioners that the RJC, funded in part by the government, has published. There is no question but that there must be clear and public standards by which restorative justice practitioners engage with victims and offenders. But in an echo of the criticisms made by Ashworth and others concerning the impact of this engagement on such other values as proportionality and consistency in sentencing, while victims' views are important they cannot be conclusive. Care must be taken, as with victim impact statements, not to raise their expectations concerning the outcome of their views (Ministry of Justice 2013a; 2013b).

It may seem churlish to cavil at restorative justice's benign worldview. But as Roche (2003, 2–3) noted, while "many restorative justice proponents take it for granted that restorative justice meetings will always bring out people's better selves, and that victims' anger and offenders' indifference will magically give way to compassion and empathy," it can "as easily provide opportunities for people to indulge their impulses for highly punitive and stigmatizing treatment." The problem is one of public accountability for private decisions endorsed by officials acting on the state's behalf for the purpose of responding to crime (Shapland et al. 2011, 84). It is symptomatic of its position as a boundary object that the government has appointed an *Experts Group (Restorative Justice)* drawn from eighteen different communities of restorative justice practice to advise on its vision for restorative justice.[27] Whether those communities' shared syntax or language will generate shared recommendations for fulfilling that vision remains to be seen.

CONCLUSION

A boundary object is a construct having the "potential to improve the uptake transfer and innovation of research findings, technology and other intellectual property across the fields of social policy, organization and management and commercial and public services" (Fox 2010, 70). When it is successful, it presents a set of terms and modes of operation that provide its communities of practice and of interest with a clear understanding of what it is they are doing when engaged in their practice. Even though they may disagree about the emphasis to be placed on any one of its aspects, they nevertheless have the capacity to discuss and to compare their practice with other practitioners, to learn from them, and maybe adapt their work for the better. The problem is that "there is no single story of restorative justice. There are diverse practices and multiple layers of explanation and theory" (Cuneen and Hoyle 2010, 101; see also Liebmann 2007). There remain competing and incomplete visions of what restorative justice means and how it is to accomplish those visions. As a partly successful boundary object, it still has work to do to achieve a "shared syntax and language."

NOTES

1. I am grateful to Professor Jack Dowie, who introduced me to the boundary objects literature. He has no responsibility for what is said here.

2. The 1970s saw the development of Mennonite and other religion-based victim-offender reconciliation programs. The Canadian School of Peacebuilding, for example, is an Institute of the Canadian Mennonite University http://csop.cmu.ca/.

3. In their succinct and reflective analysis of the definitional and issues touched on in this section Johnstone and van Ness note that the mutations and shifts in its understanding during the 1980s and 1990s "were initially resisted by some as departures from restorative justice principles and values" (2007: 8).

4. "Restorative justice is a process whereby all the parties with a stake in a particular offense come together to resolve collectively how to deal with the aftermath of the offense and its implications for the future" (Marshall, 1999: 5).

5. In his 2014 video, *A Humanistic Approach to Mediation and Dialogue*, Mark Umbreit, director of the Center for Restorative Justice and Peacemaking and one of the leading restorative justice scholars and practitioners, opens with the words, "The terminology in the restorative justice movement . . . can be very confusing at times; the term 'mediation' is used at times, or conferencing, or meetings, or circles."

6. Google Scholar counts over 65,000 hits on "restorative justice." The University of Minnesota's Center for Restorative Justice and Peacemaking lists dozens of publications under the heading *Scholarly articles* http://www.cehd.umn.edu/ssw/rjp/.

7. http://www.cost.eu/service/search.

8. See for example the definitions offered by the Restorative Justice Council of Great Britain, http://restorativejustice.org.uk, the Prison Fellowship International, http://www.restorativejustice.org/university-classroom/01introduction/tutorial-intro-duction-to-restorative-justice/lesson-1-definition/lesson-1-definition, and the Crown Prosecution Service of England and Wales, http://www.cps.gov.uk/legal/p_to_r/restorative_justice/.

9. http://www.euforumrj.org/.

10. The Australian Institute of Criminology's website contains a brief but useful discussion of the reasons for this lack of agreement. http://www.aic.gov.au/publications/current%20series/rpp/121-140/rpp127/04_defining.html.

11. Powers of Criminal Courts (Sentencing) Act 2000, s. 130(1).

12. In many countries, serious and disabling personal injuries and homicide may be compensable under their criminal injury compensation schemes (Miers, 2014a).

13. Criminal Justice Act 2003, ss. 22–17 (adults: Ministry of Justice, 2013b), Crime and Disorder Act 1998, ss. 66A-66G (young offenders: Ministry of Justice, 2013c).

14. Powers of Criminal Courts (Sentencing) Act 2000 s. 1.

15. Powers of Criminal Courts (Sentencing) Act 2000, ss. 73–75 (reparation orders) and 130–134 (compensation orders); see Miers (2014b)

16. Powers of Criminal Courts (Sentencing) Act 2000 ss. 16–32 (referral orders), Criminal Justice and Immigration Act 2008, Part 1 (youth rehabilitation orders).

17. Criminal Justice Act 2003, ss 177 and 200A.

18. Criminal Justice Act 2003, ss. 147, 177 and 199. https://www.gov.uk/community-sentences/community-payback.

19. See earlier references to the European Forum for Restorative Justice.

20. http://www.crcvc.ca/docs/restjust.pdf

21. See earlier references to the Center for Restorative Justice and Peacemaking.

22. New Zealand: http://www.justice.govt.nz/publications/global-publications/r/restorative-justice-in-new-zealand-best-practice; Australia: http://www.lccsc.gov.au/agdbasev7wr/sclj/documents/pdf/restora-tive_justice_national_guidelines_discussion_paper.pdf.

23. Section 23ZA of the Criminal Justice Act 2003 (adults) and s. 66B of the Crime and Disorder Act 1998 (young offenders), added by the Anti-social Behaviour, Crime and Policing Act 2014 c. 12, Pt 6 s. 103(1). And see the slightly different definition of a "victim" for the purpose of a rehabilitation activity requirement; Criminal Justice Act 2003, s. 200A(9).

24. http://restorativejustice.org.uk/standards-and-quality.

25. This was withdrawn on May 27, 2015 pending revision to take account of new restorative options.

26. https://www.justice.gov.uk/youth-justice/effective-practice-library/letter-of-apology-to-victims.

27. http://restorativejustice.org.uk/news/members-experts-restorative-justice-group-announced.

EIGHT

Victimhood and Transitional Justice[1]

Kieran McEvoy[2] and Kirsten McConnachie

The importance of victims and victimhood to transitional justice has been the subject of significant scholarly and policy attention in recent years (e.g., Sriram et al. 2013; Roldan 2012; UN Secretary General 2011). At the level of the international tribunals (the International Criminal Court, the International Criminal Tribunal for the former Yugoslavia, and the International Criminal Tribunal for Rwanda—hereafter ICC, ICTY and ICTR respectively) there is an ever-growing literature on victim-related issues such as reparations, restorative justice, procedural justice, the witness/victim division, outreach and education programs, and other elements of what is now a fairly well established template as to how to manage victims as part of these major institutions (McCarthy 2012; Findlay and Henman 2012; McGonigle Leyh 2011; Koomen 2013; Ramirez-Barrat 2011). In a similar fashion, hybrid tribunals (involving international and local legal actors), truth commissions, community-based or "bottom up" programs, and the myriad of other variants of transitional justice almost always seek to underline their bona fides by demonstrating their "victim-centeredness." As one of the authors has argued previously (McEvoy 2007; McEvoy and Mallinder 2011), sometimes such claims are significantly overplayed in the pursuit of larger political or social goals. What is interesting for current purposes, however, is the extent to which victims are central to the process of what Barker (2001) has termed "self-legitimation." For those who work in and seek to justify the institutions of transitional justice, victims are routinely deployed as part of the "language, etiquette and rituals of self-legitimation" (Barker 2001, 6). Justice or support for victims are often *the* reasons advanced by lawyers, judges, psychologists, human rights activists, and others for their involvement in

111

transitional justice. They are the sometimes practical but certainly always symbolic beneficiaries of the "legitimation work" (Thumala et al. 2011) that is required to account for the enormous financial, political, legal, and psychological effort to deal with the consequences of past violence in many of these societies. Without what Sandra Walklate (2007) has called the "imagined victim," more abstract justifications for transitional justice (such as securing justice, deterring others from atrocity, upholding "the rule of law" determining the "truth" about the past) might appear just too intangible.

By way of background to the fieldwork, over four hundred interviews have been conducted by the authors in a range of conflict-affected and transitional jurisdictions since 1995.[3] Those interviewed have included victims and victims' organizations, ex-combatants, lawyers, judges, politicians, human rights and political activists. In every context in which we have conducted research, debates concerning the rights and needs of "victims" and how victims have been affected by different styles of transitional justice (e.g., the release of prisoners, amnesties, international or local prosecutions, truth recovery) have been keenly contested elements of the local polity.[4]

Broadly, all of this research was informed by a view that "structured-focused comparisons" (Zartman 2005) based on semi-structured interviews with key actors provide a balance that allows for a nuanced grasp of the local and the potential for what Robert Merton (1968) termed "mid-range theorizing." Local researchers were appointed in each jurisdiction, usually on the basis of their close working knowledge of the local context. With their assistance (and that of the secondary literature), purposeful sampling methods were deployed to decide which key actors should be interviewed (see, e.g., Merriam 2009, especially chapter 4). In the case of victims' organizations, these were normally groups and individuals involved in different forms of campaigning and mobilizing work. A key criteria was that they should reflect as broad a cross-section of victim organizations as possible in terms of positions adopted, political allegiances (if any), whether they had suffered at the hands of state or non-state actors (or both), and the styles of campaigning work in which they had been involved. Obviously such an approach to comparative work cannot capture the views of those whose victimhood remains private. In addition, as ever in comparative work on justice-related matters, the challenge is to strike a balance between avoiding simplistic transpositions from the experience of one setting to another on one hand, or on the other, to resort to a form or relativism that suggests we can never know or theorize beyond local exigencies (Nelken 2003; Pakes 2004). We would argue that, in doing comparative transitional justice research of this ilk, it is possible to extract and examine broad themes and to be attuned to context-specific variables while developing interpretative and explanatory strategies which can be tested according to "cosmopolitan and not only local criteria" (Nelken 2009, 292).

In addition to that comparative fieldwork, the chapter also draws upon a range of academic and policy literature. In the section below we examine in particular the relevance of the victimology literature drawn from criminology in the UK, United States, and other long-established democracies to transitional settings.[5] The chapter also draws upon a number of other fields including feminism, sociology, philosophy, and postcolonialism. Our fieldwork and this literature are combined to explore the construction and consequences of victimhood in transitional justice organised around the themes of *voice, agency,* and *blame*.

VOICE, AGENCY, AND BLAME IN "WESTERN" CRIMINAL JUSTICE

The field that has given most consideration to crime victimization is criminology, and particularly the victimology literature. While most of that scholarship has traditionally been focused upon established democracies, there is a growing criminological interest in victimhood in transitional settings (e.g., Karstedt 2010; Rafter and Walklate 2012; McEvoy and McConnachie 2012; Hoyle and Ulrich 2014). In exploring the relevance of victimology, of course one should eschew mechanistic transpositions of the experiences of victimhood from, for example, the United States to Rwanda, or the United Kingdom to Sierra Leone. The scale and intensity of violence and suffering, the fact that organized or proxy state violence is often a key dynamic in such conflicted societies, the influence of international legal actors in the latter contexts—these and a myriad of other variables mitigate against nuanced comparisons. That said, we are persuaded by the view of some commentators that the forces at play in transitional justice are sometimes more like the "ordinary justice" of consolidated democracies than transitional specialists acknowledge (e.g., Posner and Vermeule 2003, 763). An openness to exploring the relevance of criminology, critical, and sociolegal studies, and a range of other disciplines, rather than defaulting to the exceptionalist view of transitional justice, could be viewed as an indicator of the intellectual maturation of the field (Bell 2009). Therefore we would argue that a cautious and critical understanding of the generic victimology literature does offer a useful organizing framework for exploring victimhood in transitional justice. In particular, as noted above, we have been drawn to the ways in which issues related to *voice, agency,* and *blame* are intimately bound up with the experience and politics of victimhood in both settled democracies and transitional contexts.

A full exposition of the full breadth of the victimology literature is well beyond the scope of this chapter. Summarizing for the sake of brevity, the earliest variants of victimological research were focused largely

on trying to determine the "true" nature and extent of crime victimization (Von Hentig 1948; Wolfgang 1958). Victimization work emerged as a
corrective to the traditional offender-focused preoccupation of criminology, examining questions such as unreported crime and victims' perceptions of their own experience of crime, as well as their treatment by the
criminal justice system. More sophisticated techniques were developed
from the 1980s onward to explore not just the prevalence but also the
personal impact of crime victimhood on the victim (Hough and Mayhew
1983; Van Dijk et al. 1990, 2008). Influenced in part by these technical
advances, as well as by feminist, critical, and "realist" criminological critiques (i.e., that the "official" knowledge on crime was vitiated by variables such as gender, class, and ethnicity), policy-makers became increasingly sensitive to the fact that the effectiveness and legitimacy of the
justice system was intimately bound up with the views and experiences
of victims (Walklate 1989; Spalek 2006). As a result, a long-standing axi-
om in UK and U.S. politics has been, as the Home Office (2005, 8)
summed up, "to make sure that the victim's voice is heard at the centre of
government and throughout the criminal justice system."

At a systemic level, capturing the *voice* of victims has therefore become an important source for evidence-based policy and service delivery
for the courts, police, prisons, probation, and youth justice (Spalek 2006;
Wolhuter et al 2009). Of course, efforts to capture and deploy the views of
crime victims have always been more than an academic or policy pursuit.
In the political arena, contests over the "authentic" voice of victims became increasingly deployed by political actors from both right and left
from the 1970s onward (Walklate 1989; Fattah 1991; Elias 1993). The crime
victim became a key political signifier of competing worldviews (Mawby
and Walklate 1994; Newburn 2008). On the right, the crime victim was at
the heart of calls for more extensive police powers, longer prison sentences, more punitive regimes, and so forth (Simon 2007), a central plank
in embedding what Garland (2001) famously referred to as "the culture
of control." On the left, more progressive discourses used the prevalence
and experience of victims from certain groups (e.g., women, people of
color, the poor) to frame victimhood within its broader structural context,
to highlight discriminatory policing and criminal justice practices, and to
argue for a more effective use of resources that better serve those most
adversely affected by crime (Mawby and Gill 1987; Mawby and Walklate
1994).

Across the political spectrum, opportunities for turning voice into
agency for the crime victim were often cast in terms of affording greater
"rights" to such victims in the criminal justice process. In the United
States and Canada, victims' "bills of rights" were advanced. In reality,
these tended to focus on important service delivery and procedural aspects of criminal justice rather than enforceable "human rights" as guaranteed in international law (Elias 1993; Roach 1999, 283). Indeed the diffi-

culties in rendering such "rights" enforceable itself—when compared to the more familiar protections afforded to suspects and convicted prisoners—became a rallying cry on the right, proof positive that the criminal justice system was overly concerned with the rights of the criminal to the detriment of the victim (Rock 1998a). This "zero-sum" trade-off (Zedner 2004; Drake 2012) often appeared to promote a view that the exercise of agency on the part of the victim could only be achieved through ever more punitive treatment of the offender (Maruna 2001). Even those more usually associated with the political left have shown elements of this reductive binary thinking. For example, as Bullimer (2008) has argued, long-standing efforts to have domestic violence taken seriously by the criminal justice system have (for some feminists) been co-opted by right-ist discourses. From such a vantage point, victim empowerment is judged solely by the length of the prison sentence secured, regardless of the preferences of victims themselves. A similar critique has been advanced with regard to restorative justice where, despite the vocal commitment of its advocates to empowering victims, the concurrent emphasis on offender shaming and reintegration may in some instances pressurize victims toward sympathy and even responsibility for the reform of an offender which is at odds with their own feelings or indeed best interests (Acorn 2005; Pemberton et al. 2007).

Again, as in transitional contexts, the exercise of victim voice and agency in consolidated democracies overlaps strongly with notions of *blame* and blamelessness. For example, early iterations of the victimology literature included notions of "completely innocent" and "most guilty" victims (Mendelsohn 1956) and sought to determine "victim precipitation" in their own misfortune (Wolfgang 1958). Although the crudest variants of this type of scholarship were subsequently discredited, as Sandra Walklate has argued (2007, 110), the ideal victim is still "blameless" (Walklate 2007, 110): a faultless innocent who has had crime visited upon them by a wicked perpetrator. When victims are not faultless, when they are in some sense "deviant" (Karmen 1983), they become much more problematic, both as an object of public empathy but also in terms of their entitlement to formal compensation on the part of the state. Thus drug addicts, prisoners (or indeed former prisoners), prostitutes, and other social groupings who themselves may have been involved in criminality are troublesome victims in terms of public discourse. Indeed as the UK Home Office has repeatedly stated, the criminal injuries compensation scheme for victims of violent crime applies to the "blameless" victim (CICA 2008, 4; Home Office 2005, 15). As Miers (2007, 342) has argued, "blame" in such contexts does not refer simply to a victim's actions in respect of the criminal injury but to his or her "moral worth as a person."[6]

Such issues of blame become particularly loaded when, for example, we consider that certain sections of the population, such as young black males, are likely both to be the victims of crime and to be adjudicated offenders (Coleman et al 2008; Tonry and Melewski 2008). Certain vulnerable populations, such as the homeless, may have almost daily experiences of moving between criminality (being perpetrators) and victimization (being victims) (Tyler and Beal 2010). Putting it simply, people can be either victims or perpetrators at different times depending on a whole range of variables; these are not static categories. Of course, this does not mean that every victim is also a perpetrator, or vice versa. It does mean, however, that the (sometimes literal) assumption of black-and-white distinctions between these categories does not always chime with the lived experience of real people. As we will argue below, in the arguably more "messy" contexts of conflicted societies, the limitations of such simplistic bifurcations are on occasion all the more stark.

To sum up, this literature, drawn largely from the United States and the United Kingdom, speaks directly to a number of key dynamics of relevance to the social and political construction of victimhood in transitional contexts. This includes the importance of research, policy, and practice that privileges the *voice* of victims. An overlapping political and legal commitment to victim empowerment or *agency* may be discerned that is often viewed as synonymous with victims' "rights." Finally, the voice and agency of victims is often both publicly and legally bound up both with the innocence of the victim and the capacity to *blame* the perpetrator. These factors provide the template for our exploration of the experience of victims in transitional justice.

VICTIMS, VOICE, AND TRANSITIONAL JUSTICE

As we have noted above, the procedural treatment of victims by criminal justice systems in the established democracies is sometimes referred to loosely as "victims' rights." At first blush, the centrality of human rights discourses to the evolution of contemporary transitional justice would suggest that the "rights of victims" would play a much more significant role than is actually the case. In practice, however, as Ferstman (2010, 407) has argued, if we trace the treatment of victims from the tribunals at Nuremberg and Tokyo, through the ICTY, ICTR, the Special Court for Sierra Leone to the ICC, until recently "only sparse consideration was given to victims views and concerns and only limited space was given to their engagement with such institutions other than as prosecution witnesses." The ICTY and the ICTR had only limited powers to deal with victim reparations (and these proved hard to invoke) and both institutions were frequently criticized for a range of failures concerning their treatment of victims during the conduct of their trials (e.g., Findlay 2009; Findlay and Henman 2009; McCarthy 2012). For example, Julie Mertus (2004) has described efforts to advocate for recognition of victims of sexual violence at the ICTY as like "shouting from the bottom of a well." Staggs et al. (2007) reported comparable frustrations among victims of sexual violence at the Special Tribunal in Sierra Leone. Similarly, Haslam (2011) has explored the ways in which some international NGOs interacting with the ICTR were constituted as "subjects" (important players who could influence policy and procedure) while others (some Rwandan victim and survivor groups) were primarily deemed to be objects, for example, groups to whom the tribunal imparted information as part of its "outreach" program. In short, while justice for victims was and is a key rhetorical element in the establishment of international tribunals, in practice their handling of victims has often been found wanting (Clarke 2009).

Given the significant political and financial pressures to secure the convictions of those deemed most culpable for crimes such as genocide, war crimes, and crimes against humanity, a certain institutional imperative toward the instrumentalization of victims is arguably unsurprising. Once major legal edifices are created and underpinned by an emerging body of law, it is all too easy for powerful political, institutional, and professional needs of lawyers to come to be viewed as synonymous with those of victims (Karstedt 2010). In a classic version of what Nils Christie (1977) described as the "theft" of conflict by lawyers, victims' voices are often picked out, appropriated, and then re-presented to suit the aims of the prosecution. Deciding which victims to call as witnesses, which elements of their stories to emphasise or omit, how events are framed, and the nature of support (if any) to be provided before, during, and after court are of course the quotidian challenge of any criminal lawyer (Duff et al. 2004; Wexler 2008). In the transitional justice context, however, where the scale and nature of suffering are so acute, such processes are all the more politically and emotionally charged. The ways in which the voice of the victim is "managed" by lawyers in such contexts demands great sensitivity. As one Rwandan national prosecutor told the authors:

> I have seen a failure by these prominent lawyers to apply standards that they defend. For example, during cross-examination at the ICTR, a British lawyer used techniques to destabilise the witness, psychologically. Ask him or her a lot of questions, push them around. This is how you test the credibility of a witness in ordinary situations but how, how do you use the same methods to deal with a witness who is a survivor, and who is already psychologically disturbed by the experience? Those are the failures of applying these standards as they define them.

It should be acknowledged, however, that some lessons appear to have been learned in terms of the provisions to afford greater victim participation in the workings of other international or hybrid tribunals, such as Extra-ordinary Chamber of the Courts of Cambodia (ECCC). In the ECCC, the court has adapted a novel system, drawn from the civil law tradition, wherein victims are specifically represented as "civil parties" in the proceedings. While of course welcome, these developments have not been entirely unproblematic, with cogent criticisms emerging of judicial restrictions on the way in which the civil party system has operated in practice as well as the funding, organization, and professionalization of the civil party lawyers (Killean 2015, 2016 in press). In addition, despite the institution's emphasis on its "victim-centredness," this has not prevented the most atrocious forms of victim instrumentalization from happening in that court. As one lawyer who was working in the ECCC told McEvoy regarding the conduct of another prosecutor:

> R: The lawyer was very new to the Tribunal at the time. . . . One victim was testifying that he didn't know what had happened to his wife. The prosecution had determined that she was executed at twenty-one [S 21 Khmer Rouge Torture and Execution Centre] and they proceed to reveal this to the victim on the stand. He first of all didn't understand what was happening. When the penny finally dropped, obviously he's completely devastated because he's been looking for her for thirty-five years and holding onto hope that she's alive.
> I: Nobody had briefed the lawyer that he didn't know?
> R: That was part of the point I think. I think it was because they wanted to show the impact, the emotions, I suspect . . . I think he just hadn't thought it through from the perspective of the psychology of the victim.

With regard to the ICC, it too purports to provide victims with a "voice in the proceedings" as distinct participants from the Prosecution (ICC undated, 16; Doak 2011). Again, while such developments are to be applauded it would be premature to laud them as an unqualified success. In practice, the voice of victims must be mediated through a lawyer representing their interests (Redress 2005). Some lawyers from the affected jurisdiction who are closest to the victim organizations are not entitled to address the Court because of restrictive rights of audience (Haslam 2011). In addition, while the input from such victim lawyers may afford the court greater knowledge of what occurred, it is difficult to discern how their voices actually impact the final judgment. As Claire Garbett (2013, 207) has discussed in her analysis of the ICC judgment in the *Lubanga* case,[7] there is a lack of clarity concerning how the voice of the victims contributed to the decision, no account of the individual familial or collective harms suffered by those victims and significant ambiguity as to whether their "views and concerns" were seen as having the same evidential weight as the testimony of other witnesses or whether they were seen as having a distinct function—that is, not contributing to the conviction of Lubanga but rather providing the context to the crimes being considered. Article 75 of the Rome Statute also makes it possible for the ICC to order reparations to victims and reparations hearings associated with the Lubanga case have now commenced (Moffett 2013). In sum, while in the ECCC and the ICC at least, victims' voices are beginning to emerge in the proceedings, it is as yet unclear to what extent they are being listened to or acted upon.

Of course, it is not just the retributive variants of transitional justice that raise challenges with regard to the handling of the voices of victims. Even institutions that are avowedly "victim-centered," such as truth commissions, are open to the charge of constructing victim subjectivities in particular gendered or racialized fashions. For example, Ni Aolain and Turner (2007) have argued that the exclusion of socioeconomic crimes from the truth commission in Chile and El Salvador in effect privileged "male conceptions of conflict" (at p. 238) and failed to address versions of harm, loss, and violence experienced predominantly by women. While the racialized and gendered violence that underpinned the thirty-six-year war in Guatemala saw sexual violence used as a tool of genocide against the Mayan people, many of the stories about violence perpetrated against women were related largely by male informants to the Catholic Church's Recovery of Historical Memory (REMHI) project and the UN-sponsored Commission for Historical Clarification (Crosby and Lykes 2011). For the women who did speak to the REMHI project, over half of them talked about what happened to others, their families, and their communities rather than about themselves (Nolan and Shankar 2000). Even in contexts where the significant challenges associated with helping women to come forward and to give testimony to such bodies are overcome (see Ross 2003; Theidon 2007), naming the wrongs committed as "human rights violations" (as normally occurs in a truth commission) may narrow and individualize the experience, reifying women as sexual victims of conflict and thereby obscuring the broader cultural or structural elements of patriarchy in a given society, which may well persist beyond the end of conflict. Indeed, in some instances the suffering of women may be appropriated for other grand narratives, becoming representative of the sexual violation of the nation as a whole or emblematic of the failure of men to protect *their* women and thus, potentially at least, "a narrative anchor for the remythologization of a national masculinity" (Franke 2006, 824).

In much of the writings on these and other themes on truth recovery, the notion of voice almost always features heavily. By way of illustration, voice is a central tenet in the literature on the iconic South African Truth and Reconciliation Commission (TRC). The Deputy Director of the TRC, Alex Boraine (2000), explains in some detail the care that was given to assisting victims to "break the silence" of their pain. Boraine describes how one victim, Nomonde Calata, whose husband Fort was murdered by a South African death squad, broke down and how "her spontaneous wail from the depths of her soul . . . caught up in a single howl all the darkness of and horror of the Apartheid years" (Boraine 2000, 102). Antje Krog, a journalist working for the South African Broadcasting Corporation, which repeatedly broadcast Ms. Calata's painful evidence, later called it "the signature tune, the definitive moment of what the process is about" (1998, 42). In this context, the voices of victims like Mrs Calata become both emblematic but also, at times, just too excruciating. Indeed, Boraine (2000, 103) notes that many people later told him they found the broadcast "unbearable" and switched the radio off.[8]

As Wilson (2001), Moon (2009), and Cole (2010) have all discussed, with regard to the TRC, the decisions as to which victims' voices were heard, and the ways in which those voices were recorded, edited, performed, or broadcast all reflected *choices* by those managing the process. In particular, each suggests that voices cannot be understood without a keen grasp of how broader political and social narratives are framed. For example, within the context of the TRC, the eulogizing by the Commission of reconciliatory or "forgiving" accounts by victims (and the parallel presentation of more retributive views as somehow discordant) resonated with the social and political mood music driven by the prevailing elites in South Africa. While there may well have been sound political reasons for such an emphasis, the methods adopted by a transitional justice mechanism and the context within which it operates, are key in determining what Brandon Hamber (2009, 130) has termed "the quality of voice." As its enabling legislation makes clear, the South African TRC was established explicitly to promote *reconciliation*. The voices of victims who wished to "speak truth to reconciliation" (Gready 2011, 156)—challenging the desirability of such a purpose, its viability, or even the operating procedures designed to achieve it—went largely unheard. As one victim activist in South Africa summed up to the authors:

> they didn't listen, they refused to listen when we shouted and said you cannot have a process which is one year long. And then they extended it by another six months. Bullshit. And so the human rights violation hearings were for one and a half years and then they closed the door. And how many thousands of people were left out of the process?

At one level, it is hard not to be sympathetic to the logistical challenges of managing a transitional process such as a truth commission where it is impossible to "do justice" to all of the voices of victims affected by past violence. The challenge for foreign correspondents in war-torn regions— famously illustrated by Edward Behr's (1985) story of a journalist shouting at a group of women and children refugees fleeing the horror of the then Belgian Congo "anyone here who has been raped and speaks English"—echoes the hard choices which must be made by those who staff transitional justice mechanisms in seeking to capture "representative voices" to highlight the truth of past violence.

However, understanding the realities of managing complex transitional justice processes is not an excuse for hubris. As one of us has written elsewhere, transitional justice arguably requires a greater degree of *humility*. From such a vantage point, it is irresponsible to promise to victims that they will have their voices heard or, even more grandiosely, that these processes can end impunity, deliver justice, establish *the* truth, or lead to healing and reconciliation (McEvoy 2007). Rather, we would argue that what is required is a sympathetic but measured approach to promises made to victims. As is discussed further below, with regard to issues such as gender, race, class, sexuality, and other variables (often key to the construction of victims' voices), what Ni Aolain (2012, 220) has recently termed some "complex interweaving" is required by transitional justice scholars and policy makers to minimize the dangers of either silencing or essentialism. At the very least, we would advocate an honest self-awareness among those tasked with the design and implementation of transitional justice—communicated directly to victims themselves—that *power* and *choice* are in fact being exercised in the construction of victim voices by such institutions.

VICTIMS, AGENCY, AND TRANSITIONAL JUSTICE

The complex intersection between voice and agency has been much discussed across a range of disciplines. Social constructionists, anthropologists, educationalists, literary scholars, postcolonial scholars, feminists, and others have all addressed the tensions manifest in determining the extent to which voices are chosen, listened to, reproduced, and actioned (see Jackson and Mazzei 2008 for an overview). Postcolonial and feminist scholars have perhaps best captured the dynamics at work for current purposes. Spivak (1988, 304) for example, asks "what can the elites do to watch out for the continuing construction of the subaltern," calls for a systematic unlearning of privilege in order to speak to (rather than listen to or speak for) the historically muted subaltern subject (1988, 305) and concludes, rather forlornly, that despite such Western feminist sensitization, the subaltern still cannot speak. bell hooks (1990, 24) makes the same point, critiquing Western academics' approach to the subaltern subject, informed as it is by the view that only Western expertise can provide the appropriate tools for both knowledge and praxis. Her words are worth reproducing:

> No need to hear your voice when I can talk about you better than you can speak about yourself. No need to hear your voice. Only tell me about your pain. I want to know your story. And then I will tell it back to you in a new way. Tell it back to you in such a way that it has become mine, my own. Re-writing you I write myself anew. I am still author, authority. I am still colonizer the speaking subject and you are now at the center of my talk.

The central problematic for transitional justice is that, in practice, it is often what Madlingozi (2010) refers to as "transitional justice entrepreneurs" who are involved in the process of either reproducing or speaking on behalf of victims in transitional justice processes. The risk of prosecution lawyers appropriating the voice of victims for their own institutional and professional purposes was discussed above. In ways that are again reminiscent of what Barker (2007) memorably termed "the politics of pain" concerning criminal justice debates in mature democracies, one often sees local political actors claiming to know and speak for the victims of past atrocities in transitional settings. As one local victims' spokesperson in Northern Ireland recounted:

> Those politicians who are opposed to the peace process always play the victims card. They are always speaking on behalf of victims or with victims at their side, so long as the victim takes the political line that they want. I always found it very distressing seeing victims paraded in this fashion. Of course if a victim like [name omitted] starts to find their own voice, which is a different point of view, then they are dropped like a hot potato. It has taken some years but I think many in the victims sector have got wise to these tactics and see them for what they are but not all.

However, even those who see themselves as *genuinely* representing the views and interests of victims in transitional justice sometimes fail to sufficiently problematize the power relations at work. As is discussed within development studies (Munck and O'Hearn 1999; Veltmeyer 2011 and critical work on human rights activism, e.g., Kennedy 2002; Merry 2006), this problem is often particularly discernible among international NGO activists and academics. In many instances progressive interlocutors, infused by moral outrage at past abuses and a genuine empathy for the plight of victims, can all too readily "steal the pain" of victims (Razack 2007; cited in Madlingozi 2010). Such a process risks resilencing victims negating their potential for agency, and reproducing the sense of powerless, which is much discussed in writings on victimhood in the developed democracies (e.g., Lamb 1999). As one prominent community activist in Northern Uganda told one of the authors:

> Some of the big international human rights NGOs who have done work on Northern Uganda have not really listened to voice of the community. The community here was in favour of the amnesty because they saw the soldiers in the LRA [Lords Resistance Army] as victims, as their children. Yet the NGOs came here, they did their surveys, pushed for the ICC and they said, the community does not want this amnesty. They said that because they wanted to promote international law which forbids amnesties. But that is not what the community was saying, I don't believe it!

Does this mean therefore that only victims or survivors themselves can legitimately become involved in advocacy work? Of course it does not. The reality is that many victims may be traumatized, lack relevant skills or capacity, have little access to power, resources, and so forth. Many victims do need help and support from those with skills or resources.

However, as with lawyers who staff international tribunals, victim advocates and activists also need to be very aware of the challenges of what Linda Alcoff (1991–1992) referred to as *the problem of speaking for others*. Unlike Spivak's essentially pessimistic conclusion, Alcoff (1991–1992, 24) suggests that speaking for others remains the "best possibility" in some contexts and advances a number of ways designed to "lessen the dangers." She urges (24) that those who are in a position to speak for others do so after "a concrete analysis of the particular power relations and discursive effects involved" and by engaging in a series of "interrogatory practices." Her message is also of value for transitional justice practitioners: not to be paralyzed by the political challenges of providing help and assistance to victims, but rather to be aware of and informed by such dynamics.

It would of course be wrong to suggest that transitional justice activists and scholars are oblivious to these concerns. Diane Orentlicher (2007, 19), one of the most influential commentators in transitional justice, has acknowledged that in authoring a major UN report on transitional justice (United Nations 2005), while she recognized "the primacy of a victims' perspective," she did not "reflect the emphasis I would now place on victims' agency in defining their own interests and preferences and in participating in national processes aimed at designing policies of transitional justice." The participatory developments discussed above with regard to the ICC, and indeed the emerging, if uneven, emphasis on supporting the participation of victims at the Extraordinary Chambers in the Courts of Cambodia (Elander 2013) also suggest a much greater awareness at least of the importance of victim agency at the elite level.

In more grassroots-oriented programs, Lundy and McGovern (2007, Northern Ireland), Arriaza and Roht Arriaza (2008, Guatemala), Clark (2010, Rwanda), Madlingozi (2010, South Africa), Kent and Robins (2011, East Timor), and others have all engaged in different ways with the challenges of working with victims in transitional justice. A common theme that runs through this work is that there is a real potential for forms of mobilization among victims and other key actors which seeks to maximize community ownership and participation while simultaneously challenging the assumption that only "state-like" legal institutions can "do" transitional justice (see McEvoy and McGregor 2008). Such a perspective does not require the suspension of critical faculties or a naive or overly romanticized notion of community or civil society. Indeed a cold-eyed assessment of the potential for exclusionary practices, unequal power relations, or even political hubris among and within groups including victim organizations (discussed further below), is specifically required. Nonetheless, an orientation toward maximizing victim agency, a pragmatic assessment of the risks and capacity which that orientation entails, and a greater self-awareness of the dangers of "speaking for" victims, is precisely what is required for effective praxis in transitional justice.

VICTIMHOOD, INNOCENCE, AND BLAME

> There are innocent victims and there are terrorists and I find it offen-
> sive that anyone would seek to equate the two. People make choices to
> become involved in paramilitary groups and if they were killed, that
> was the choice they made. They didn't give their victims any such
> choice.[9]

The final issue we wish to address is the space available is the relationship between victimhood, innocence, and blame. We have argued previously that, like the construction of the crime victim in established democracies, a phenomenon is apparent in many of the transitional justice societies that we have studied wherein it is *only* those designated as "innocent" who may lay claim to the term victim (McEvoy and McConnachie
2012). Summarizing for current purposes, a hierarchy of victims is often
apparent, where those who consider themselves or are considered by
others to be "innocent" victims dispute the "deservingness" of other
"bad" or "impure" victims (Madlingozi 2007; Meyers 2011) to recognition. Of course such victim hierarchies often map closely onto the national political sphere. As noted above, there are often close relationships
between political constituencies and victims' groups, which may in turn
be linked to disputed interpretations of the violence of the past and its
justifiability.[10]

As we and others have argued, transitional justice appears to find it
difficult to contend with victims who are not in fact entirely blameless
(Bouris 2007; Moon 2008). Of course, in the lived experience of conflicted
societies, not every victim will fit neatly into such boxes and, as argued
above with regard to crime victims, individuals may move between these
categories. By way of illustration, one of the authors has conducted interviews with hundreds of ex-combatants and, almost universally, they
speak of experiences of victimhood in the form of violence visited against
them, their families, or communities by other organizations, the state, or
indeed the armed groups to which they belonged (Shirlow and McEvoy
2008). The two categories of perpetrators who are most readily recognized as victims in the transitional justice literature—child soldiers and
female members of armed groups—are again defined by the lack of voice
or agency in their involvement in violence (Moser and McElwaine 2001;
Drumbl 2012). Their claim to "innocence" and their lack of agency is
precisely what renders them eligible to the title of victim. For the rest of
those directly involved in violence, they are usually deemed blameworthy. As the spokesperson for one reconciliation group in South Africa
suggested:

> I think that's the huge mistake that victims make, is that they don't ask
> themselves you know, a lot of deeper questions on, what would make
> somebody join a group of militants and to commit certain acts? What

has shaped them to believe in what they do? . . . when people begin to reflect upon that they will be able to understand that as much as the victims have suffered but so too have people involved in the struggle gone through challenges and difficult things. They haven't just thought, OK, let's go and attack that particular group of people, you know. There are causes and things that shape them to become the people that they are.

Aside from noting the complexities of the "perpetrator as victim" issue, we are particularly interested here in process of blaming. Before looking at that in more detail, it is important to make a number of preliminary points. We take as a given the fact that there are numerous instances where unjustifiable violence is inflicted upon civilian populations who can in no sense be "blamed" for their victimhood. Indeed, a much-discussed phenomenon of so-called "new wars" is precisely the deliberate targeting of civilians for political, economic, or ethnic reasons (Slim 2010; Rothbart et al 2012). The unjustifiability of such violence and the prerogative of those wronged to declare themselves victims or survivors (if they so wish) are also axiomatic. In addition, of course, there are real dangers in the kind of moral relativism—nicely described by Meyers (2011, 255) as "there is blame all-aroundism"—which seeks to negate individual or structural responsibility for wrong-doing. Indeed, a key raison d'être of what McEvoy (2007) has previously termed a "thicker" understanding of transitional justice, is precisely to provide a more rounded account of past conflict, one which can capture individual human agency and hurt as well as the broader causes, context, and consequences within which violent acts occurred.

With those axioms in mind, we are interested here in the ways in which certain variants of "innocence" are politically constructed and deployed in transitions. In particular, we would argue that innocence, based upon the reality of past and indeed current suffering, may at times be used as a shield by some victim advocates. Innocence may allow some victim groups to disavow that the positions adopted are inherently political but also to render critical interrogation of such positions (even of the most reactionary or exclusionary discourses) very difficult without appearing callous or indifferent. In particular, the strong tendency in such discourses toward blame is, for us, problematic. As noted above, in many of the contexts we have examined, blame is directed (unsurprisingly) at the "perpetrators" of violence for being entirely responsible for all of the ills of the past. It is also on occasion fixed upon the "other" community (however defined regardless whether individuals therein were actually responsible for past violence) or indeed other victims who adopt a different political perspective. In short, the blame net is sometimes cast widely and, as we explore further below, the positionality of those victims casting that net often goes unquestioned because of their past suffering.

There is a rich literature on the notion of blame to be found in philosophy, theology, criminology, social psychology, and other fields, much of which is beyond the scope of this chapter. However, below are a number of overlapping themes in that literature, which we think are of particular relevance and which were reflected in our fieldwork.

First, we should acknowledge the power of the "urge to blame." Nietzsche, in his critique of religion, pithily remarked, "'I suffer: someone must be to blame for it'—thus thinks every sickly sheep."[11] In a similar fashion, Mary Douglas (1992, 4) has charted the shifts and durability of blaming techniques from "primitive societies"—wherein blame could be attributed to "miscreants for spoiling the weather, killing with lightning, or causing storms at sea"—to contemporary forms of blame and blaming which claim to be based upon an "objective basis in knowledge" (7). As theorists of punishment have long argued, the institution which most lends weight and authority to the "scientific" process of distinguishing between the "innocent" and the "blameworthy" is of course the legal system. However, the punishment of crime and the inherent blaming of the offender are never simply technical affairs. As Durkeim (1933, 86) observed, regardless of the claims of law to rationality, order, proportionality, and so forth, in reality "passion is the soul of punishment." Crime provokes what Garland (1990, 30) has termed "a sense of outrage, anger, indignation and a passionate desire for vengeance . . . a shared emotional reaction caused by the criminal's desecration of sacred things." In the contexts in which transitional justice operates, the crimes are often egregious and accompanied by a lack of effective legal redress through corrupt or inept justice systems. It is perhaps little wonder that the compulsion to blame is all the more compelling in such societies. In such places, blame offers sharper distinctions between the wicked and the righteous, given the basic premise of transitional justice that "in all cases, public airing of the dark past assigned blame to the perpetrators while giving due credit to the victims, survivors and successors" (Tilly 2008, 11).

Second, in retributive variants of transitional justice—again in a fashion which is strongly reminiscent of crime victims in the established democracies—many victim organizations become fixated upon the degree of blame attributed (and indeed the efficacy of their own advocacy skills), measuring this exclusively by the harshness of punishment (Doak 2011). As one rather exasperated international advisor to the Officer of the High Representative working in Bosnia summed up:

> R: The argument of so many of the Victims Associations about the lightness of the sentences, whether here or in The Hague, are predictable and depressing . . . if you sentence a 60 year old former Republic of Serbska army officer to 20 years, you're sentencing him to life, what difference does it make if you don't give him life, if you don't give him 40 years. There's an awful lot of professional moaning, a lot of these

victims' associations have actually had a good thing out of being perpetually outraged, hurt, damaged . . .

I: In what way, financially?

R: Yes, and always being in the media spotlight, they've become professional keeners . . . in a Greek sense. My own impression is that outfits like the [name omitted] and other rival outfits, they all try to out-do each other in being the most strident in their demands. I think they've been in a sense institutionalized in a way, which is actually not necessarily very helpful for people who do have extremely legitimate cause for complaint.[12]

A third problem with simplistic blame discourses in transitional justice is that they often lead to an *individualizing* of responsibility for violence onto *only* those who took up arms (Steinhert 2008; Jamieson 2012). The individualization of culpability in such contexts fails to capture what Osiel (2007, 200) has termed "complicit and benefitting bystanders" who may also bear some responsibility for past abuses. Certainly the public visibility or performative aspects of retributive justice in such contexts — what Douglas (2001) termed in relation to the Nuremberg trials as the "spectacle of legality" — has the effect of shining a bright light on the villains while the audience, or indeed those who choose not to watch, can remain safe in the darkness. An Argentinian lawyer (who works for a very active human rights NGO which advocates for trials of those associated with the military junta) expressed it thus: "the trials against perpetrators in some way acquitted everyone. Different sectors of the society — I mean different sectors like business, the Catholic Church, regular people, I think felt a relief with this, kind of okay, we already found the guilty people, we'll deal with this." Such individualization of blaming is not restricted to the retributive variants of transitional justice. In South Africa, for example, while it attempted to address institutional and structural culpability, the TRC has been accused by some critics of being far too gentle toward the white community, which benefited from the Apartheid legal and economic order but whose response was often framed in terms of their noninvolvement in direct violence (Posel 2002; Fullard 2004). As the same victim advocate in South Africa quoted above told the authors with regard to the Truth and Reconciliation Commission:

the major problem with the TRC was that it didn't get to the root causes of violence and it didn't exercise its powers to lay the buck where it needed to be laid. I mean their political testimonies were pathetic, absolutely pathetic. They didn't take on business, local and international — these are the culprits actually. I was at the political testimonies and FW de Klerk was the person who has a Nobel peace prize — for God's sake, please — and he said he didn't know what the military were up to. [. . .] And so the real perpetrators are sitting very pretty out there, all systems in place, no dent on their lives at all and the people who pay the

> price are the poor people who bore the brunt of the bullets and the
> whips and the torture.

Finally we would argue that in some instances the establishment and reproduction of blame for past hurts might actually obfuscate culpability for either historical or contemporary wrongs, which were actually inflicted by victimized communities. In a remarkably prescient account written in 1946, Hanna Arendt wrote to Karl Jaspers wondering about the long-term consequences of Jewish innocence and German guilt for the atrocities committed during the Second World War. Arendt argued that, in comparison to the inhumanity that was visited upon them by the Nazis, even the least sympathetic of Jewish victims was blameless: "the most revolting profiteer [was] as innocent as a new born child" (Arendt Jaspers 1992, 56). In the same letter, she also suggested that if the Germans were burdened with hundreds of thousands who could no longer be punished adequately by the legal system, "We Jews are burdened with millions of innocents who make every Jew today feel like innocence incarnate." As Ben Meir (2013) has put it more recently, "Does the Jewish people's unprecedented historical suffering somehow transform them from 'victims' to 'Victims,' guaranteeing them, and by extension the State of Israel, an unconditional status of moral untouchability?"

Of course, the linkage between a strong sense of historical victimhood and a lack of empathy and failure to take responsibility for atrocities committed by one's own side is far from unique to either Jews or the state of Israel. As Cohen (2001, 56) has well captured, such versions of denial are clearly discernible in some Palestinian discourses, in the Balkans, in Northern Ireland and, we would argue, in many other contexts where transitional justice is done. This version of blame allocation, and the parallel claiming of innocence is part of the age-old tradition of scapegoating (Girard 1972, 1989), whereby locating blame in the "other" also absolves "us" of any semblance of guilt or responsibility. For Girard (1977, 24), the emergence of the legal system to replace messy forms of communal sacrifice offered a version of scapegoating that is "holy, legal, and legitimate." Law formalizes blame, both practically and symbolically. Those who have committed wrongs against fellow human beings, once formally adjudicated as blameworthy by a legal process, are by definition the most plausible of scapegoats for *all* of the ills of the past.

To recapitulate, to understand the urge to blame in transitional justice, one must recognize and acknowledge its particular power in societies which have experienced violence; one should be cognisant of the tendency in some contexts for the effectiveness of blaming to be measured solely by the degree of retribution visited on the perpetrator; one should acknowledge the risks associated with the individualization of blame in terms of failing to countenance broader realities of culpability and the closely associated dangers that the versions of innocence that are constructed and reproduced in such circumstances may themselves sow the seeds for continued or future violence or repression. In addition, we would argue that to make victimhood contingent upon blameless "innocence" is as disempowering as being silenced by the most arrogant of international lawyers or "spoken for" by the most overzealous victims' rights advocate.

CONCLUSION

As we noted in the introduction to this chapter, victims serve a key practical and symbolic role in the "legitimation work" (Barker 2001) of almost all of those who work in the field of transitional justice. For many in this field, victims are the stated reasons why we do what we do. They play a central role in underpinning what Clarke (2009) has termed the "fictions" of justice in transitional settings—the cultural meaning ascribed to key themes such as justice, accountability, truth, and so forth—as well as the institutions which are established to achieve these objectives. In navigating how the variants of voice, agency, and blame are constructed and enacted in such contexts, we outline the political and ideological factors at play that are familiar in settled democracies. Of course, in societies which have experienced extreme communal violence and state repression, victimhood is inevitably mapped onto competing narratives of community, nation, and the contested past all the more starkly. There is perhaps one more controversial notion that we would also argue should be part of the more nuanced appreciation of victimhood in transitional justice.

As noted above, crime victims in settled democracies have increasingly utilized rights language in their mobilization strategies. In the context of transitional justice, efforts by victims and victims' groups to "mobilize empathy" (Wilson and Brown 2009) similarly occupy the terrain of international human rights law rather than general "rights talk." As a result, they are faced with the dialectical consequences of "human rights-claims making" (e.g., Falk 2008). Human rights require, at a quite fundamental level, an acknowledgment of the rights of the "other." For example, as has been argued elsewhere with regard to armed groups that highlight human rights abuses against their own members while simultaneously engaging in abuses themselves (McEvoy 2000; Dudai and McEvoy 2012), resorting to such rhetorical and practical forms of mobilization have what Hunt (1993) has referred to as a "constitutive" effect on the individual and social actors involved. Actors and organizations are often forced to reflect critically on their own language and mobilization strategies through human rights talk (Scheingold 2004). For those armed groups or their political wings which do not, the mismatch between their rhetorical commitment to human rights values, and the practices and exclusionary discourses and styles of campaigning in which they engage, becomes clear. Bluntly put, what is sauce for the proverbial goose is sauce for the gander.

Racist, sectarian, sexist, reactionary, or other such discourses and practices—whether directed against other victims or victims' organizations, former combatants or political opponents—can and should be challenged. Acknowledging and respecting the pain suffered by victims does not entail a suspension of critical faculties once such individuals and groups have entered what Brewer (2010, 162) has termed "public victimhood."[13] For us, the variant of both voice and agency, which is legitimately claimed through human rights in transitional justice, comes at a price. That price is that victims and victims' organizations will be subject to the same level of respectful critical inquiry that ought to be applied to all relevant actors in a postconflict context. Together with an informed understanding of the complexities of voice, agency, and blame, an interrogation of the positionality of victimhood is also crucial in transitional justice.

NOTES

1. A previous version of this chapter was published in *Social and Legal Studies* (2013), 22, 4. 489–513. It is published here with permission.

2. The authors would like to thank Cheryl Lawther, Louise Mallinder, Lorna McGregor, Ron Dudai, and Maeve McCusker for comments on a previous version of this paper. Kieran McEvoy also received useful feedback on versions of the paper presented at different seminars at the Universities of Edinburgh, Lancaster and the Alliance for Historical Dialogue and Accountability Conference Columbia University New York in December 2012. We would also like to thank Ian Loader for pointing us toward the utility of Barker's work. Finally, the quotes cited are drawn from projects funded by: Atlantic Philanthropies (Transitional Justice from Below); The Arts and Humanities Research Council (Grants AHRC *AH/E008984/1* Beyond Legalism: Amnesties, Transition and Conflict Transformation and *AH/J013897/* Amnesties Prosecutions and the Public Interest) and the Economic and Social Research Council (*ES/J009849/1* Lawyers, Conflict and Transition).

3. The methodology deployed in these projects has been replicated across a number of studies, all focused on overlapping aspects of political transition from conflict. The first of these was a study on the release and reintegration of politically motivated prisoners in South Africa, Italy, Spain, Israel and Palestine (1995–1996) conducted by McEvoy (with Gormally). In 2006–2008 (with Mika) the current authors conducted fieldwork in South Africa, Rwanda, Colombia, Sierra Leone, Colombia, and Northern Ireland on the theme of transitional justice from below. In 2008–2011 (with Mallinder and Dickson) McEvoy led another project exploring the use of amnesties in transitional contexts—South Africa, Uganda, Uruguay, Argentina, and Bosnia-Herzegovina. More recently, in 2013–2016 he has conducted further interviews with a range of victims' organizations on matters related to dealing with the past in Northern Ireland and with lawyers, victims, and others in a comparative project on lawyers in conflict in transition in Cambodia, Israel, Palestine, Chile, Tunisia, and South Africa (with Mallinder, Requa, and Bryson).

4. It should be noted that there have been significant developments in recent years concerning the exploration of historical injustices in settled democracies such as Aus-

tralia, Canada, Ireland, and elsewhere which have borrowed explicitly from transitional justice discourses. The issues examined have included the racist treatment of indigenous people, "stolen generations" of aboriginal children and institutional, religious, and sexual abuse of children and vulnerable adults. While some of the victim-related themes discussed in this chapter may resonate, such sites were not part of the original fieldwork and we make no claims of expertise in such contexts. For a discussion on the applicability of different elements of the transitional justice "tool kit" to such settings see Cellemajer and Kidmann 2012, Nagy 2013, and McAlinden 2012.

5. McEvoy (2007) has argued elsewhere that the lack of a criminological perspective on transitional justice is one of the reasons for the dominance of the type of legalistic thinking in transitional justice which sometimes contributes to the instrumentalization and disempowerment of victims. There are of course other historical, social, and political factors at play in the legal processes which may instrumentalize victims in transitional contexts. These include the "seductive" qualities of legalism, which are especially prevalent in transitional states. In contexts where the past may have been characterized by violence, disorder, and corruption, the "rule of law" provides a particularly compelling way of imagining an ordered and rational alternative. In addition, the often unquestioned prevalence of human rights discourses in transitional contexts, often framed as apolitical bulwarks against the messy business of political compromise, may lead to an emphasis on the punishment of perpetrators above all else and sometimes, as Dembour and Haslam (2004), Karstedt (2010), and others have described as "silencing" certain victims whose narratives do not fit in the pursuit of such objectives. Finally, a tendency toward what the anthropologist James C Scott (1988) has referred to as "seeing like a state"—the belief that top-down state and state-like institutions are the best ways to deliver transitional justice—rather than giving appropriate prevalence to "bottom-up" community or civil society initiatives which may in fact be better placed to work with and campaign on behalf of the victims of past violence (See further Baxi 2002, McEvoy 2007, Clarke 2009)

6. In the United Kingdom people with a criminal record will often have any award refused or reduced as a result of their criminal record, regardless of whether that record is relevant to the injury in question (Criminal Injuries Compensation Authority 2008). Similar provisions exist in the equivalent state compensation schemes in many European countries as well as many of the states in the United States (Greer 1996, Miers 2007).

7. The Lubanga case was the first trial undertaken by the ICC and the first case upon which a legal judgment has been delivered. The victims in this case were predominantly the child soldiers that Thomas Lubanga Dyilo has been found guilty of conscripting and enlisting into the armed forces and using to participate actively in the hostilities in the district of Ituri in the Democratic Republic of the Congo. One-hundred twenty-nine such victims were authorized to be represented in the proceedings. In July 2012 Lubanga was found guilty of the "crimes of conscripting and enlisting" child soldiers and sentenced to fourteen years imprisonment. The Prosecutor v. Thomas Lubanga Dyilo. ICC-01/04-01/06.

8. We encountered a similar experience in conducting fieldwork in Sierra Leone in 2006. At that time the then president was involved in a very public dispute with a prominent victim activist concerning the payment of reparations. The individual concerned, who was leader of one of the principal amputee organizations in Sierra Leone had apparently suffered his amputation in trying to defend his daughter from being raped. When we asked another victim how the president could afford to be in dispute with such an obviously "sympathetic victim," he replied "sometimes the amputees are shunned in Sierra Leone. Their terrible physical injuries are an unwanted reminder of the past. Also, because they are so badly traumatized by what happened to them people just don't listen—they shout too loudly."

9. Interview with Unionist victims' group spokesman March 2010, Belfast. The interviewee was responding to a suggestion (since abandoned) by the British government-appointed Consultative Group on the Past that the families of all of those killed

during the Northern Ireland conflict (i.e., state security forces members of and non-state groups and civilians) should be treated as "victims" and receive a one-off payment in recognition of their loss. For further discussion of those recommendations see Lundy (2010).

10. Thus for example, in interviews conducted by one of the authors, iconic victims organizations in Argentina such as the Madres de la Plaza Mayor or the Abuelas refused to countenance the notion that the family members of security force personnel killing during the junta years might also be deemed victims. In Northern Ireland, an important British government-sponsored initiative which recommended the establishment of a Legacy Commission (in effect, a truth commission) was scuppered among chaotic scenes at the document launch in Belfast by the recommendation that the family members of Republican and Loyalist paramilitaries killed during the conflict should also receive a one-off payment in recognition of their loss.

11. Interestingly for current purposes, in a manner reminiscent of early "victim blaming" research in criminology, Nietze (1996:106) goes on to argue that the political dangers of such destructive resentment are negated by religious leaders who urge the masses to look at their own sinfulness as the cause of their suffering.

12. The Office of the High Representative (OHR) is an ad hoc international institution responsible for overseeing implementation of civilian aspects of the Peace Agreement ending the war in Bosnia and Herzegovina. Previously a very powerful political position (the most prominent holder of which was Lord Paddy Ashdown), it was created under the General Framework Agreement for Peace in Bosnia and Herzegovina, usually referred to as the Dayton Peace Agreement.

13. For Brewer, the "publicness" of victimhood is underpinned by a number of overlapping processes including; the communal nature of the violence which they have experienced; the fact that their suffering and sense of wrong is done in public (through campaigns, media work, mobilization, and so forth) and, in many instances, that their public assertion also entails a claim to saying who else is, and is not, entitled to the status of victimhood which they assert.

NINE

A Change for the Better or Same Old Story?

Women, the State, and Miscarriages of Justice

Annette Ballinger

For social science scholars committed to developing critical perspectives on the relationship between the state and victims of crime, the publication of *Critical Victimology* by Rob Mawby and Sandra Walklate in 1994 had a fundamental impact. Placing the state at the forefront of analysis, this volume provided an in-depth critique of positivist victimology, exposing the shortcomings of the key features associated with it, such as its focus on conventional crime occurring in the public sphere, and its inbuilt tendency to blame individual victims at the expense of an exploration of the wider, capitalist, hetero-patriarchal social order shared by both victims and perpetrators.

Critical Victimology also maintained that the mantras associated with left realism—producing an "accurate victimology," taking the "victim of crime 'seriously' and understanding problems as people experience them" (Mawby and Walklate 1994, 15)—nevertheless failed to offer an adequate analysis of the state (Mawby and Walklate 1994, 17). Addressing this inadequacy, Mawby and Walklate (1994, 21) defined critical victimology as a perspective that strives to:

> Examine the wider social context in which some versions of victimology have become more dominant than others and also to understand how those versions of victimology are interwoven with questions of policy responses and service delivery to victims of crime. It constitutes an attempt to appreciate how the generative mechanisms of capitalism

133

and patriarchy set the material conditions in which different victims' movements have flourished.

The inclusion of this wider context was, and remains, an extremely important feature of critical victimology, because it allows us to render visible and name "processes and experiences which were once unspoken and hidden" (Mawby and Walklate 1994, 19). Critical victimology thus provides the tools necessary for questioning the social construction of reality by exposing processes that usually "go on behind our backs" (Walklate 1989, 19). These tools have been particularly welcomed by feminist scholars, whose work constitutes a substantial strand within the critical victimology perspective, not least due to Mawby and Walklate's (1994, 177) insistence that "the feminist movement should no longer be marginalized by 'victimology.'" Instead, they emphasized that "the kind of state under discussion is a patriarchal state" (Mawby and Walklate 1994, 184). In turn, this involves a recognition that the various agencies of the state—including the criminal justice system and law itself—also work "from within a system which operates from a deeply embedded patriarchal framework" (Mawby and Walklate 1994, 185). In other words, we cannot assume the state to be a neutral arbiter inevitably working in the interests of its people. Thus, while key agencies within the state such as the legal system, presents itself as "objective" and "rational," merely "concerned with the facts" (Mawby and Walklate 1994, 185), "male power [within it] is systemic" (Mackinnon cited Mawby and Walklate 1994, 185). This insight forms one of the starting points of this chapter.

Another key focus within *Critical Victimology* was the immense power of the law and the state to oppress. That is to say, the state and its agencies are well placed to play a role "in the production of victims" (Mawby and Walklate 1994, 14). Thus, a second starting point in this chapter is concerned with the fact that the state itself can be understood to be directly responsible for an extremely serious and damaging form of victimization against its own citizens—that of miscarriages of justice. While it is a fact that both men and women have been, and still are, victims of miscarriages of justice, I shall focus on women as victims of injustice, the purpose being to illustrate the close relationship between these two starting points.

In the remainder of this chapter I therefore trace the modern history of miscarriages of justice through a number of case studies that have occurred immediately before and since the creation of the Court of Criminal Appeal, whose key function is to allow evidence to be heard that materializes following the conclusion of a trial, thereby offering an opportunity for victims of miscarriages of justice to have their case heard after their conviction.

HISTORICAL CONTEXT: TRACING CASES OF
MISCARRIAGES OF JUSTICE

The establishment of the Court of Criminal Appeal in 1907 has been widely regarded as a result of "the most dangerous verdict that has ever been recorded" (Sir Charles Russell quoted in Ryan and Havers 1977, 201)—the guilty verdict that concluded the Florence Maybrick trial in 1889. Cases involving the defendant standing trial for murder by poisoning, as Maybrick was, inevitably relied on circumstantial evidence during the nineteenth and early twentieth centuries. In the Maybrick case, this type of evidence was particularly problematic, as the victim, her husband James Maybrick, was widely known to have both purchased and regularly and deliberately ingested for medicinal purposes arsenic, the substance which eventually caused his death. Lacking evidence that Florence had administered arsenic to her husband, the case against her was based on little more than malicious gossip and largely unfounded suspicion by disgruntled servants, and an ex-partner of James who felt that she ought to have been his rightful wife.[1] It would appear that state servants were well aware of this, for in the absence of a Court of Appeal, Florence's death-sentence was remitted by the Crown due to the Home Secretary declaring *"that there was the most grave and serious doubt as to whether any act of Mrs. Maybrick had brought about the death of her husband"* (Ryan and Havers 1977, 270, italics added). Yet, despite the Lord Chief Justice recommending that she be released immediately, she spent nearly fifteen years in prison, due to the "mishandling" of her case by the Home Secretary, who nonetheless maintained that this "most grave and serious doubt" about her guilt, did "not wholly exclude a reasonable doubt." He subsequently decided that she was guilty of a *failed* attempt to murder her husband—a crime with which she had never been charged, and thus had never been convicted of (Ryan and Havers 1977, 270–271). With such a wide margin of discretion being exercised by a politician, the creation of the Court of Appeal would seem to have been overdue at the end of the nineteenth century.

The establishment of the Appeal Court did not however, save the life of Edith Thompson, executed in 1923 for a murder she did not commit and had not participated in. Edith and her husband, Percy, were walking home when Edith's lover, Freddy Bywaters, suddenly appeared and stabbed Percy to death. As in the Maybrick case, there was no direct evidence that Edith had participated in this crime, or that she had prior knowledge of Percy's intent. On the contrary, Freddy himself repeatedly stated that he was solely responsible for the crime, spending two thirds of the limited space available on his petition for his own life reiterating Edith's innocence. He also asked the Home Secretary "to accept my word sir, or perhaps you can show me some way in which I can prove to you that I am speaking the truth" (HO45/2685 cited in Ballinger 2000, 254).

When this appeal was ignored, he asked his mother to send this statement to the Home Secretary:

> I swear she is completely innocent. She never knew that I was going to
> meet them that night. . . . She didn't commit murder. I did. She never
> planned it. She never knew about it. She is innocent, innocent, absolutely innocent. (cited in Ballinger 2000, 254)

This was to no avail since Edith Thomson was widely regarded as having stood trial "for her immorality" rather than for murder (Sir Henry Curtis-Bennett cited in Ballinger 2000, 225)—that is to say—despite the evidence against her amounting to nothing more than insinuation, suspicion, and speculation, her adulterous behavior ensured that she was deemed to be guilty, despite the lack of evidence. Her adultery *was* the evidence.[2]

Freddy was a sailor and during their fourteen-month affair, when he was at sea, he and Edith would play a fantasy game, expressed through letters and revolving around killing Percy. Edith's defense counsel argued her letters were inadmissible since they discussed the possibility of poisoning Percy or feeding him ground glass in his food. Both methods were dismissed by the pathologist, who was adamant there was no evidence to support either. Nonetheless, the judge allowed the inclusion of the letters, and the prosecution proceeded to select only those letters which contained incriminating passages, quoting these passages repeatedly and out of context, thus succeeding in "presenting a false picture to the jury in which the correspondence appeared to rise to crime in an accelerando of incrimination" (Broad 1952, 195).[3] In short, highly ambiguous, and often innocuous passages such as "you'll never leave me behind again, never, unless things are different," were interpreted as evidence of murderous intent, or incitement to murder (Exhibit 50 cited in Ballinger 2000, 227). Other passages singled out involved reference to a poison Edith had read about in a novel, despite the fact that she was not standing trial for poisoning. These passages therefore merely served to consolidate insinuation and suspicion, since they played no part in supplying evidence of the actual stabbing (Exhibit 22 in Ballinger 2000, 227).

Ironically, the Court of Appeal played a crucial role in *consolidating* her guilt in a case that is now recognized as a miscarriage of justice by virtually all those who have examined it, although not by the judiciary itself.[4] While space does not permit an analysis of all seven grounds on which the Appeal was heard, one ground was that the judge had failed "to direct [the jury] that there was no evidence that the Appellant was a party to or had knowledge of the attack upon Percy Thompson" (HO45/2685). Bresler has argued that the judge did in fact include this in his instructions to the jury—hence it was they, rather than the judge, who had acted wrongly in convicting Edith. He further argues that The Appeal Judge *realized* she had been wrongly convicted, hence to ensure the verdict fitted the evidence, he used the Appeal Court to *redefine* the case:

> The real case against Edith Thompson was that the letters were evidence of a protracted continuous incitement to Bywaters to commit the crime which he did in the end commit. . . . It was not necessary to prove that the knifing occurred by arrangement with her. It was enough that she had continuously incited Bywaters to murder her husband . . . (cited in Ballinger 2000, 246).

The appeal judge went a step further when, discussing Edith's appeal, he argued it was *irrelevant* whether Edith's letters had been true or false:

> So far as the persuasive effect of incitement was an issue, it depended not upon the question whether the statements were true, but upon the question what they were intended and likely to cause the reader to believe (*Criminal Appeals Reports* 1922, 71).

Thus, not only was Edith convicted on evidence for which she was not standing trial (poisoning), but that evidence did not have to be true. However, there was not a single piece of evidence to support the indictment she *was* charged with. Therefore the only possible reason for presenting evidence relating to poisoning would be to cause suspicion by implying that her letters made it *more* likely she was involved in Percy's murder. In other words, because there was no evidence of Edith's involvement in Percy's murder, the Crown utilized "evidence" of a crime *which had not been committed* (poisoning) to prove she was guilty of a crime which *had* been committed (Ballinger 2000, 247). Consequently, her counsel, Curtis-Bennett, had concentrated on proving the letters were based on fantasy, only to be told by the Appeal Court judge that it was "of little importance whether Mrs. Thompson was truly reporting something which she had done or falsely reporting something which she merely pretended she had done" (Criminal Appeal Reports cited in Ballinger 2000, 246). In short, the Appeal Court had been used to redefine the case to ensure the evidence fitted the verdict. The case therefore provides an early example of the Appeal Court's failure to prevent a miscarriage of justice. On the contrary, the purpose of this court was arguably, *subverted* to the point where an unsafe conviction was *consolidated* into a miscarriage of justice as a result of being heard in the Court of Appeal.

CRITICAL VICTIMOLOGY AND FEMINISM

In line with Mawby and Walklate's (1994) insistence that a gendered perspective should be at the forefront of the victimological agenda, feminist scholars have contributed to critical victimology by demonstrating the manner in which, not only the state, but also the law and the legal process within it is gendered. Thus, far from being a neutral arbiter, in possession of the tools necessary to identify the "truth," feminist scholars maintain that law pays great attention to gender. More specifically, within the courtroom, discourses relating to femininity such as those of motherhood, domesticity, respectability and sexuality have been exposed as playing a crucial role in defining the "good" woman—"someone who by *nature* is maternal, caring, gentle, modest, unselfish and passive" (Ballinger 2007, 67). Furthermore, this work has demonstrated how traditional phallocentric knowledge about women can have specific, and immensely detrimental, consequences for female defendants because they are judged according to double standards; that is, not only according to their crimes, but also according to their feminine conduct and behavior, particularly in relation to these four discourses. Within this context, feminists have identified those women who fail to fulfill gender role expectations and who also break the law as "doubly deviant" (Smart and Smart 1978, 3; Morris 1987; Naffine 1990; Kennedy; Ballinger 2000).

Thus, critical scholars shifted the focus of analysis onto the terrain of "the differential impact of law on distinct categories of women," a strategy which allowed a recognition of other factors such as the specific *type* of woman being judged (Ballinger 2007: 460). Indeed, as Carlen has stated, "the majority of women . . . are sentenced not according to the seriousness of their crime but primarily according to the court's assessment of them as wives, mothers and daughters" (1988, 10), with those who are deemed to have failed to live up to acceptable feminine conduct likely to experience "judicial misogyny" (Carlen 1985, 10).

From this perspective it is unsurprising that Florence Maybrick and Edith Thompson suffered victimization at the hands of the state in the form of miscarriages of justice, since they were both the *kind* of women who posed a threat to the established hetero-patriarchal social order. Both women had severely transgressed acceptable and appropriate standards of femininity by ignoring the discourses of respectability, sexuality, domesticity, and motherhood surrounding the "good" woman. Flouting Victorian propriety and respectability, Florence left her children in the care of others in Liverpool, while she travelled to London to conduct a passionate affair with "a tall, bearded and handsome gentleman"—Alfred Brierley—who was several decades younger than her husband (Ryan and Havers 1977, 35). Such was the scandal surrounding Florence's immoral conduct that it could not be ignored by her counsel who acknowledged that "this lady fell. She forgot her self-respect. She forgot her duty to her husband." However, he also appeared to be aware of the harsh consequences for women who 'forgot their duty' when he continued: "Because she sinned once is she, therefore, to be misjudged always?" (cited in Ryan and Havers 1977, 175).

Yet, her transgressions paled significantly compared to those committed by Edith Thompson, who not only continued working after her marriage,[5] commanding a salary higher than her husband's, but also kept her maiden name for business purposes. After several years of marriage she had failed to display a desire for motherhood, opting instead for an affair with nineteen-year-old Freddy Bywaters, eight years her junior (Ballinger 2000, 244). All these factors combined to ensure that Edith was perceived as a scheming, wicked, and sexually insatiable female—a seducer of young men like Freddy who consequently could be presented as the *real* victim in the case, despite having carried out the actual stabbing of Percy:

> As a youth of 19, of previous good character, he was exposed for many months to the malign influence of a clever and unscrupulous woman 8 years older, who . . . wrote him numerous letters, inciting him to help her in getting rid of her husband. . . . An impressionable youth of that age would need to be of unusual strength of character to resist such solicitations. . . . Bywaters fell a victim to her machinations. (Committing Magistrate Eliot Howard, cited in Ballinger 2000, 251)

In the absence of their husbands, the state—via the criminal justice system—can therefore be understood as having taken over the responsibility for disciplining "uppity," uncontrollable, and transgressive wives like Florence and Edith, whose transgressions against the hetero-patriarchal social order could not be formally punished by law. The women were instead punished for crimes they did not commit, leading to an almost universal recognition that they were victims of an intertwined set of patriarchal discourses that led directly to their death at the hands of the state (Ballinger 2000; Broad 1952; Lustgarten 1960; Ryan and Havers 1977; Weis 1990).

THE FEMINIST CRITIQUE OF OFFICIAL DISCOURSE AND EXPERT KNOWLEDGE

When analyzing the production of miscarriages of justice by the criminal justice system, issues around the social construction of official discourses produced by the state, as well as the power behind expert knowledge, should also be considered. In line with Mawby and Walklate's (1994) emphasis on the importance of questioning "what is real," such a consideration is able to expose legal, official truths as being socially constructed through complex power relationships between state servants and expert knowledge.

The criminal justice system presents itself and communicates through the very discourses on which legitimacy for the law is founded—neutrality, objectivity, reason, and rationality (Lacey et al. 1990, 152). These discourses hold the promise of a correct interpretation of events, "or even a direct access to the truth which avoids the problem of human interpretation" (Smart 1989, 11). Moreover, while law is not a science, it is nonetheless able to present itself as if it is, setting "itself apart from and above other discourses in the same way that science does" (Smart 1995, 73). However, following Mawby and Walklate's (1994) strategy of questioning "what is real" and what "goes on behind our backs," we are able to expose both legal and scientific discourses as socially constructed, and therefore, no more "objective" than other forms of knowledge.

OFFICIAL DISCOURSE VERSUS SUBJUGATED KNOWLEDGE: THE CASE OF LOUIE CALVERT[6]

The subjective and partial nature of official discourse generated by the state is highly visible in the Louie Calvert case, which also stands as a direct challenge to the legal principle of equality before the law, and instead illustrates that not everyone has equal access to the tools of knowledge production. On the contrary, "the state symbolically dominates society through maintaining a monopoly over the means of producing the truth" (Inglis 2003, 3). In the Louie Calvert case, that monopoly resulted in the ultimate form of victimization by the state—her execution—following what must, at the very least, be considered an unsafe conviction.

In 1926, Louie Calvert was found guilty and sentenced to death for the murder of Lily Waterhouse—a woman in whose house she had been living for the previous three weeks.[7] Official discourse produced by different state servants about Louie displayed little ambiguity about the *type* of woman she was. Home Office personnel described her, and the circumstances of her crime, in these terms:

> The prisoner . . . has been known as a prostitute of a low type in Leeds for some years. She has also a bad record of theft and housebreaking since she was 15. . . . She has had two illegitimate children aged 9 and 6. . . . The prisoner is of idle and very dirty habits. (HO144/6012)

Those in a position to construct the official "truth" about Louie Calvert therefore firmly identified her as a woman who had failed to conduct herself according to appropriate discourses around femininity, and hence, as falling within the "doubly deviant" category outlined above.

While awaiting execution, Louie wrote her "Life Story" which included the following account of events surrounding the death of Lily:

> I got into the company of the young woman with whose death I am charged . . . we used to go out at night and visit the public houses with the intention of get old [*sic*] of any man who had money and get them drunk then rob them of whatever money they had left and leave them and the last Sunday I was there this woman brought a man home supposed to be a soldier from Becketts Park hospital for wounded soldiers and after he had been there a few days we began to quarrel about him she wanted him and he wanted me but I wanted neither I wanted to leave them and go home again as it was beginning to get a little bit to [*sic*] hot the detectives were on our tracks and we could not go out with them pulling up and getting us fined well on the Wednesday night the day I was going to leave her we went out and had a few

drinks with this man and he fetched half a dozen pint bottles of beer and stout home and when we had been home about half an hour we all started to quarrel and it got to fighting oh the drink it is the ruination of everything for we do lots of things in drink and temper that we are most sorry for after well he said something nasty to her and she landed out with her fist at him and they both rolled on the floor when she got up and struck out again I picked up the poker which happened to be the nearest thing to me and my intention was to strike the man and make him leave of hitting her but instead it struck her on the head through him dodgeing [*sic*] out of the road and she fell dead at our feet he went mad then and got hold of her belt strangled her and carried her upstairs I got out and got home God knows how I did it I don't. (Calvert 1926, HO144/6012)

Louie's account of events is noteworthy for its specificity about the man alleged to be present. A Home Office memo confirmed that legal person-nel had knowledge about his existence *prior* to her trial:

The police, when they visited Calvert . . . *the day after the murder*, had found in a handbag a paper with the [Canadian] address of a man called Crabtree . . . and . . . careful inquiry was made as regards the movements of a miner named Frederick Crabtree. . . . This man was in fact an out-patient at Becketts Park Hospital. (HO144/6012; emphasis added)

Despite this indisputable evidence provided by the police themselves, when the Prison Governor passed Louie's "Life Story" to the Home Of-fice *after her conviction,* a state servant noted that "this is the first time the prisoner has told this story." The inaccuracy of this statement is sup-ported by the Home Office's own documents. For example, one memo stated that the prosecutor, Mr. Lowenthal:

had F. Crabtree ready in C[our]t with all evi[dence] as to his alibi but there was no justification for calling him as there was a mere sugges-tion that someone other than & stronger than the pr[isomer] might have killed the woman in the kitchen and carried her upstairs. Mr. Lowenthal was quite satisfied that the verdict was right. (HO144/6012)

It is unsurprising that Mr. Lowenthal was satisfied with the verdict as he was the *prosecutor* in the case. More surprising, however, is the fact that Mr. Lowenthal had this man waiting to be called as a witness in the court, which begs the question why Home Office personnel claimed never to have heard Louie's story before. In fact, the same memo demonstrates knowledge of Fred Crabtree's existence from the very beginning of the investigation, as illustrated in the quotation above.

Furthermore, Lily's neighbor, Emily Clayton, testified that "the previ-ous Sunday" a man had come to her "house and asked for Mrs. Water-house":

Mr. Chapple: Could you describe the man?

> He was tall. . . . He looked to be well built, and he said he was in Becketts Park Hospital, and he was going back to Canada the same week. (HO144/6012 Trial Transcript, 18)

It would appear that the trial judge, Mr. Justice Wright was aware of the potential significance of Emily's testimony, for he referred to it in his "Judge's Notes":

> On the Sunday about 9 a man came to my house and asked for Mrs. Waterhouse. He . . . said he came from Becketts Park Hospital and was going to Canada the next month. (HO144/6012)

The "Judge's Notes" also referred to Detective Officer Chester's testimony that he had found "papers with [the Canadian] address of man called Crabtree" in Louie's handbag when she was first interviewed. Finally, providing indisputable proof that Louie had discussed Fred Crabtree the very first time she was interviewed by police, the judge noted Detective Superintendent Pass's statement, taken the day after Lily's body was found:

> She said that Lily was expecting a man named Fred Crabtree to come and stay with her that night. I asked who Crabtree was. She said he was an ex-soldier from Becketts Park Hospital who is going to Canada on Saturday, and that Crabtree had been there last Sunday and stayed all night. (HO144/6012)

Indeed, the state's concern about any potential connection between Fred Crabtree and Lily's murder resulted in him being traced and interviewed:

> He appears to have been able, however, to satisfy the Police that he could not be the man who left his address at Mrs. Waterhouse's house and who is the man to whom the prisoner now refers in her "Life Story." . . . According to the witnesses whose statements were taken he had a complete alibi. . . . The only suspicious circumstance was that on the 1st April he had a slight cut just below his eye, but this was accounted for by . . . a bat [which] had hit him in the face [at work]. (HO144/6012)

Nonetheless, despite the considerable amount of evidence indicating a connection between Louie, Lily, and Fred Crabtree, the Home Office Permanent Under-Secretary concluded:

> I have today discussed this fully with the Directors + they both agree that prisoner's story of the presence of a man etc *now told for the first time* is incredible on the evidence + may safely be disregarded. (HO/144/6012, emphasis added)

He further concluded that the details of the Fred Crabtree found in Louie's bag:

> was *another* patient at the Becketts Park Hospital, and that it seems *probable* he either borrowed Frederick Crabtree's name or that he was of

the same name. Fred Crabtree the miner, has a sister in Canada. . . . I do not *believe* the prisoner's story, that a man was present when she struck the deceased woman with the poker, and that he subsequently strangled her and carried her body upstairs. (HO144/6012, emphasis added)

Apart from questioning the likelihood of there being two men called Fred Crabtree living within close proximity of each other, who both attended the same hospital, were both ex- or current servicemen and both had Canadian connections, it would also seem appropriate to question the Under-Secretary's use of the words "believe" and "probable." In a capital case, it would seem to be of crucial importance to move *beyond* probabilities and beliefs. In this case, it would have meant carrying out a thorough investigation to establish the identity of this man who had been observed by an independent witness going into Lily's house—and whose details were found in Louie's bag upon arrest. However, as Gilligan and Pratt (2004, 2) have noted:

> official discourse is . . . very wide ranging in its scope: it can be designed to bring closure to controversial incidents . . . and it can seem little more than simple documentation of the work . . . of a particular criminal justice bureaucracy, written by its chief executive. What such discourse does however, is to provide an official, objective truth about crime, criminal justice and punishment which puts a particular stamp on the available beliefs that individuals and social groups have of such matters.

This process of "truth-production" engaged in by state servants was facilitated by Louie's failure to conform to dominant discourses of acceptable femininity. As "a prostitute of a low class," "bad character," and "very dirty habits" with thirteen previous convictions and two illegitimate children—one of them in care—she had broken every convention associated with domesticity, motherhood, respectability, and sexuality, and as such, became the target of "judicial misogyny" (Carlen 1985, 10). As a doubly deviant woman, she was precisely the *type* of woman who could easily be discredited as a witness. Thus, her attempt to produce "truth"—based on lived experience and memory in the form of her *Life Story*—could be relegated to the very bottom of the hierarchy of knowledge, until she was dismissed altogether as a liar. Svensson (1997, 89) has noted:

> The usual way of piling up a criminal's life in the court records, as well as in the newspapers, is to refer to his [sic] life as if it simply consisted of his [sic] crimes. . . . The person is described as the symbol of evil . . . criminals are regarded as ruthlessly calculating individuals deliberately committing their crimes. There is no regard for the fact that most crimes are committed by people under the influence of drugs or alcohol, often frightened and under stress, or that these acts are often badly planned or unpremeditated . . . [by the] socially vulnerable. Since their voice has been taken away from them they cannot really be heard.

In Louie's case, this dominant portrayal of the defendant was exacerbated by her failure to comply with any of the discourses that contribute toward acceptable femininity. Meanwhile, "establishment forces" were located at the top of the hierarchy of knowledge—largely as a result of their ability to forge official truth into something which "simply fit[ted] the authorities' preconceived ideas of what really happened" (Gilligan and Pratt 2004, 5). This is further exemplified by Home Office communications such as: "The excuse of the murder I do not believe and the law must take its course," and: "The prisoner did not give evidence and the circumstantial evidence of her guilt is overwhelming." Hinting at the doubly deviant nature of Louie's crime, a third state servant responded: "I agree. It is the sort of crime that men frequently commit but women very rarely" (HO144/6012).

The state's success in producing "'truth' in official discourse . . . [is] something that has come to be largely taken for granted," as indicated by its ability "to deny or nullify alternative truth accounts" (Pratt and Gilligan 2004, 9) such as that presented by Louie. Within the context of this "unequalled ability to marshal the available judicial resources . . . and to use them effectively to win their case" (Inglis 2003, 178), an attempt to launch a battle "on behalf of the truth" (Foucault 1980, 132) was unlikely to be successful by powerless, uneducated, and transgressive women like Louie Calvert.

Once again it is also noteworthy, that, despite having existed for nineteen years at the time of Louie's trial, the Court of Appeal did not ensure that the contradictions within the evidence identified above were problematized. However, in the spirit of Mawby and Walklate's (1994) insistence that critical scholars should challenge "what is real," a critical victimological perspective applied to cases such as Louie's can make visible that which has hitherto remained invisible and give voice to those who have been silenced by official stories generated by state servants. Furthermore, while space does not permit a full account of other evidence that supports Louie's version of the truth, even an analysis of the disputed evidence outlined above, provides justification for arguing in favor of an extension of the definition of a victim of the state to include cases of unsafe convictions that have not officially been classified as miscarriages of justice.

CREATING VICTIMS THROUGH EXPERT KNOWLEDGE: THE SALLY CLARK CASE

Within Enlightenment discourses, a claim to "scientificity" is a claim to speak the truth, drawing on this claim therefore further reinforces the credibility of the legal process. However, as noted above, a critical victimological perspective can expose such claims as social constructions by questioning official truth generated by state agencies. Such exposure reveals that far from stemming from scientific methods as advocated by positivist victimology, "the authority to identify 'empirical truths' and to interpret observable, testable 'facts' is dependent on existing power relations within given social contexts" (Faith in Ballinger 2003, 219). Moreover, within the legal system, these claims to "scientificity" and "truth" disguise and mystify the subjugation and transformation of the defendant's account, as illustrated in the case of Louie Calvert.

Enlightenment principles and values have also been responsible for creating a hierarchy of knowledge dominated by "experts"—"judges of normality"—who can lay claim to 'truth' as a consequence of having produced "scientific" and "objective" knowledge (Foucault 1977, 304). Yet, from a critical perspective, scientific knowledge—despite its privileged position at the top of this hierarchy—can be deconstructed and therefore, like legal knowledge, also be exposed as socially constructed. Nowhere is this better illustrated than in the Sally Clark case, which has been described as "one of the greatest miscarriages of justices in recent times" (Osborne 2004, 1; see also Chapman and Broster 2003, 6). In 1999 Sally was found guilty of crimes that had never occurred—her children had died of natural causes. That these "imaginary murders" (Sweeney in Batt 2004, 305) could result in an innocent person receiving a life sentence and subsequently losing her appeal, was almost entirely due to the presentation in court of speculative, incompetent, and misleading evidence by experts, as well as the withholding of results from a postmortem test.

Having initially ascertained that Sally's firstborn son Christopher had died of natural causes, Home Office pathologist Allan Williams altered his own findings with regard to the cause of his death after he had performed an autopsy on Sally's second son, Matthew. Despite the fact that almost none of the other experts giving evidence were prepared to support Williams's claim that Matthew had been murdered, he now decided that with respect to Christopher, there was a "possibility that the child was smothered . . . a possibility in a broad range" (cited in Judgement 2003, para57).

Only one other expert supported Dr Williams's claim that these deaths were unnatural; *all* other defense *and* prosecution expert witnesses agreed that the causes of death were unascertained. This other expert was Professor Sir Roy Meadow, who gained notoriety with his claim that in a family like the Clarks',[8] there was a 1 in 8,543 risk of SIDS.[9] Therefore, in order to calculate what the chances are of two SIDS occurring in one such family:

> you have to multiply 1 in 8,543 times 1 in 8,543 . . . it's approximately a chance of 1 in 73 million . . . in England, Wales and Scotland there are about say 700,000 live births a year, so it is saying by chance that hap-

pening will occur once every hundred years. (Meadow in Judgement 2003, para96)

These statistics were not only inaccurate, but also irrelevant, since neither Sally nor her defense claimed the babies had died of SIDS. Nonetheless Meadow elaborated:

> it's the chance of backing that long odds outsider at the Grand National, you know; let's say it's an 80 to 1 chance, you back the winner last year, then the next year there's another horse at 80 to 1 and it is still 80 to 1 and you back it again, and it wins. Now here we're in a situation that, you know, to get to these odds of 73 million you've got to back that 1 in 80 chance four years running, so yes, you might be very, very lucky because each time it's just been a 1 in 80 chance and you know, you've happened to have won it, but the chance of it happening four years running we all know is extraordinarily unlikely. So it's the same with these deaths. You have to say two unlikely events have happened and together it's very, very, very unlikely. (cited in Judgement 2003, para99)

Yet, even Professor Meadow, whose statistical evidence arguably was to prove decisive in the jury returning a guilty verdict, conceded "there was a lack of research on shaking of babies and it was *no more than guess work*" (Judgement 2000, para59 emphasis added). Nonetheless, despite challenges to Meadow's testimony, the Appeal Judges ruled that there was "overwhelming evidence of the guilt of the appellant" (Judgement 2000, paras 256, 254), and the convictions were upheld.

Following the dismissal of her appeal, Sally's husband Stephen, succeeded in retrieving test results of Harry's blood, which had not been disclosed at either the trial or the first appeal. The report indicated Harry had suffered from an infection "that had spread as far as [his] cerebral spinal fluid" (CSF). This led to an investigation by the Criminal Cases Review Commission (CCRC) who referred the case back to the Court of Appeal. The non-disclosure of the report became the first ground of the appeal. The tests had been ordered by Dr. Williams, who had known the results "since February 1998. He had kept the results secret" (Skeleton Argument, henceforth SA 2003, 1). After disclosure of these results, experts who had given evidence during the trial now confirmed the crucial impact this infection would have had on the cause of death. Professor Berry stated it "would have had a significant impact on his opinion as to the cause of Harry's death" (SA 2003, 3). Dr. Rushton concluded: "on the basis of the reports now available . . . the death of Harry was due to staphylococcal infection" (SA 2003, 4). Professor Luthert—one of the experts the appeal judges—had referred to as having provided "overwhelming evidence" of Sally's guilt (Judgement 2000, para223)—"described the . . . non-disclosure as 'blood-chilling'" (SA 2003, 4). He was one of several experts to confirm that in the light of the new disclosure, evidence that had previously been presented to indicate Sally had harmed Harry was likely to have arisen in connection with this infection (SA 2003, 4).

Given the grave consequences of withholding such evidence, the second appeal reflected on Williams's conduct:

> It is clear that Dr Williams appreciated that this was information that needed to be considered before a final conclusion was reached on the cause of Harry's death. . . . However, [he] made no reference to these results, not even to having submitted these samples for examination. (Judgement 2003, paras140, 142)

His failure to do so led the appeal judges to conclude that "he had fallen a very long way short of standards to be expected of someone in his position upon whose evidence the court was inevitably going to be so dependent" (Judgement 2003, para164). Following their criticism, they offered "him the opportunity . . . to explain his apparent shortcomings"—he declined to do so (Judgement 2003, para165; see also Nobles and Schiff 2004, 239).

The judges upheld the appeal on the nondisclosure of evidence alone, but chose to respond to what would have been a second ground—Professor Meadow's statistical evidence. They agreed with the first appeal judges that he had failed to qualify his statistics which themselves represented an "illegitimate over-simplification" of the chances of two SIDS deaths occurring in one family (Judgement 2003, para102).[10]

The Sally Clark case demonstrates the continued relevance of the feminist challenge to legal theory and practice, together with critiques of the symbiotic relationship between law and expert knowledge (Smart 1989; Heidensohn 1995; Allen 1987; Ballinger 2005), by demonstrating how traditional phallocentric knowledge about women can have specific and immensely detrimental consequences for female defendants, because they are judged, not only according to their crimes, but also according to standards of femininity. That is to say, while women's status has undeniably changed in recent decades and formal equality between the sexes has been achieved—with these "new types of freedom," new forms of oppression have also emerged (McNay 2004, 171). Moody notes that "changes in the status of women may have had an impact on judicial attitudes" (1995, 223), and evidence of this can be observed in Sally's trial, where the very equality she represented—a highly educated, financially independent working lawyer—could be used against her to suggest a lack of maternal feelings. Thus, the first question put to her in cross-examination was, "You were not cut out to be a mother, were you?" (cited in Kennedy 2005, 77). She was described as "career-obsessed," and portrayed "as a baby-murderer whose motives for killing her babies were that she resented the interference with her career" (Batt 2004, 198).

The strategy adopted by the prosecution in Sally's case thus suggests that "the courtroom remains a gendered space which frequently functions as a key arena" for reinforcing traditional discourses of femininity, for it is inconceivable that a man would be considered an unfit father as a result of being a successful lawyer (Ballinger 2016, 144). Her very success, her lack of helplessness, her rejection of overly feminine attire in court—instead appearing in business suits—exemplified her failure to act according to traditional discourses of femininity and ensured she did not cut a sympathetic figure (Batt 2004, 97). Instead, "she was repeatedly described as a career woman who had a luxury, dream-home, as though there was clearly no place for babies in her world" (Kennedy 2005, 78).

EXPERT KNOWLEDGE AND STATE POWER

Professional misconduct of expert witnesses offered the opportunity to individualize the "cause" of this miscarriage of justice by identifying rogue individuals as being the sole culprits. Allowing the wider legal structures within which experts like Williams and Meadow operated to remain unexplored, arguably contributed toward the stability of the legal process at a time when it potentially faced a crisis of legitimacy. However, according to Naughton (2007, 42), far from being aberrations, miscarriages of justice are endemic within the legal system:

> [Official figures] show an annual average of 4,496 quashed convictions at the Crown Court . . . given by magistrates between 1986–2005. . . . If this average is added to the CACD[11] annual average . . . the official miscarriage of justice iceberg, is increased to an annual average of 4,733 cases.

Furthermore, estimates indicate that approximately "3,000 people are currently imprisoned in England and Wales who are innocent" (Naughton 2007, 134). Such statistics raise serious issues about the systemic ability of the state to generate victims. For example, the Criminal Procedures and Investigations Act (1996) has restricted the defense's ability to check withheld material, and therefore, "no one knows how many wrongful convictions and/or miscarriages of justice are being caused simply because no one knows how much material is being withheld" (Naughton 2007, 76).[12] Thus, while high-profile cases such as that of Sally Clark undeniably caused a crisis of legitimacy for the criminal justice system, its response has always been to argue that individual "errors" in the legal system, in individual cases, were responsible. Hence, while the Court of Criminal Appeal was created in response to the Maybrick case, and the CCRC was established in response notorious cases such as that of the Birmingham Six, the state has failed to address structural issues that give rise to miscarriages in the first place. Instead, official inquiries established following a high-profile case is tasked with identifying the specific "error" that was responsible. As Burton and Carlen (1979, 48) observed:

> The task of inquiries into particular crises is to represent failure as temporary, or no failure at all, and to re-establish the image of administrative and legal coherence and rationality. One of the political desiderata of official discourse is therefore to retain the intellectual confidence of parties, elites and functionaries within the state apparatuses. To create a discourse of unity and cohesion between parties . . . [thus] demonstrating the state's sovereign reason.

The state's success in achieving this goal can be measured by the fact that "the production of 'truth' in official discourse . . . [is] something that had come to be largely taken for granted," as indicated by its ability "to deny or nullify alternative truth accounts" (Pratt and Gilligan 2004, 9). In the Sally Clark case this "unequalled ability to marshal the available judicial resources . . . and to use them effectively to win their case" (Inglis 2003, 178), was reinforced by expert knowledge, and combined, they generated a case built on "judicial misogyny" to the extent crimes against an innocent woman were invented.

However, Inglis reminds us that "institutions and experts who claim to speak the truth should be treated with wariness and critical reflection" (2003, 3), and this case therefore also illustrates that even the most powerful truth producers can be challenged. Yet, arguably, the overturning of Sally's conviction can also be understood to have reestablished legitimacy for a system that appeared to possess the correct tools to rectify "errors" within it. Consequently, it is vital that the feminist critique of the state and its laws is not seduced by the legal system's eventual recognition of Sally's innocence, for it can be understood to have merely remedied a problem it itself had created, a process which ultimately restored its legitimacy, and arguably, increased its own power "by confirming that it is the most appropriate body to establish the truth" (Ballinger 2012, 20). It is thus the power of law itself—together with its symbiotic relationship with expert knowledge—which should be challenged, for without a decentering of both, their "superior position at the apex of the hierarchy of truth production will be maintained" (Ballinger 2012, 20). Once again, the relevance of Mawby and Walklate's (1994) insistence on the examination of structures, rather than individuals, is relevant, and the ongoing need for a feminist critique becomes particularly poignant when reflecting on subsequent events in relation to those who were responsible for the construction of the knowledge upon which Sally was convicted. While Williams and Meadow both faced charges of professional misconduct, the consequences for them were temporary in nature. While Williams lost his accreditation to carry out post mortems for the Home Office for a period of three years in 2005 (Dyer 2005, 10), an Appeal Panel reinstated him in 2007 "on the basis that he had made an honest albeit serious error, which was not likely to be repeated and which he had not sought to conceal" (Campbell and Walker undated, 32).

Having been struck off the medical register after being found guilty of "serious professional misconduct" by the General Medical Council in 2005, Professor Meadow regained his license in 2006 after Mr. Justice Collins justified overruling the Council's decision with these words:

> This case was presented by the media as Prof Meadow's evidence having caused a miscarriage of justice. That's unfair, manifestly unfair. . . .
> It may have contributed to it—who knows?—but the suggestion that it caused it is wrong and always has been. (*Guardian*, February 18, 2006)

Thus, the symbiotic relationship between law and expert knowledge had been restored. The price for these experts' wrongdoing was to be paid by the victim of their misconduct, for Sally was not to enjoy the privilege of such an unproblematic return to her former existence. She died in 2007, aged forty-two. She had endured severe post-traumatic stress disorder and "protracted grief reaction" during the four years after her release, and "never fully recovered from the effects of this appalling miscarriage of justice" (BBC News UK 22 November 2007).

The aftermath of Sally Clark's conviction, and indeed of the other cases analyzed in this chapter, raise issues around the relationship between miscarriages of justice, wrongful convictions, and social harm. For example, while the creation of the CCRC is to celebrated, and it must be emphasized that Sally's conviction was overturned as a direct result of her case being referred to this commission, Naughton (2007) has identified important limitations inherent to its operation, arguing that only those cases that pass the "real possibility" test are likely to be referred back to the CACD. That is to say, only cases which are considered to have a strong chance of being overturned according to *legal* procedure, will be reviewed. Hence, even the most compelling cases, such as that of John Roden,[13] cannot be referred to the CCRC because the very "evidence that indicates his innocence was available at his original trial, and thus does not satisfy the CACD requirement" (Naughton 2007, 77). In short, even though this is almost certainly a miscarriage of justice, it is not a wrongful conviction, as *procedures* were adhered to. This demonstrates the CCRC's focus on miscarriages of justice as defined in criminal law, as opposed to the possible wrongful conviction of the innocent as expressed in public/ political discourse:

> It operates entirely within the parameters of the criminal justice process to uphold the integrity of due process, but does not question the possibility that due process procedures can cause miscarriages of justice and/or the wrongful convictions of the innocent (Naughton 2007, 77).

CONCLUSION

This chapter has demonstrated that miscarriages of justice and wrongful convictions continue to be generated uninterrupted from one century to another, because structural critiques, as advocated by Mawby and Walklate (1994), are undermined by a focus on "individual error," thereby perpetuating and reproducing dominant discourses within the legal system.

At a different level, adopting a social harm approach (Hillyard et al 2004) to the cases examined above can provide "a more holistic understanding of the harmful consequences engendered, which have not previously been . . . subjected to critical appraisal" (Naughton 2004, 111). The untimely death of Sally Clark has already been noted, and a small glimpse of the impact of her conviction on her husband Steven and their surviving son became visible when Steven stated that "my honest, law-abiding family has just been crushed by the machinery of the State" (cited in Batt 2004, 207). Becoming a widower and a motherless child must also count toward the social harm generated by actions of the state.

Louie Calvert also left behind a distraught family. When her six-year-old son Kenneth visited her the day before her execution, he "pathetically appealed to his mother to come home" (cited in Ballinger 2000, 140).

After her release Florence Maybrick returned to the United States, where she lived in severe poverty as a recluse for the rest of her life. She died alone in a wooden shack in 1941 and was never to see her children again (Colquhoun 2014).

The execution of Edith Thompson and Freddy Bywaters left two families devastated by the loss of much loved son, daughter, and sister, and her executioner, John Ellis, resigned from his post ten months after her execution. Following a failed suicide attempt in 1924, he eventually succeeded in committing suicide in 1932, an act that several commentators attributed to Edith's execution. One of those commentators included his son, who stated: "Dad had not had a good night's sleep for many years. We all knew what prevented him from sleeping" (PCOM 9/1983 XC2662).

While the state is not formally accountable for this level of victimization and secondary victimization, this level of social harm raises questions about redefining the state's role in generating victims. One way of formalizing the state's responsibility for such victimization could be through a redefinition of "crimes of omission" (McLaughlin 1996, 286). That is to say, the state's failure to carry out an adequate investigation can be understood as "omission," while the social harm generated as a consequence of such omission, can be understood as "commission" (Ballinger 2003, 237).

There is little contemporary evidence to suggest an improvement in the environment wherein miscarriages are generated. Thus, nearly a decade after Sally's conviction Home Office pathologist Freddy Patel "had his earlier work condemned by the General Medical Council" and was criticized for his finding that Ian Tomlinson died of coronary heart disease, when his death was in fact due to "internal bleeding," after being struck by a police officer (*Guardian*, March 15, 2011). Prior to that, Home Office Pathologist Michael Heath had faced a "disciplinary tribunal into his professional conduct," after his "flawed evidence clear[ed] three of murder" (*Guardian*, June 20, 2006). Paradoxically, it was predicted that cases which rely on complex forensic evidence to prove a miscarriage of justice would find it considerably more difficult to obtain such evidence following the closure of the *Forensic Science Service* (*Guardian*, September 9, 2011). Meanwhile, Richard Foster, the Chair of the CCRC, told the House of Commons Justice Committee that the CCRC had suffered "the biggest cut that has taken place anywhere in the criminal justice system . . . [while] there has been a 60 percent increase in applications compared to the previous 10 years" (The Justice Gap).

Through their development of a critical victimology in 1994, Mawby and Walklate provided scholars committed to social justice with the tools to question "what is real," who has the power to define that reality and how that definition operates in relation to the social order. Referring to MacKinnon's work, they noted the patriarchal framework within which law and the state operate, and therefore emphasized the importance of foregrounding feminist work within a critical perspective. More than twenty years later, not only is Mawby and Walklate's (1994) analysis of the relationship between gender, the state, and victimization still relevant, MacKinnon's analysis of a feminist jurisprudence also remains poignant. Advocating a new relationship "between life and law" Mackinnon (1989, 249, emphasis added) elaborated:

> Law that does not dominate life is as difficult to envision as a society in which men do not dominate women, and for the same reasons. To the extent feminist law embodies women's point of view, it will be said that the law is not neutral. *But existing law is not neutral.* It will be said that it undermines the legitimacy of the legal system. But the legitimacy of existing law is based on force at women's expense.

The case studies presented in this chapter in relation to women who have been victims of the state through either miscarriages of justice or unsafe convictions demonstrate that these issues remain as relevant to the twenty-first century as they were in the nineteenth and twentieth centuries, reminding us of Weedon's observation that legal equality "has not proved any great threat to the balance of power in a society where patriarchal relations inform the very production and regulation of female and male subjects" (cited in Smart 1989, 88). More recently, Fraser (2013, 210 original emphasis) has noted that "second-wave feminism has wrought an epochal cultural revolution, but the vast change in *mentalities* has not (yet) translated into structural, institutional change." Both observations eloquently capture the eternal struggle between continuity and change, and crucially, both lead to the conclusion that despite substantial progress in women's legal status, critical scholars, and activists are still faced with the task of developing further critiques of the state's role, and the power of the criminal justice system, in generating and sustaining gender oppression in the twenty-first century.

NOTES

1. For a full account of the case see for example Ryan, B. and The Rt Hon The Lord Havers (1977) *The Poisoned Life of Mrs Maybrick London*: Penguin Books.

2. For a full account and analysis of the Edith Thompson/Freddy Bywaters case, see Ballinger, A. (2000) *Dead Woman Walking*.

3. Space does not permit a full deconstruction of the letters and critique of the evidence against Edith. For a full analysis, see Ballinger, A. (2000) *Dead Woman Walking*.

4. Lawyers, philosophers, scholars, and journalists have examined this case and concluded this was a miscarriage of justice. See for example: Weis, R. (1990) *Criminal Justice*; Young, F. (1923) *Trial of Frederick Bywaters and Edith Thompson*; Lustgarden 1960; Broad, L. (1952) *The Innocence of Edith Thompson*; O'Donnell, B. (1956) *Should Women Hang?*; Twinning, W. (1990) *Rethinking Evidence*.

5. The 1920s was a period where, for example, London County Council enforced a jobs ban on married women (Past Notes in *Guardian* February 17, 1997).

6. Extracts from this case study appear in Ballinger, A. (2011) and is reproduced by kind permission from Routledge.

7. For a detailed account of the Louie Calvert case see Ballinger, A. (2016) *Gender, Truth and State Power: Capitalising on Punishment,* Ashgate.

8. The Clark family were considered to be a low-risk category due to being non-smokers; having a wage-earner in the family and the mother was over twenty-six years old (R v Clark 2003 para96).

9. Sudden Infant Death Syndrome.

10. See for example a critique of Meadow's statistics by *Royal Statistical Society* 23 October 2001.

11. Court of Appeal (Criminal Division).

12. The Law Society and the British Academy of Forensic Sciences have produced a list of over two-hundred examples of wrongful conviction caused through nondisclosure (Naughton 2007: 76).

13. For a full account of the John Roden case, see Eady, D. (2010) "The Failure to Live up to its Stated Values? The Case of Michael Attwoll and John Roden" in Naughton (ed.) (2010).

TEN

Hierarchical Victims of Terrorism and War

Ross McGarry

During the past twenty years the position and attention afforded to victims of crime have undergone significant changes within criminal justice systems in the West. David Garland (2001) has previously noted that the role of victims within criminal proceedings were at one time functional and offered the victim no agency; the victim of crime did not stand in direct contrast with the offender as having or receiving less from the process of justice. Instead, the role of the victim was as "testis" (Agamben 1999): third parties giving evidence in judicial proceedings pursued in the *public interest*. For Garland (2001), this changed somewhere in the late 1980s to early 1990s and emerged fully within UK policy during the early twenty-first century following a recurrent and powerful rhetoric which included "centering" the victim of crime throughout the justice process. Within the UK, the 2001 "Justice for All" white paper (see Criminal Justice System, 2001) set the political scene for a shifting emphasis aimed at balancing the "needs" of victims of crime with services to deliver their *procedural* "rights" (see Goodey 2005; Walklate 2007). In the years that followed, other policy surfaced to facilitate this process of "centering," including the "Domestic Violence, Crime and Victims Act" (HMSO 2004), the accompanying "Code of Practice for Victims of Crime" (Home Office 2005), and a review of victim services, "Getting it Right for Victims and Witnesses" (Ministry of Justice 2012a). Broadly speaking, central to many of the concerns of these policies has been the recognition of the emotional impacts of crime upon victims and the support required to be provided in the aftermath of such events. An emphasis on the need to hear the "voice" of the victim though "victim allocution" (qua Walklate 2007) and recognize their "trauma" within the processes of justice is another popular trope within such policies. More recently, following in the footsteps of the European Commission's pursuit of enforcing a minimum set of standards to victims of crime through European Union directives (see European Commission 2013), a new victim policy is currently in train within the UK that will aim to resolve the tensions between victim "needs" and "rights" by "guaranteeing" the entitlements of victims set out in the "Code of Practice for Victims of Crime" republished during 2013 (see Ministry of Justice 2013).

These policy issues are well established within victimological literature (see Bottoms and Roberts 2010), and the victims of crime are now not only central to criminal justice concerns, they are said to be used frequently in the *political interests* of the state, eliciting feelings and emotions from the public in a bid to ratchet up punitivism by juxtaposing the "otherness" of offenders with the vulnerability of victims (Garland 2001). This way of thinking about the victim is part of the concerns of critical victimology, a perspective that emerged from tensions toward the main preoccupations of positivist and radical elements of the discipline (Walklate 2007). For positivism, Martin Wolfgang's (1958) concept of "victim precipitation" attracted a problematic legacy from feminist scholars following Amir's (1971) later attempts to develop his mentor's work. Amir (1971) suggested that women were in some ways responsible for their own sexual assaults, an approach to understanding violence against women that was rightly lambasted as "victim blaming." Further concerns have been cast over radical victimology's lack of attention to violence against women. The focus on state victimization is said to have overlooked crimes that were lesser in scale, frequently more pervasive and disproportionately experienced by women (i.e., rape, assault, and abuse) (Walklate 2007). Against the backdrop of such concerns, the growth and influence of feminist criminology (see Smart 1977) gave way to radical Left Realism (Lea and Young 1984): a criminological perspective that sought to engage with the intricacies of the "crime problem," particularly those experienced by women and others in positions of relative deprivation, with the intention of influencing policy. Walklate (2003) reminds us however that offering a *critical* alternative to studying victims of crime is not simply to assume that it is an area of study dominated by concepts of "precipitation" and "malestream" views of what is harmful. It is also related to the ways in which the "scientific" measurement of victimization is employed within the discipline (Walklate 2003). The version of critical victimology I am concerned with during this chapter is developed from this school of thought—a victimology informed by feminism and Left Realist criminology that questions the labels afforded to those juxtaposed to one another as "offenders" and "victims" and challenges the political conditions under which the victim is constructed and seen to operate.

Constituted by such issues, Mawby and Walklate's (1994) critical victimology acknowledged the need for objective scientific measurement of victimization, but in conjunction to the pursuit of a depth of meaning achieved through an appreciation of the interplay between structure and agency. For Mawby and Walklate (1994), this includes the victims we "see" as well as the ones we do not, recognizing that the victim is a human agent who can be active as well as passive; those who can make choices and whose identities are not fixed to one particular identity (McGarry and Walklate 2015). This way of victimological thinking also means questioning what the term "victim" means and understanding the patterning of criminal victimization within a theoretical framework that is sensitive to the role of the vested interests of the state in producing it (Mawby and Walklate 1994). From this perspective the centering of the victim within recent criminal justice policy making in the UK urges us to question the processes by which this has occurred, the myriad consequences it presents for the justice process, and the role and influence acquired by crime victims as a result.

Although still not all encompassing in the decade or more since Garland (2001) made the above comments, the scope of who *might* be considered a victim within justice proceedings has broadened. Following the terrorist attacks in North America on September 11, 2001 (9/11), it is with increased frequency that victims of crime have featured within the criminal justice process alongside those who Mendelsohn (1974) would have described as the products of a "danger complex": the victims of terrorism and war. Understanding how these victimological "others" come to be situated within state mechanisms of justice proceedings is the focus of this discussion.

This chapter will illustrate how victims of terrorism and war have been contemporarily rearranged in political and cultural processes to present a complex hierarchical arrangement of victimhood. It will do so by presenting a discussion in three parts. In the first section of this chapter, victims of terrorism in the United States and UK will be discussed in relation to policy and victim compensation to illustrate how some victims of terrorism are politically situated as "unique," while others become more "routine" features of victim policy. In the second section, soldiers and civilians are presented as two quite different types of victims of war that further complicate how we understand those harmed during war as "unlikely," "ideal," or "non" victims. Within the third section, the various victims of terrorism and war presented in the first two sections are arranged into a hierarchy of victimization to provide an illustration of how each can be constructed and perceived quite differently within both political and cultural practices of imagining victimhood. The chapter finishes by drawing some brief conclusions relating to victim "credibility" and the value of critical victimology to develop such lines of inquiry further to examine victims less obviously placed with domestic criminal justice interests.

THE RISE OF THE VICTIMS OF TERRORISM

Two of the most significant incidents of terrorism to occur in the United States and UK during the twenty-first century include the deaths of over three thousand people in New York, Pennsylvania, and the Pentagon following the terrorist attacks of 9/11 and the deaths of fifty-two people in London following the terrorist attacks on the London transport system on July 7, 2005 (7/7). At this opening juncture, let us first consider these events in relation to the attendant policy that catered for victims of terrorism within domestic criminal justice processes. To do so requires us to reflect upon the uses of crime data and victim compensation awards.

"UNIQUE" AND "ROUTINE" VICTIMS OF TERRORISM

Much like the production of the "Crime Survey in England and Wales" by the UK Home Office, the Federal Bureau of Investigation (FBI) produces Uniform Crime Reporting (UCR), gathering statistical data on crimes committed against the person and property (including rape, robbery, assault, burglary, theft, motor vehicle theft, and arson). This data is arranged within several publications (i.e., Crime in the United States, Hate Crime Statistics, and Law Enforcement Officers Killed and Assaulted) produced annually for the purposes of documenting crime in official record and providing a snapshot of criminal activity across North America (see FBI 2004). There is not the space here to begin unpacking the methodological problems of documenting the *experience* of victimization in this way (see Hope 2007), however, as has been noted elsewhere (Leighton 2002; Young 2011; McGarry and Walklate 2015), the accounting of 9/11 victims requires some critical scrutiny.

Although the deaths caused on 9/11 were classified as murders within UCR definitions, the FBI (2001, 303, *my insert*) declared that they did not belong in UCR publications:

> The statistics of September 11 are not a part of the traditional Crime in the United States publication because they are different from the day-to-day crimes committed in this country (*the United States of America*).

Instead data concerning the victims of these mass murders were published in a special report documenting the "murder victims of 9/11/2001 terrorist attacks" (see FBI 2001) within which it is reasoned that:

> The murder count of September 11 is so high that combining it with the traditional crime statistics will have an outlier effect that skews all

types of measurements in the Program's analysis. (An outlier is any extreme value, either large or small, that substantially deviates from the rest of the distribution.) (FBI 2001, 303).

At first glance this helps illustrate some nuances in the official documentation of terrorist violence. However, for Leighton (2002), excluding those murdered as victims of 9/11 from UCR has more underhand effects than maintaining the analytical neatness of crime data, a point we will return to shortly. Next, however, let us contrast this with attendant policy related to victims of 7/7, a category of victims also murdered as a result of terrorism who were included in UK crime reporting (see Walker et al 2006).

Despite the classification of the victims of 9/11 being excluded from UCR, the U.S. state made quick moves to victim reparation. Under the specifically constituted "9/11 Victim Compensation Fund" (see http://www.vcf.gov), over $7 billion is said to have been paid out in state-funded compensation to direct, indirect, secondary, and tertiary victims of the attacks, including those injured physically and psychologically, families and relatives of those who were killed, and others "representing the deceased" (Letschert and Ammerlaan 2010). This treatment was markedly different to those who had experienced violence during the terrorist attacks in London during 7/7. Rather than have an "unlimited" set of funding made available to claimants (as with the specially commissioned "9/11 Victim Compensation Fund") for those who were victims of the London Bombings on 7/7, £15 million in state compensation awards were made available under the preexisting "Criminal Injuries Compensation Authority" (CICA) (Letschert and Ammerlaan 2010). However, this was not without controversy. The headline complaints levied against the CICA in the aftermath of 7/7 was that the compensation payment process was protracted, slow to pay requisite sums of money to victims, and had capped claims for the most seriously injured at £500,000, setting at a limit of £11,000 for bereavement payments (Miers 2006). The disruption to compensation arrangements for 7/7 victims illustrated a deficiency with how victims were dealt with which fell far from the "center" of the criminal justice system as intended within UK victim policy. Compared with the average compensation payment of $2.1 million received in death benefits following 9/11, Letschert and Ammerlaan (2010, 228) state that for victims of 7/7, "these tariffs follow the tariffs as applied to bereaved families of a victim who died because of an 'ordinary' murder." This tariffed award merely reflects recognition in official crime reporting that each death is situated alongside other murders committed during the same reporting period. As such, rather than placing a "unique" emphasis on victims of terrorist murder as experienced in the United States following 9/11, murder as a result of 7/7 was instead seen as "routine," in both policy and statistical terms.

THE UNEQUAL PENAL COUPLE

Both of these opening examples illustrate that victims of terrorism can be articulated quite differently within criminal justice policy. Those who lost their lives as a result of 9/11 and 7/7 are victims of murder caused by acts of terrorism, but—as noted above by Leighton (2002)—there are other deleterious issues that unfold around the policy construction of terrorist murder as "unique" or "routine."

The policy responses that followed the 7/7 bombings created differently problematic constructions of victims and offenders. The aftermath of 7/7 for the CICA witnessed the publication of the "Compensation for the Victims of the London Bombings of 7 July 2005" booklet which, although not changing the compensation arrangements of monies awarded to victims, instead explained the scheme within the context of the events of 7/7 and "was also written in a slightly more compassionate style, addressing these particular victims" (Letschert and Ammerlaan 2010, 228). Subsequently the Criminal Justice System (see Home Office 2005) published a review of criminal compensation awards in "Rebuilding Lives: supporting victims of crime," influenced by the issues experienced by 7/7 victims and playing into the established political agenda of pursuing a more "central" role for victims of crime within the justice process:

> The tragic events of 7th July 2005 also raised concerns about whether the Criminal Injuries Compensation Scheme (CICS) is operating effectively for those victims most seriously affected (Home Office 2005, 5).

According to Miers (2006) this review looked to reconsider the variety of people who should be classified as victims and the range of injuries that could be compensated by the state as the result of crime. Emerging alongside the "victimagogic activities" (Davies 2011, 161) noted earlier to "center" the victim within UK criminal justice processes for victims of crime (including terrorist crime), "The Victims of Overseas Terrorism Compensation Scheme" (see Ministry of Justice 2012b) was established to ensure that those experiencing terrorist violence while outside of the UK could also claim state compensation as victims of violence.

It would, however, be a mistake to think that all victims within such policies are equal, even victims of terrorism. One of the inequalities embedded within these UK compensation arrangements is that it has the capacity to either reduce or revoke compensation for victims of terrorism if currently serving unspent criminal convictions. This does not depart from the practices of other compensation awards to victims of crime, but comparisons can be drawn between the previous compensation arrangements of 7/7 victims under the CICA. As Miers (2006, 8 *my insert*) observes:

> there need be no causal connection between the applicant's bad character and the injury sustained. Both the Authority and the Home Office

assert that the (*CICS*) Scheme applies to the "blameless" victim. But "blame" in this context does not refer to a person's actions in respect of the criminal injury, but to his moral worth as a person who should properly be the beneficiary of public money. This disentitling condition is one of the touchstones of the Scheme, which is to compensate only the "innocent" victim of crime.

Next, returning to the thoughts of Garland (2001), reconceptualizing victims of terrorism as being unequal actors with differing "moral worth" encourages us to situate the "blameless" victim of terrorism in contrast and opposition to those who committed these acts of violence as terrorist offenders. Codifying the violence experienced on 9/11 as both normative crimes (murders caused by interpersonal violence) but differentiated from "day-to-day crime" (murders caused by terrorism), the victims of 9/11 and the offenders responsible are ascribed with a "bulimic" quality (qua Young 2003). The violence of 9/11 was at once both accepted as being victimizing to the social body of the U.S. public and state, while at the same time rejected as an act disassociated with violence recognized by the sovereignty of the law. As an "outlier," acts of murder from terrorism when committed on U.S. soil are not only separate from normative experiences of crime as narrowly defined by UCR, they also need to be considered differently in terms of measurement and policy responses. The violence of 9/11 was recognized as creating victims proximate to the emotional center of a vulnerable U.S. citizenry caused by a "foreign" form of violence that required more "exceptional" treatment (qua Agamben 2005) than would be afforded by domestic responses to murder. The ratification of the US PATRIOT Act and execution of extrajudicial treatment of terrorist suspects as "enemy combatants" in Guantanamo Bay are now widely known testaments to such "exceptional" circumstances.

What this initial analysis of terrorism victims does is introduce the "penal couple" (qua Mendelsohn 1963) as a central part of our concerns. It highlights at the outset a relationship that has partners with unequal status and illustrates that there exists a tension between victims when exposed to the "unique" and indiscriminate nature of terrorist violence. Undergirding this tension are policies that construct some circumstances of terrorism as more "unique" within the policy process and considers some victims of terrorism to be more worthy of a victim status than others. Having outlined these policy provocations in this way within the domestic contexts of the United States and UK, we now turn our attention to the context of war. This change in focus begins to highlight a different set of tensions in defining victimhood for those who perpetrate and experience violence in extremis.

ENTER THE VICTIMS OF WAR

Achieving a different analysis for victims in contexts less regularly regarded as the criminological landscape requires us to think differently
about victimhood. As the popular quotation from Richard Quinney
(1972, 321) reminds us, by doing so we must "expand or at least revise
our image of victimization . . . we would begin to conceive of the victims
of police force, the victims of war, the victims of the 'correctional' system,
the victims of state violence, the victims of oppression of any sort."

However, this invitation raises its own ambiguities of who constitutes
a "victim of war" and under what circumstances. It was Friedrichs (1981)
who later offered this further clarity suggesting that those who have
historically been exposed to violence but not considered so in terms of
the law include both civilians and soldiers experiencing war. Despite
some conceptual messiness, civilians suffering as a result of war are perhaps more easily conceived of as "victims of war" through being harmed
and killed by violence they did not instigate nor encourage. The victimhood of those who perpetrate "legitimate" state violence within the same
context are altogether trickier to comprehend and often the most unlikely
to be conceptualized as victims at all. It is to this group we turn to next.

UNLIKELY VICTIMS OF CRIME AND WAR

The ways in which victims of war have come to feature within the criminal justice system in the UK illustrates how the domains of war and
criminal justice policy have begun to gently fold in to one another. Returning our attention back to the UK, British soldiers serving at war have
undergone a process of redefinition when it comes to how their injuries
and deaths have been considered in relation to criminal justice. Despite
giving their lives and risking injury under the "unlimited liability" of the
Military Covenant (Ministry of Defence 2000), two particular issues arose
in the years following the invasion of Iraq that began to draw their status
into the "central" lexicon of victim policy and victimology. Due to the
changing nature of warfare fought against non "warring factions" in Iraq,
British soldiers killed as a result of violence waged during activities not
considered a part of "war operations" can be defined as victims of "criminal" violence (see Rayment 2006). Since its introduction in 1979, the
"Criminal Injury Compensation (Overseas) Scheme" (CIC(O)S) has
equipped the criminal justice system with the ability to pay criminal
compensation to victims experiencing crime outside of the UK (Ministry
of Justice 2003). As applied to members of the British military:

> The intention of the scheme is to provide, as nearly as possible, com-
> pensation equivalent to that for which members of the Armed Forces
> would have been eligible (under the terms of the Criminal Injuries

Compensation Scheme) if the criminal act had been committed in Great Britain and to exclude such injuries the risk of which members of the Armed Forces undertake as a result of their serving in a combatant or peace-keeping capacity. (Ministry of Justice 2003, para. 1)

Exclusions of this scheme for members of the military serving under an "unlimited liability" include death and injuries that were caused either by preparing for or participating in "war operations" (Ministry of Justice 2003). The identity and motivation of the "perpetrator" also dictate exclusions under these conditions making the relationship between the penal couple more complex. Those representing "warring factions" as part of an identifiable force, "exercising such control over a part of the state's territory as to enable it to carry out sustained and concerted military operations," would exclude soldiers from being considered as victims of crime (Ministry of Justice 2003, para. 3b). So too would those acting on behalf of some "other force" fighting to achieve "ideological or political aims" against another opposing authority (Ministry of Justice 2003, para. 3b). However, death or injury caused to a member of the British military would be considered criminal if caused by an individual acting on their own motivations or circumstances such as:

Internal disturbances and tensions which lead to riots, looting, sporadic outbreaks of violence or terrorism or other such incidents is unlikely to amount to military activity by warring factions. However an incident can involve the commission of a criminal offence and still be excluded — the two are not mutually exclusive. (Ministry of Justice, 2003, para. 3b)

The deaths of several British Paratroopers executed in a large-scale riot in Majar al Kabir, Iraq during 2003 are a prime example of this type of criminal incident at war (see Nicol 2005). Soldiers at war can therefore find themselves at the "center" of the criminal justice system as victims of crime through policy established to provide a means of equitable reparation provided by the CICS. There are however other ways in which British soldiers have been conceived of as "victims" that fall a little further from the confines of the CIC(O)S.

For those injured as part of activities that fall outside of the CIC(O)S and are considered to have been caused by "war operations," other mechanisms to compensate for injuries and the loss of life can be pursued under the "Armed Forces Compensation Scheme" for soldiers harmed as part of their "unlimited liability" to the state (see Ministry of Defence 2015). However, following a number of deaths and injuries experienced by British soldiers fighting in Iraq, it quickly came to public attention that the lives of some military personnel were being unnecessarily put in danger beyond their commitment of an "unlimited liability." These circumstances included deficiencies and inadequacies in their kit and equipment (McGarry et al 2012; McGarry 2014) and avoidable accidents experienced within the "workplace of war" (McGarry 2012). Within the UK, this way of conceptualizing soldiers as "victims" falls under claims within the Human Rights Act (1998) to an inadequate protection from the state to the "right to life." Such claims have often been raised retrospectively against the Ministry of Defence (MoD) by bereaved relatives and spouses of those killed at war under circumstances that could be considered negligent and unnecessarily putting the lives of service personnel at risk beyond what is reasonably expected (McGarry 2012). Key exemplars of this include deploying military personnel to Iraq without adequate body armor, inefficient communications equipment, and in vehicles that are not robust enough to protect the lives of soldiers from explosives (McGarry et al. 2012).

Claims to victimization under these conditions are now judged on an individual basis and considered by the Supreme Court as civil cases raised against the MoD. The "soldier as victim" (qua McGarry and Walklate 2011) therefore poses some conceptual difficulties and policy provocations that force us to rethink who we consider as being vulnerable in the context of war and terrorism. Men perpetrating violence on behalf of the state do not readily fall within our victimological imaginations but they do provide a valuable contrast to the "ideal victim" (Christie 1986), which is where we turn our attentions to in our final example.

UNIMAGINED, "IDEAL," AND NONVICTIMS OF WAR

Occurring subsequently to the terrorist attacks on 9/11 and concurrent with the violence of 7/7, the U.S. and Coalition Force's invasion of Iraq has not been without controversy. Within criminological literature—alongside a range of other indictments—the conduct of this war has been accused of being illegal in relation to international conventions of war (Kramer and Michaelowski 2005) and tantamount to corporate crimes (Whyte 2007) and genocide (McGarry and Walklate 2015). Despite this latter exception the controversies of this war have generally had less consistent attention paid to them within victimological literature. This is perhaps due in part to its lack of proximity for victims within criminal justice practices and some conceptual difficulty for victimology to readily define those who are harmed at war as being victims of any sort.

There are of course other contexts within which violence has raged over the past decade following the invasion of Iraq. Much less attention has, for example, been afforded within criminological and victimological scholarship to victims of war and terrorism in Afghanistan and Pakistan. To offer this some consideration, we now turn our attention to Malala Yousafzai,[1] a high-profile victim of terrorism.

Malala Yousafzai is a female teenage activist from Pakistan. Known for speaking out in favor of educational rights for women and children in her home region of Swat, during 2012 Malala was confronted by a member of the Taliban while sitting on a school bus and shot several times (see Yousafzai 2013; Husain 2013). Following her attempted murder she woke up in a hospital in Birmingham, England, within the embrace of a health and welfare system more than five-thousand miles away. In a trial shrouded in secrecy and controversy, two of Malala's attackers were subsequently charged with attempted murder and terrorism offenses in Pakistan (see BBC 2015) and she and her family were given asylum in the UK. Since her ordeal, Malala has gained international notoriety; she continues to be an activist and pioneer of educational and women's rights and became the youngest person ever to be awarded a Nobel Peace Prize (see Yousafzai 2014). The brutality of this attack and courageousness of Malala is without question, but her case poses a different set of critical issues for our understanding of victims of terrorism and war in contrast to those we have already discussed. In Pakistan, those killed and injured through the attendant terrorist violence of the war in Afghanistan are perhaps a lesser known quantity than other regions exposed to war post 9/11. To date, over 150,000 civilians are reported to have been killed in Iraq due to violence caused or instigated by war (Iraq Body Count 2015) and in Afghanistan, tens of thousands of civilian deaths and injuries have been recorded in Afghanistan since 2007 by the United Nations Assistance Mission in Afghanistan (2007; 2008; 2014). Malala is therefore not the first or only civilian victim of such violence since 9/11, so it is worth considering what singled out Malala from thousands of other civilian victims of terrorism and war.

Taking stock of Malala's circumstances and the characteristics of her experience assists in finding at least one theoretical answer to this question. Malala is female and at the time of her attempted murder was a child in a much less powerful position physically, violently, and culturally relative to her male attacker in Pakistan. She had not instigated her victimization in Pakistan, nor could she be blamed for living in her home region of Swat in the midst of the violence emerging around her. Malala's attack was also not random; she was targeted for carrying out a "good deed" by publicly advocating for the rights of girls and women to education in Pakistan. Taken collectively, this constitutes many of the key characteristics of Nils Christie's (1986) "ideal victim," a status that is known to more easily gain public and political support for *particular* types of harm experienced by *particular* types of victims. Considering Malala's status and achievements further following her victimization, she has since become a globally renowned figure for the rights of women and girls, emulating that the ideal victim is someone able to find a voice and gain public support for their victimization (Christie 1986). However, much like the victims of 9/11, Malala's victimhood was aided by these cultural notions of her vulnerability, innocence, and blamelessness held up in a unique set of circumstances following her attempted murder. The

Pakistan government had fully funded her treatment in the New Queen Elizabeth Hospital in Birmingham (BBC 2012), but this is a passage to the "center" of health services in the UK made possible by circumstances of terrorism and war. Following mounting public and political pressure to better cater for the needs of injured British soldiers as victims of war as described above, the trauma facility of the Royal Centre for Defence Medicine in Birmingham where Malala was treated had been especially implemented in 2010 to receive and treat repatriated British military personnel who had suffered traumatic combat injuries (Adams 2015; *Telegraph* 2012). As such, Malala's presence as a victim of terrorism within the UK has ultimately been made possible by the development of health specialism for treating injured soldiers as victims or war. If we take our attention back to the position of soldiers as victims within the criminal justice system in the UK, there is a final paradox to observe here.

In 2011 a member of the British military, Sergeant Alexander Blackman, was found guilty of shooting and killing an injured "unknown member of the Taliban" (Blackett 2013). Sergeant Blackman was tried in a military court martial in the UK, sentenced to ten years imprisonment for murder and dishonorably discharged from the Royal Marines. Although a perpetrator of crime rather than a victim in the ways outlined earlier, his status as a member of the British military had been reconstructed in various ways to help provide rationales for his crime. Public perceptions ranged from calls for the exoneration of his crime on the grounds that he was simply doing his job protecting the UK from a "terrorist," to what has elsewhere been described as "military victimhood" (McGarry 2015). This latter construction placed emphasis on his professional judgment as a soldier at the time of the murder being impaired due to long and cumulative exposure to violence in Afghanistan: consequences of war that have recently begun to be more widely recognized (see for example Mac-Manus et al 2013). His military victimhood was also situated in a particular context that had witnessed concerted efforts from across the political spectrum to more firmly position the military within civic life (see Ministry of Defence 2008). Concomitant with this context were the emergence of public displays of private grief for British soldiers who lost their lives in Afghanistan and Iraq. In the rural town of Royal Wootton Bassett in the UK, thousands of people had taken to mourning the British war dead in large public gatherings between 2007 and 2011 by lining the routes where funeral processions would pass to pay their respects (see Walklate et al. 2015). Couched within this wider context that elevated Sergeant Blackman to a vulnerable status as an "undeserving offender" (qua McGarry 2015), another pressing question was overlooked: what of Sergeant Blackman's murder victim?

Despite his victim being identified as an "enemy" combatant, Sergeant Blackman was still convicted of murder under the Criminal Justice Act (2003), meaning that he was embroiled in the most intimate of relationships as one actor within the penal couple. However we know nothing of his victim, addressed in court sentencing summaries only as "an unknown member of the Taliban" (Blackett 2013). We are therefore left to assume the gender, nationality, ethnicity, and age of the person he had killed, all of which has been neutralized, affording Blackman's victim with no credibility or passage to the "center" of the criminal justice system due to being in the throes of violent terrorist activity prior to his murder. Similar to the classification of the CICA for victims of 7/7 with unspent convictions, it appears that within the context of war there are also some victims of crime who are more worthy of victimhood than others.

CHOOSING SIDES

What has been outlined throughout this chapter are various actors who are at one time or another articulated as victims of terrorism and war in the domains of policy or public perception. So in what ways does this leave us with a critical understanding of victims of terrorism and war?

Some of those who have been described throughout this chapter readily attain a "deserving victim" status, easily attracting public and political sympathies and are a comfortable enough fit with our ideas of an ideal victim; others are less easily welcomed into victimhood. For critical victimologists, however, there is not the convenience to ignore or prioritize one type of victim over another, instead—as Howard Becker (1967) urged—this way of thinking requires that we "choose whose side we are on" to aid our critical understanding of those considered criminal and deviant. What this means for critical victimologists is opting to view victimization across a spectrum that will include victims of various sorts (often the most unlikely) and work to recognize how their "credibility" (qua Becker 1967) is arranged and mobilized within social, cultural, and political life. So it is that we once again turn our attention back to the context of UK victim policy to consider how the victims of terrorism and war as described here might be arranged when considered collectively.

HIERARCHIES OF VICTIMHOOD

Addressing the continued emphasis placed upon the criminal justice system to treat victims as "customers" at the center of their services, like Garland (2001), Duggan and Heap (2014) observe a continued neoliberalization of victim services in the UK. Recent reforms to victim policy under the UK Coalition government "redefined hierarchies of need which aligns with new considerations of vulnerabilities" that increasingly included political attention cast toward victims of antisocial behavior and hate crime (Duggan and Heap 2014, 93). Victims experiencing such politically expedient crimes (i.e., antisocial behavior and hate crime) are said to be conceptualized in public and political imaginations by "group affiliation" with those considered most vulnerable prioritizing support under the guidance of the 2013 Victims Code of Practice; the least vulnerable, however, "may be so low down this hierarchy as to almost be considered unworthy of note, or are off the radar altogether" (Duggan and Heap 2014, 98). Drawing our attention to crime and disorder, Carrabine and colleagues (2004) state that those in the pit of such a hierarchy are "low status" and "powerless" groups such as the homeless, those unemployed, or substance abusers. These are people who are themselves often the most vulnerable, but liable to be overpoliced, less likely to report their victimization, and have their victim "credibility" (qua Becker 1967) ranked low in public and political perceptions of victimhood (Carrabine et al. 2004). What this means is that victims of *crime* are arranged into a hierarchy laden with identity politics mediated between the public and policy domains.

Within the context of our broader discussion during this chapter, this hierarchical arrangement of victims has significant omissions. Carrabine and colleagues (2004, 161) continue that this "hierarchy of victimization is shaped by international politics and conditions of war," a remolding of victimization that needs to be considered alongside a hierarchy of victims of "street" crimes (i.e., antisocial behavior, hate crime, and disorder). Acts of war and terrorism often unexpectedly position "ordinary citizens" at the top of a hierarchy of victimization due to being thrust into environments where they are vulnerable to indiscriminate violence, human rights abuses, and displacement (Carrabine et al. 2004). However, so too can these same conditions inversely reposition those once considered as vulnerable with stereotypes as "noncitizens" isolated from the protection of foreign and social policy (Carrabine et al. 2004). The change of context from *crime* to *terrorism and war* proposes similar challenges to those presented by transitional justice for how we as critical victimologists imagine victimization. As McEvoy and McConnachie (2012, 532) note:

> What is more interesting from our perspective, however, is the view propagated by some actors that it is only those designated as completely innocent who can be considered to be victims at all. A hierarchy of victimhood, predicated on distinctions between what Madlingozi (2007) has termed "good" victims and "bad" victims.

Drawing upon the victims of terrorism and war outlined in detail above, table 10.1 arranges these into a hierarchy that situates their victim status in relation to their political (i.e., policy) and cultural (i.e., public) environments as suggested by Greer (2007) and their "good" and "bad" victim identity as noted by Duggan and Heap (2014) and McEvoy and McConnachie (2012).

When arranged into a hierarchy between the public and policy domains within which they have been imagined we begin to see that victims of terrorism and war undergo a "calibration of suffering" (McEvoy and McConnachie 2012, 532). Those considered culturally as innocent and blameless for their victimization are placed near the top of this hierarchy as "ideal victims." Victims that we can identify within terms of proximity to our own occidental identities in the West or those succumbing to violence as *individual*, "ideal victims" are more easily subsumed into deserving victimhood than large homogenous civilian groups victimized by war; these are much more difficult to imagine due to their scale and distance from the criminal justice process. Others fighting in war and perpetrating violence are also trickier to place within the cultural imagination. The popularized notion of soldiers being vulnerable due to their war experiences perhaps fall short of being "ideal" due to a tangential understanding of an "unlimited liability" attached to their role and identity, but they are still afforded some semblance of sympathy and "military victimhood" nonetheless. A victimhood much harder to reconcile is that of soldiers experiencing *crime* "out there" (at war) in *similar* ways to what the public may understand it "in here" (at home). After all, war occurs at a distance and has significantly less proximity to everyday life than acts of terrorism no matter how infrequent they may be.

Within victim policy, however, the arrangement of this hierarchy looks somewhat different. In contrast to victims of crime, the "ideal victim" of war and terrorism is perhaps less likely to feature in the policy

Table 10.1.

Victim status	Political / policy	Cultural / public	Good / bad	Group affiliation
Unique	Civilian group	Individual civilian	Good	Terrorism
Ideal	(9/11)	Civilian group (9/	Good	Terrorism
Routine	Individual	11)	Good	Terrorism
Unlikely	civilian	Civilian group (7/	Good	Terrorism
Nonvictim	Civilian group	7)	Good	Terrorism
Unimagined	(7/7)	Soldiers	Good	Terrorism
	(no or spent	'Enemy'	Good	Crime
	conviction)	combatant	Good	War
	Soldiers	Civilian group	Good	War
	Soldiers	Soldiers	Bad	Terrorism
	Civilian group		Bad	War
	(7/7)		Good/Bad	War
	(unspent		Good	Crime
	conviction)			
	Enemy			
	combatant			
	Civilian group			

domain as there are calculated choices to be made over what constitutes violence and tariffed conditions under which compensation can be awarded. Those harmed as victims of terrorism and war can be squarely catered for as "routine" actors within victim policy alongside other victims of crime, meaning that *some* victims of terrorism are exposed to an inequality embedded within victim policy if dually considered as "offenders." For others whose violence has been deemed too extreme to be adequately catered for within routine policy, new ground is opened up to accommodate for their unique circumstances experienced as a result of war and terrorism. These are victims who attain "ideal" victim status culturally, but transcend this identity in relation to policy as more "unique" victims afforded exceptional treatment and compensation. However, this has direct implications for the context of war. As McEvoy and McConnachie (2012, 532) state, "the 'innocent' victim is placed at the apex of a hierarchy of victimhood and becomes a symbol around which contested notions of past violence and suffering are constructed and reproduced." Those who are held aloft by the state as unique due to the violence they have experienced as a result of terrorism and war help to reestablish a binary between innocence ("us") and the "enemy" ("them"). Those cast as the "enemy" are unilaterally "bad" nonvictims, even when succumbing to victimization identified within criminal justice legislation as murder. Following Walklate (2012), this hierarchical positioning will only ever result in a "zero sum" relationship for the penal couple that fosters responses from the public and the state, which are punitive, vengeful, and imbued with emotion (qua Karstedt 2002).

CONCLUSION

This chapter has aimed to draw victims of terrorism and war into a critical victimological discourse by presenting several case studies of victimization. By setting the scene of the "unique" and "routine" ways in which victims of terrorism can be constructed in policy terms, some common assumptions have been challenged about "ideal" victimhood in the policy process. By identifying a pathway between terrorism, war, and the domestic criminal justice setting, those who are harmed in war as "legitimate" or "illegitimate" perpetrates and innocent civilians have been embraced within a similar critical framework. This chapter has established that although often hard to place within victimological discourse, victims of war have a place "central" to our concerns in ways equal to that of victims of crime. Illustrating this throughout this analysis has made it clear that although some victims of war are difficult to place within the cultural imagination, unique and ideal victims in the political domain serve to reinforce binaries between the "innocent" and the "enemy." As such, following Garland (2001), this chapter avers that within the post–

9/11 context, victims of terrorism and war have taken on a punitive (albeit unwitting) role in social control similar to the victim of crime within the criminal justice setting. Being mindful of the tenets of a critical victimology that is invested in drawing attention to choice and agency for victims whose identities are often appropriated for political gain in this way, it is worth asserting that "choosing sides" (qua Becker 1967) in the ways advocated within this chapter does not constitute an "underdog" victimology any more than it does of criminology. As critical victimologists with an interest in social, cultural, and policy issues that influence perceptions of the penal couple, we need to continue posing challenging questions of those we are encouraged to see laterally as "victims" and "offenders" of terrorism and war. We must also seek to continue making connections with victim policy to illuminate how the violence of terrorism and war has routinely become a central feature of domestic criminal justice practices.

NOTES

1. My thanks to former University of Liverpool student Emma Cawtheray who brought Malala's biography to my attention during her assessment in May 2015.

ELEVEN

Bereaved Family Activism in Contexts of Organized Mass Violence

Jon Shute

There is, sadly, no shortage of "data" for the scholar of lethal violence. Recent estimates suggest, for example, that 475,000 non-combat-related homicides[1] were committed globally in 2012 (World Health Organization 2014), and around 125,000 fatalities produced in contexts of organized violence[2] in 2014 (Uppsala Conflict Data Program 2015). Naturally, each death presumes one direct victim, however, the effects of an untimely and violent death on the networks of actors connected to the deceased by ties of family, friendship, and work are often profound and enduring. This chapter analyzes the effects of violent bereavement on family members—defined as any self-identifying relation by blood or partnership—and attempts, among the normal range of responses, to understand the organized attempts of some to address publicly aspects of their experience: what will be termed "bereaved family activism." We begin with a brief review of the relatively sparse literature on bereavement and lethal violence in "peacetime" and discuss some of the typical experiences of family members who do and do not resort to activism. The discussion is then extended to contexts of lethal and organized *mass* violence—defined here as forms of inter- and intrastate armed conflict—to consider both quantitative and qualitative differences in bereaved families' experience. Particular emphasis is given to contexts of mass violence that feature the murder and concealment of primary victims and where surviving family members must contend with profound *absences*: of official acknowledgment, information, disposal site, and body. This peculiarly harrowing set of privations understandably pushes many beyond their capacity to cope, however, organized family member responses have occurred with quite profound effects both locally and beyond. This is illustrated with regard to two contexts studied as part of a major research program on the material human remains of mass violence. First, the almost paradigmatic case of post-Junta (1976–1983) Argentina is described, in particular, the phenomena of the "Mothers," "Grandmothers" and "Children" of the "Disappeared," who evidence globally influential but surprisingly complex and contested histories of discourse and action. The second case is of postwar (1991–1995) Bosnia, where a unique combination of perpetrator actions and subsequent political-administrative conditions have supported unique and still-developing forms of bereaved family (re-)action. The case studies, taken together, illustrate a little of what is to be gained from a victimological engagement with those who search and speak for the dead and highlight, inter alia, the strength and purpose that can be gained from collective defiance, the influence of family activism in post-conflict society building, and the tragic elusiveness of personal and collective "closure."

"PEACETIME" BEREAVEMENT AND LETHAL VIOLENCE

"Peace" is a relative and slippery term, used here to denote the kind of circumstances that obtain domestically in nation states *not* actively engaged as primary parties in the forms of inter- or intrastate armed conflicts. States nominally "at peace" under these definitions can and do, of course, experience sporadic terroristic violence, engage in systemic political repression, execute criminals, and facilitate extraterritorial armed conflict through the legal (and often profitable) exchange of military intelligence, training, and materiel. That most of these forms of violence are not captured in indices of conflict points to their definitional limitations; that they are not recorded in official statistics or victim surveys points to some essential limitations of traditional criminology (Green and Ward 2004). These caveats accepted, we will, for the sake of argument, retain this essentially negative (absence-focused) and incomplete definition of variably peaceable "peace."[3]

In such conditions, and as a fundamental part of the human condition, bereavement occurs for the most part due to age-related illness and has a predictable range of culturally inflected effects on individual family members, for example, an acutely increased risk of mortality, physical and psychological morbidity (Stroebe, Schut and Stroebe 2007), and a stressed reevaluation of relationships in the family system as a whole (Hayslip and Page 2013). While agonizing and incapacitating for many, most people with time and social support, adjust to loss and often experience some level of "post-traumatic growth," such as strengthened relationships, increased self-awareness, and capacity for resilience (Michael and Cooper 2013). Contemporary Western models of bereavement echo this positive perspective, having moved from the Freudian position that a "healthy" response to death requires emotional detachment to a constructivist emphasis on meaning-making, continuity, and an ongoing relationship with the deceased (Rothaupt and Becker 2007).

The process and relative success of adjustment is, of course, affected by many variables, not least among them, the circumstances of death. Sudden, unexpected death due to lethal violence[4] presents particular challenges to the normal grieving process of family members. Most obviously, "peacetime" homicide is to a significant extent *intra*familial: of the 526 homicides committed in England and Wales in 2013/14, 35 percent of victims were female, 72 percent of whom were killed either by a current or ex-partner, or another family member (Office for National Statistics 2015). Fifteen percent of male victims were killed by a partner or family member. As Jack Katz (1988) has shown in his analysis of U.S. court records, such crimes are often committed after a long history of relationship dysfunction and are proximately the result of intoxicant-facilitated, in-the-moment, "righteous" fury in response to a perceived grievous humiliation. Homicides of this nature introduce complexity into familial grieving processes due to a likely connectedness to both victim and perpetrator, and there are other characteristic experiential features that distinguish this form of bereavement (Paterson et al. 2006; Rock 1998b; summarized in Condry 2010). These include the difficulties of coming to terms with the shock of the unexpected event, the motivated malice or recklessness of the assailant, the horror of the real and imagined details of the killing, a general and pervasive sense of powerlessness, and extended forms of suffering attendant on the often insensitive responses of criminal justice and an intrusive media (Condry, 2010). Recent systematic reviews of the clinical effects of homicide on family members—also termed "survivors," "co-victims," and "secondary victims"—confirms the general picture of serious disturbance, with high rates of chronic post-traumatic stress disorder (PTSD), depression, complicated grief, and substance abuse (Connolly and Gordon 2014; van Denderen et al. 2015).

While these experiences represent common and debilitating features of violent bereavement, it is notable that there is also considerable variation in what family members feel able to *do* with their trauma. In recent decades, and as part of a systemic politicized emphasis on increased participation of victims in criminal justice (Garland 2001; Walklate 2012), the right to make a "victim impact statement" at the point of sentencing has been extended to family members in homicide cases. In England and Wales, an evaluation of early trials of this as part of the Victims' Advocate Scheme (VAS) indicated that a high proportion of families both appreciated and took the opportunity to make a statement, although the emotional demands of doing so meant that it was mostly read by someone other than the author(s) (Sweeting et al. 2008). English judges stressing judicial independence and steeped in the common law tradition of distinguishing *obiter dicta* (contextualizing details) from *ratio decidendi* (details direct pertinent to the legal ruling) were rather more ambivalent about its impact. Their position—that statements should not and would not affect the legal decision—is somewhat at odds, however, with a rather more extensive U.S. psycholegal literature (for example, Myers and Greene 2004; Paternoster and Deise 2011) that suggest family statements of this nature tend to promote more punitive decisions, which themselves have potentially lethal consequences in states that retain the death penalty.

Another acknowledged but little-studied way in which bereaved family members engage their trauma is via public activism. High-profile campaigns—for example regarding community notification of sex offenders—instigated by and gaining legitimacy from the bereaved are familiar features of late modern discourse on crime and punishment (Garland 2001), and, as a number of English writers have detailed, "grassroots" mobilization of self-organized *groups* of family victims also exert influence (Rock 1998b; Scraton 1999). Paul Rock's (1998b) study describes the formation, development, and co-relations of several such groups, including the still-active Support After Murder and Manslaughter (SAMM[5]). The work is notable for its sensitive phenomenological account of the ontological predicament of the bereaved and also makes clear the "imperative for organization" (Rock 1998b, 133) felt by many as they attempt to impose personal and collective order on their suffering and make something positive of it. Scraton's work with the Hillsborough Family Support Group (HSFG) differs in that the deaths in question relate not to murder but to the negligence of police, local government and stadium officials that led to ninety-six deaths at a major football match, followed by a major cover-up and trial by media. The example is instructive for our overall purposes, however, in that it illustrates the spontaneous formation of a group focused on a single traumatic set of events, initially for self-help but taking on a campaigning role in relation to perceived and systemic injustice. The campaign also illustrates something of the discord and disagreement that can arise in perpetually emotionally charged settings such as these—the founding group split due to arguments about the acceptability of campaigning for *living* survivors—and also the long and fractured process of achieving recognition in the face of official denials (Scraton 2013): fresh inquests into the causes of death are ongoing at the time of writing, some twenty-six years after the original tragedy. These are themes to which we will return.

In sum, family bereavement as result of "peacetime" lethal violence is seen, with some justification, as a special category of suffering that produces intense and debilitating effects. Deaths are not infrequently the result of intrafamilial violence which may add further layers of incomprehension and ambivalence into the process of grieving. Studies of families have moved on from a clinically oriented description of symptoms, syndrome, and course to highlight the rupturing and remaking of meaning and identity attendant on bereavement. It is in this light that both greater participation in criminal justice and family activism can be seen as a renegotiation of an ongoing relationship based on advocacy for, and responsibility to the dead. Such participation is "risky" and contested, however, and brings few guarantees of resolution.

EXTENSION TO CONTEXTS OF ORGANIZED MASS VIOLENCE

We now leave the chimerical "Anglo-America" of so much criminological homicide literature—where well-funded studies describe relatively rare and well-recorded events in essentially stable democratic societies—and turn to the experiences of families bereaved in conditions other than "peacetime." As in the preceding section, "conflict" is surprisingly difficult to define meaningfully and inclusively and is often best discussed in relation to concrete case studies. For general clarity, however, we may say that the contexts of interest require human agency (excluding, therefore, natural disasters and technological accidents), a high degree of co-operative organization (excluding, therefore, lone shooting "sprees"), and mass near-simultaneous fatalities involving battle and/or massacre. The Uppsala Conflict Data Program (UCDP) usefully distinguishes between "state-based conflict" (inter- and intrastate armed conflict where the government is a combatant), "nonstate conflict" (between organized militia groups such as Islamic State and Kurdish irregular forces in Syria) and "one-sided violence" (civilian massacres committed by state or nonstate groups), conservatively estimating 125,000 fatalities across such forty such conflicts in 2014 (Melander 2015). We are certainly interested in these phenomena, but, as a matter of emphasis, are particularly interested in the intentional (as opposed to collateral) killing of unarmed civilians—captured partially but not wholly by the UCDP's "one-sided violence" category—and that entail commission of the international crimes of genocide, crimes against humanity, and war crimes. This is not to say that the families of either armed combatants or civilians unintentionally caught in crossfire are not worthy of consideration or devastated by their losses (they are), but rather that our focus is on the most vulnerable, intentionally targeted populations without access to protection or compensation. In sum, then, we discuss here the experiences of families bereaved as a product of "organized mass violence" in this special, if convoluted, sense.

The next task is to convey something of the quantitative and qualitative differences of bereavement in these contexts while making clear (1) the absolute validity of "peacetime" experiences and (2) the assumption that the psychological process underlying them are likely identical regardless of context by virtue of common humanity. Reliable and valid data are notoriously difficult to obtain in active conflicts, however, one preeminent dataset may be used by way of illustration: the Atrocities Documentation Survey carried out in 2004 by a U.S. State Department funded team with a representative sample of 1,136 Darfurian refugees (see Hagan et al. 2005; Hagan and Rymond-Richmond 2009; Kaiser and Hagan 2015). The refugees were then resident in camps in Chad, and had fled attacks by both Sudanese government and Janjaweed militia pursuing a racialized eliminationist ideology. Based on this data in combination with a separate WHO mortality survey of the same camps, Hagan and colleagues (2005) estimated nearly 400,000 deaths in the period 2003–2005, nearly 143,000 of these due to lethal violence; the remainder to disease and malnutrition. Underlining the frequently gendered nature of mass violence, 60.6 percent of respondents reported at least one male family member killed and 15.5 percent reported a female member killed. Despite severe social cultural stigma relating to the disclosure of sexual violence, 7.6 percent of respondents reported that a family member had been raped, and 65.9 percent reported at least one family member had been killed or raped. Dehumanizing racist epithets were overheard by 37 percent of respondents where the content expressed the intention to use rape as a genocidal tool—"we will kill all the men and rape the women. We want to change the color" (Hagan et al. 2005, 526). In separate analyses of the same data (U.S. Department of State 2004), 80 percent of respondents stated they had had their livestock stolen, and 81 percent their village destroyed. These horrifying statistics make clear not only the huge scale of family bereavement in this kind of "asymmetric" violence but that it often forms part of a wider constellation of systematic and intentional sexual violence, property appropriation, and destruction. Though, for reasons of ethical sensitivity and data quality, respondents were not asked about their personal victimization, it is evident by their testimony and general situation as refugees that they were also primary victims.

If these statistics give a sense of the scale of collectively imposed and collectively experienced trauma attendant on mass murder, there is one further form of mass violence that can be said to create its own particular family trauma dynamics: the abduction, murder, and *clandestine* disposal of relatives. As a strategy of aggression, this can be traced at least to Hitler's 1941 "Night and Fog" decree that used these methods to suppress resistance in occupied western Europe, and in doing so, not only eradicated the abductee but among those connected to him/her, also sowed terror and fundamental uncertainty regarding their whereabouts and vital status (USHMM 2015). Patrice McSherry (2005) analyzes the development of this strategy postwar, and its consolidation as a key tool for the repression of Marxist political groupings in Latin America during the 1970s and 1980s. As we shall see, the state of not knowing, fearing the worst, but not daring to relinquish hope or give oneself permission to grieve has been shown to be particularly debilitating for surviving family members.

Bereavement in these contexts has well-described and perhaps unsurprisingly severe effects on the mental health of survivors, with particularly high levels of psychiatric disorder such as major depressive disorder (MDD), post-traumatic stress disorder (PTSD), and complicated grief (CG) observed (Kristensen et al. 2012). As an illustration, of sixty war-bereaved Kosovar civilians who had lost a first-degree relative, 38 percent met the criteria for CG and 55 percent for PTSD a full seven years after the death event (Morina et al. 2010). The prolongation of grieving attendant on having a "missing" relative has also been shown to elevate measures of traumatic grief and major depression relative to those with confirmed bereavements, fifteen years or more after the trigger events (Barakovic et al. 2013; Powell et al. 2010).

In sum, human psychology dictates that while inward grief is likely to be experienced similarly—albeit with significant cultural loading regarding its outward expression—mass violence associated with the commission of international crimes has a greater capacity to overwhelm as the cumulative stress of primary victimization, multiple traumatic bereavement, and potential loss of an entire way of life takes its toll. How, then, can families thus affected possibly organize themselves to exert effects in peri- and postconflict society?

STUDYING ORGANIZED MASS VIOLENCE: THE "CORPSES OF MASS VIOLENCE AND GENOCIDE PROGRAM"

The case studies described in the following sections begin to answer these questions and formed part of a four-year European Research Council funded program "Corpses of Mass Violence and Genocide."[6] The program's aim was to examine through a multidisciplinary lens, the ways in which diverse societies do and do not come to terms with a legacy of mass violence through their relationship with the dead. Combining historical, anthropological, criminological, and sociolegal insights, the program developed methods centered around "brief team ethnography": immersive and intensive (one–two week) field visits prefigured by extensive literature review and access negotiations; and where fieldwork consisted of semistructured professional interviews with a wide range of actors (for example, forensic archaeologists, state prosecutors, psychologists, artists, and funeral directors), commemorative and archival site visits, opportunistic encounters, and cultural and academic events. A variety of data—field notes, photographs, court documents, secondary datasets, and more—were collected, pooled, and analyzed both collectively though team debriefs and through individual thematic analysis. Emerging findings were also informed by secondary analysis of existing documentary sources and by reciprocal longitudinal engagement with the networks of fieldwork participants who later participated in annual academic workshops in the UK, France, and Switzerland. Fieldwork was conducted in contexts designed to provide variation in time, place, and form of mass violence: Argentina and Uruguay (2012), Belarus (2013), Bosnia (2013 and 2015), Rwanda (2014), Spain (2014), Latvia (2014), and Poland (2015).

Family activism proved to be a strong emergent theme from the program as a whole. In Argentina, the subthemes emerging from professional interviews were triangulated with family survivor data from fieldwork and from examples in the literature and media, and focus here on survivor narratives. In Bosnia, we focus in on insights gained from professional interviews and related literatures.

ARGENTINA: CONTESTED FAMILY RESPONSES TO "DISAPPEARANCE"

As McSherry (2005) has analyzed in detail, the "national reorganization process" instigated in the 1976 coup by the heads of the Argentinian army, navy, and air force, had its origins in "Plan Condor," a Cold War era, U.S.-backed strategy to coordinate the repression and eradication of anti-Marxist political opposition in Latin America. The strategy involved the division of the country into operational zones in which plain-clothed paramilitary squads in unmarked cars pursued "wanted" leftists, abducted them from streets and homes, and transferred them to a network of clandestine detention centers (CDCs) where they were interrogated, tortured, and killed. Bodies were disposed of in illegal burials and cremations, and dumped in so-called "death flights" over the Rio de la Plata (CONADEP 1986, 209–233). This process came to be known as "disappearance," and its victims the "disappeared" ("desaparacidos"). Junta leaders denied it absolutely, and the use of paramilitary actors enabled the authorities to respond to both informal and formal (habeaus corpus) requests for information with feigned ignorance and a veneer of legitimacy. Disappearance was most intense during the "hot" period 1976–78, and after the Junta's self-dissolution in the wake of the Falklands/Malvinas defeat, the subsequent 1984 truth commission ("CONADEP") established just under nine-thousand missing for the entire period.

Families of the disappeared were affected in obvious and less obvious ways. The CONADEP report—"Nunca Mas" ("Never Again") details that during the "hot" period, family members were used as hostages in order to secure surrender of "suspects," were co-detained and tortured, and indeed, entire families were themselves disappeared (CONADEP 1986, 321–328). For those who were not also primary victims, the paradigmatic ontological predicament became centered around *not knowing*:

dread at the thought of what might be happening to loved ones, but a wall of official silence and denial in response to repeated requests for information.

Most of the missing were in their twenties and thirties and, to a great extent due to the "traditional" maternal role in this conservative Catholic society, mothers tended to be the family members most active in searching for information (Guzman-Bouvard 1994). In this way, women in identical predicaments—waiting in police stations—met and began to self-organize in order to highlight their common plight and to demand information. In April 1977, and borrowing from the civil and human rights tradition of the public demonstration, the first march around the main government square of Buenos Aires was held, and over the course of the year, evolved into an iconic weekly ritual of the "Madres of the Plaza Mayo" involving linked-hands procession, slogan-chanting, and the presentation of photographs of the disappeared. Madres wore the white *panuelo* (headscarf), designed to resemble a child's diaper on which the missing person's name was written. In this way, members of the movement symbolically underlined their core identity, not as victims or survivors, but primarily as *mothers*. This, of course, was literally true but by emphasizing the strongest of familial bonds and responsibilities, the women conveyed their sense of visceral upset while avoiding an overtly ideological stance that might have threatened their own safety.[7]

During the Junta period, the slogan "return them alive" (*aparicion con vida*) pithily described the movement's core demand while articulating the innermost fear that they were *not* alive. However, this phrase took on new significance after the fall of the dictatorship. Limited prosecutions and the CONADEP commission were set up in the immediate aftermath, but it quickly became clear that a pact of silence obtained and that no further information on the disappeared would be released. The reaction of the Madres is captured well by Guzman Bouvard (1994, 138): "Initially, many of the women believed that their children might actually be living. . . . As a matter of policy, though, the Mothers refused to consider their offspring dead because they viewed this acceptance as a way of burying the past and, more important, giving up the pursuit of justice." Practically speaking, this entailed a continuation of established protest tactics, and a complete boycott of the CONADEP,[8] preliminary investigations and exhumations. The strain of this uncompromising position began to tell, however, and the organization split in 1986. In doing so, the two resulting organizations offered a collective metaphor for the processing of traumatic bereavement.

The original group retained its name and continued to pursue an agenda of resolute *denial* of their children's death. Through the successive periods of selective prosecution and amnesty (the Alfonsin regime of the 1980s), of pardon and impunity (Menem in the 1990s), and of more meaningful mass prosecution for crimes against humanity (the Kirchner regimes of the 2000s), the Madres have maintained their initial positions but been transformed into an overtly political movement that keep their children alive in memory, most particularly through the pursuit of their radical ideals. Pursuing the metaphor of the mother, they have described their missing children as "giving birth to them" as activists, and in supporting the antiestablishment politics of the next generation, describe themselves as "permanently pregnant" (Guzman-Bouvard 1994, 15).

The group Mothers of Plaza Mayo—Founding Line, however, adopted a more *acknowledgment*-based mode of activity, accepting the realpolitik of the post-Junta settlement, and attempting to find their own methods of locating, identifying, and burying the remains of their children. Among other things, this led to investment in and cooperation with the developing science of human forensic anthropology as applied to human rights investigations, an entirely new field pioneered in Argentina by the U.S. scholar Clyde Snow. Snow established basic exhumation protocols and procedures and built local capacity by founding the Argentine Forensic Anthropology Team (EAAF). Founding Line have also been instrumental in founding DNA data banks required to identify remains accurately (Moon 2013).

Family activism in Argentina stretches beyond the single generation link, however. A subgroup of the Madres had had their pregnant daughters disappeared or infant grandchildren abducted along with their parents and had therefore named themselves the "Grandmothers [Abuelas] of the Plaza Mayo." Echoing strategies used by Nazi Germany in occupied Europe and in Francoist Spain, children were given to ideologically "pure" pro-Junta families to raise as their own. The Abuelas, in general, allied with the Founding Line position, and were again, instrumental in developing dedicated forensic science in the country. As the decades wore on and the abducted children themselves gained maturity, a self-organized group known as H.I.J.O.S[9] also formed in connection with and support of the Abuelas. "Hijo/as"[10] were either eventually told of their family origins by their appropriating families, or through their own suspicions, had this confirmed by submitting themselves to DNA analysis.

Of particular interest here, are the public narratives of both Abuelas and Hijo/as. There has, in criminology as well as many other disciplines, been a "narrative turn" (Brown 1994; Presser 2015) in research over the last few decades as interest has grown in subjective identity-related discourses of continuity and change, and their implications for (criminal) action. One of the best known of these is Maruna's (2001) distinction of "redemption" and "condemnation" scripts in relation to desistance from crime. While the relative positionality of Maruna's "peacetime" perpetrators and the family survivors of lethal mass violence is both obvious and clear, analysis of the narratives of the latter (here, Abuelas and Hijo/as) suggests cognate "identity work" is performed through reflective speech in what will be characterized as "family survivor scripts." Here, however, reflections do not relate to one's own immoral behavior, but to the losses attendant on the lethal and secretive behavior of state perpetrators. The core identities in question obviously differ—for the Abuelas, the nested identities of "mother," "activist" and "grandmother," and for the Hijo/as, "son/daughter" and "grandson/grandaughter"—but both sets of scripts describe the longitudinal identity dynamics inherent in the breaking and making of affective family ties. There seem to be three forms of script.

The first might be termed a "quest/yearning" script which might be seen as the default activist position produced in everyday discourse by Abuelas who continue to search for their grandchildren. The predicament of not knowing gains poignancy as other cases are successfully identified: "It is exhausting because every time the Grandmothers find a child, I think it could be her [own grandchild]. So I'm suffering so much inside for my loss but at the same time I hold so much hope [of finding her]" (Stockwell 2014, 51). Here, grief is unresolved: the mother-child bond is broken, and while there is the awareness of the possibility of a new bond, it has not yet materialized and may not materialize. There is continuity only with the initial rupture of maternal identity and relationship. The sororal bonds of the Abuelas themselves seem energizing, however, with their collective successes experienced as sustaining for both activist identity and personal hope.

The second script might be termed a "redemption/resolution" script, which, perhaps because of its narrative completeness, tends to be the best publicized. This develops the "quest" script to encompass the excitement and trepidation of DNA analysis, concludes with an emotionally demanding but joyful (re-)union, and portrays a remaking of identity where separate and separated histories are weaved into a narrative whole with a past, present and future. The paradigmatic example of this narrative is the celebrated dyad of the (Hijo/a) Ignacio Hurban and (Abuela) Estela Barnes de Carlotto, a founding member and president of the Abuelas organization. The following selective quotes illustrate the general arc of de Carlotto's public redemption narrative: "When I turned 80, I begged God not to let me die before I found my grandson. . . . I didn't want to die without hugging him . . . all the love I'd kept for him came over me, to tell him how much I loved him, how much I'd looked for him . . . the only thought I had was: Laura can rest in peace now. I felt Laura said to me: '*mother, mission accomplished*' (*Guardian* 2015, italics added). Likewise, her kidnapped and reunited grandchild, Ignacio Hurban, produces a sympathetic narrative: "'there was always this background noise. I didn't look like my parents. . . . I was home . . . when I got the call. I was Estela de Carlotto's grandson! . . . Meeting my two grandmothers was the most moving thing because it was like 'Bam!' there it is—*we won, we did it*, we're here, seeing each other, talking. . . . It has been a beautiful experience. I've met so many relatives. It's a big family'" (*Guardian* 2015). Such scripts describe a *continuity* of relationships with significant figures of the past (the murdered daughter/mother; Ignacio's adoptive parents), significant identity *rupture* for the grandchild,[11] but a rewarding and redemptive availability of *new and positive* family identities that also have a wider social significance. There is a sense of "triumph through adversity," of collectively actualized but dyadically focused social justice, and of a "quest" completed.

A third script might be termed the "rejection" script and centers on the *adverse* reaction of the grandchild to the news of their possible or actual status as an abducted Hijo/a, together with the ramifications for the seeking Abuela. Here the identity rupture for the Hijo/a is found to be unassimilable and profoundly disruptive of an existing positive family relationship, albeit one rooted ultimately in deceit and serious crime. Our meeting with an Abuela at their Buenos Aires headquarters described initially a common "quest" script of bereavement, activist protest, and the long, supported struggle for information. It then proceeded to incorporate features of the "redemption script," specifically, the anticipatory excitement of establishing a potential "match" for her grandchild. This woman's script then diverted to describe the identified young adult's resistance to submit to DNA procedures, the eventual establishment of a positive match, but the continued resistance of the grandchild to establishing a relationship with her biological grandmother. At the time of interview, contact had been made and maintained between the parties but was described as "difficult" and with "much work to do." This script promises resolution but ultimately offers only successive emotional barriers and either a fragile, strained, and distant relationship, or no relationship at all. Such cases arguably not only perpetuate existing identity ruptures and psychological conflict (on the part of the Abuela) but also create further sets of problems (on the part of the grandchild and their adoptive families) without the short-term possibility of resolution. They strike a melancholy, bittersweet narrative chord and have provoked wider debates on the right of the alleged or actual grandchild *not* to know their identity (Peluffo 2007).

In sum, the Argentinian case illustrates, among other things, how long and psychologically complex a shadow is cast by lethal mass violence, not only on its direct victims, but also on the families who cope with its varied effects. One set of organized family responses has evolved spontaneously out of the needs of women culturally configured to best represent the interests of the "missing." As will be developed further in the next section, family activism has had not only national but also global effects by offering both a portable model of initially "apolitical" political activism, and a social catalyst for the science of forensic anthropology. But in the context of ongoing postconflict societal rancor, it is clear these gains have been achieved at considerable cost to activist members. Collective action provides support and purpose for its members but is physically and psychologically demanding, has consequential effects on wider family life, and, for the individual, the ultimate goals of truth, justice, or reconciliation may be thwarted by the natural death of the aging activist, or, as with the case of the Abuelas and Hijo/as, be rejected and denied either partially or totally. The "family survivor" scripts of these latter parties capture something of the individual possibilities for longer-term meaning- and identity making in relation to destroyed family bonds. More broadly, the collective positions of the differing groups of mothers and grandmothers illustrate contrasting modes of brokering relationships between the dead and the living; a major point to which we will return.

BOSNIA: INDIVIDUAL, COLLECTIVE, AND SOCIETAL CONTEXTS OF BEREAVED FAMILY ACTIVISM

The complex interethnic, inter- and intrastate Bosnian War (1992–1995) claimed over 100,000 lives, and produced 31500 missing persons— the majority of whom were Bosnian Muslims ("Bosniaks")—and led to the displacement of 2.2 million people, that is, over half of the prewar population (ICMP 2014). The war was infamously characterized by epic sieges, the establishment of concentration camps, widespread forced population transfer ("ethnic cleansing"), mass rape, and numerous massacres of men and boys. One such set of massacres centered on the predominantly Bosniak town of Srebrenica in an enclave on the eastern border with Serbia. After becoming a major regional refugee destination and several years of siege, Bosnian Serb and irregular Serbian forces occupied the town in mid-July 1995, forcing Muslim women, children, and elderly to flee to the local UN base at Potocari, and a column of fifteen-thousand men and boys to attempt to trek though forest to reach the Bosniak-held town of Tuzla, one-hundred kilometers to the north. After capitulation by Dutch "peacekeepers" and a failure of UN high command to call in air strikes, Serb forces captured the base and among serious violence, separated men from women. Over the next week, as a result of this action and ongoing harassment of the Tuzla-bound column, some eight-thousand men and boys were shot dead and deposited in mass graves. In the weeks and months that followed, Serb forces returned to further conceal their crimes by excavating and reburying the remains in a series of secondary and even tertiary graves scattered about the region.

The war staggered to a negotiated conclusion that created a dual-entity state where boundaries reinforced the violence of population transfer and left Srebrenica in the new entity of Republika Srpska (RS). The surviving family members of the then "missing" (*nestali* in Bosnian) found themselves expelled from their homes and in insanitary refugee camps in the non-Serb entity ("the Federation") at Tuzla and elsewhere. From this desperate situation, and as documented by the remarkable ethnographic work of Sarah Wagner (2008), Selma Leydesdorff (2011), and Elissa Helms (2013) women began to self-organize and begin the process of searching for their male relatives. As noted by Wagner (2008), the first collective action as the "Women of Srebrenica" (*Zene Srebrenica*, hereafter, "the Women") after the war was to begin a Madres-style march every eleventh day of the month in Tuzla, with name-embroidered pillowcases substituting for *panuelos*. The Women opened offices in Tuzla and Sarajevo where the organization's strategy could be planned, potential donors received, and bereaved women support. Over the following years, these and other groups exerted strong civil society effects several interlinked ways.

First, the Women provided important impetus to the developing international criminal justice response. John Hagan, in his work charting the contested early operational history of the International Criminal Tribunal for the Former Yugoslavia (ICTY), describes a transformative meeting between incoming ICTY Chief Prosecutor Carlo Del Ponte and the Women which helped to clarify the extent and nature of their losses and is attributed as giving motive force to the leadership of the prosecution (Hagan 2004, 219). Hagan (2004, 167) also describes the emotive direct address of a bereaved mother to General Krstic[12] during the course of his trial which is portrayed as a key moment not only for the substance of the testimony provided, but for its apparently strong emotional effect on the accused.

Second, in their role as advocates for bereaved families, the Women, in league with cognate women's associations, influenced the shaping of Bosnia-Herzegovina's 2004 Law on Missing Persons (ICMP 2014), the first of its kind. This guaranteed (Article 3) the family's "right to know" about their disappeared relative(s), established the framework for providing state welfare and burial support (Articles 11 to 18) and prioritized assistance to family associations (Article 19).

Third, the Women shaped the technical and social processes of identification of the dead. In the immediate aftermath of the war, there were a number of ad hoc attempts to begin systematic searches, exhumations and identifications with contributions from the International Committee of the Red Cross (ICRC), Physicians for Human Rights (PHR), Clyde Snow, and EAAF members. Separate entity-level bodies were created to oversee the process and using traditional "presumptive" techniques of identification via recovered clothing, personal possessions, and dental/medical records, modest numbers of the Srebrenica dead were identified (ICMP 2014). It was not until the International Commission for Missing Persons (ICMP) was created in 1996, however, that the process began to change fundamentally. Set up as an international NGO by U.S. President Bill Clinton, the organization's stated purpose was to assist in the investigation and recovery of the missing, which it did in two chief ways. First, it engaged bereaved family organizations like the Women via its Civil Society Initiative, organizing and providing fora for discussion on key matters and also direct funding in the form of small grants. By building capacity in this way, the organization supported family organizations to participate in the process of drawing up the Law on Missing Persons. Second, it also co-opted families into the development of a radically different approach to identification of the dead. "Presumptive" methods had seemingly achieved good results in the early days of exhumations; however, a persistent set of concerns were aired over the accuracy of identification, highlighting the frequency with which mobile refugees exchanged clothes and identification papers, together with the further problems of disarticulated remains spread across several grave sites. This raised the prospect of false identifications and the disruption of any apparent resolution achieved by the family, arguably a further form of victimization. To overcome this, it was proposed to focus on the fast-developing science of DNA sequencing-and-analysis capable of very high (>99 percent) accuracy when reference samples from human remains are cross-matched to archived samples from relatives. The Women assisted this process in two ways: first, by placing pressure on ICMP and its founders to establish technical facilities in Bosnia (ICMP 2014), and second, by establishing, promoting, and participating in a substantial DNA-gathering exercise and resulting data bank of reference samples. By combining these two innovations, families and their institutional supporters created a domestic "industry" at the forefront of the science and with the highest material throughput of its type in the world. In the aftermath of Srebrenica, to date over twenty-four-thousand skeletal samples have been processed from more than forty primary and secondary graves, representing nearly seven-thousand positive identifications (ICMP 2014, 97).

The further significance of these processes can be seen in the unique rituals of return and reburial developed by family associations, and which we observed in full. Since 2003, the several hundreds of remains identified that calendar year are transferred from their Tuzla repository to the Visoko mortuary center northwest of Sarajevo. Here, they are placed with care and respect into individually identified coffins and loaded onto convoy vehicles bedecked with the Bosnian flag. The vehicles proceed from Visoko via Sarajevo, where the convoy vehicle is festooned with flowers, to the distinctive cemetery at Potocari outside Srebrenica. This site, acquired by the Office of the High Representative (OHR) is itself a product of the lobbying of bereaved families wishing to stress communal suffering at a symbolic site now deep within ethnically cleansed territory (Leydesdorff 2011, 193). The convoy arrives on the eve of the main rituals and the coffins are unloaded and stored in buildings on the former UN base. Here, private communal prayers are held. On the morning of July 12, the coffins are deposited in the main cemetery ritual area across the road from the base and relatives take their places next to excavated graves. The site is a highly social space, not solely because of the tens of thousands of people present, but also because families, friends and former neighbors take the opportunity to "visit" each other and to pay their graveside respects. The restrained by tangibly warm reunions clearly function to renew and maintain frayed social bonds. After political speeches and brief communal prayers that end in a profound collective silence, the coffins are interred by family members accompanied by prayers. The crowds then dissipate to begin the long journey away from their former homeland.

Across these four sets of activities, we see then, how and to what extent bereaved family organizations led by women have radically shaped postconflict efforts at society building in Bosnia-Herzegovina. Much like the Argentinian case, this has and continues to be a contested and difficult process characterized by disagreement, rancor, and the limitations of the postwar political and economic settlement. The official acknowledgment and status afforded to families of the missing, along with the unprecedented levels of identification and reburial of murdered relatives testifies, however, to the undeniable progress made in this context. Our final comparative observations can now be made.

DISCUSSION AND CONCLUSION

This chapter has made a case for extending the victimological gaze to the family survivors of lethal violence, not just in peacetime, but in contexts characterized by organized mass violence. We have argued that sudden, unexpected bereavement born of dehumanizing and eliminationist ideology can exert widespread and enduring effects on mental and physical health, particularly when it is combined with primary victimization and, in the case of major international crimes, the destruction of property, community, and a way of life. We have also argued that particular forms of clandestine killing and bodily disposal can impose additional burdens on surviving family members as, in the face of official denials, they cope long-term with the absence of information or a body to begin the process of grieving. These arguments have been illustrated in relation to case studies of major systemic conflict in Argentina and Bosnia and we have also shown how often multiply bereaved family members exhibit Rock's (1998b) "imperative to organize" by forming activist associations that achieve clear, if hard-won, gains both during and after the cessation of overt conflict. A number of concluding comparative points can be made.

First, in the spirit of critical victimology, the case studies problematize the clear definition of primary and secondary victims: very often, family members are both and struggle to free themselves from the chronic effects of both forms of victimization decades after the source events. Family survivors of mass violence, like their peacetime equivalents, may gain a form of purpose and personal sense of "mission" through activism but there is no guarantee that they will achieve the sorts of "redemption/ resolution" scripts typified in the Hurban/de Carlotto case. In fact, absent the possibility of new family bonds, it is questionable whether this form of script can be formed when "resolution" might mean the confirmation of a death and the return of partial human remains. Indeed, in the example of the Srebrenica massacres, even burial of identified remains may not represent the end of the trauma journey: new identifications of body parts scattered across secondary graves, together with the ongoing resolution of early misidentifications are increasingly leading to *re*-exhumations for the purposes of skeletal reassociations, together with further family disruption. This example makes clear how fragile the psychological gains of apparently successful family activism can be, and further illustrates how the "disappeared" corpse can radically extend in space and time, the trauma associated with violent bereavement (Shute 2015).

A related point can be made regarding the complex and unpredictable interactions of individual (micro), collective (meso), and societal (macro) variables that constrain the kinds of "successes" achieved by family organizations at particular points in their history. Scraton's (1998, 2013) study of the Hillsborough Family Support Group shows how members had to endure organizational splits and three decades of macro-level marginalization and vilification before changes in political and media sensibilities enabled personal and collective vindication. In an analogous way, the energy of individual family survivors during the Argentinian Junta was initially harnessed by the formation of the Madres, however, the interaction of personal and collective values and those of successive political regimes forced organizational splits, divergent aims, and impacts that were felt differentially across the following decades. By contrast, the more wholesale destruction and reshaping of Bosnian society promoted a well-funded international effort to create political institutions (for example, the OHR) and NGOs (for example, the ICMP) that were capable of empowering family associations on an unprecedented scale and timescale. That family bereavement in Bosnia might have been *prevented* by sustained international military and diplomatic action on a comparable scale is an irony not lost on families and wider society. Clearly, a mature appreciation of the possibilities of family activism requires a multilevel and diachronic set of perspectives.

A third comparative point can be made in relation to the role of gender in the nature, functioning, and achievements of family associations in these examples. Helms (2013) notes that by portraying themselves primarily as mothers and wives, female activists in Bosnia have used "positive [gender] essentialisms" to create an effective space for public engagement traditionally denied to women. Paradoxically, however, those same essentialisms have also prevented them from being taken seriously in the more substantive arena of male-dominated parliamentary politics, and limit the possibilities for longer-term gender equality. Similar observations might be made with regard to the at least initially "apolitical" nature of the Madres' protests and claims, and although the political position of women may be relatively advanced in comparison to Bosnia, authors (for example, Peluffo 2007) continue to link the broader acceptability of the continuing movements to their relative degree of publicly expressed femininity.

Finally, in processes that have their origin in Argentina but have reached their contemporary apogee in Bosnia, a co-developed alliance of bereaved family activism and forensic anthropological/archaeological science has formed a movement that, alongside human rights and international criminal justice movements, offer increasingly substantive and globalized counterflows to the long-globalized networks of arms, military training, and trade that continue to fuel organized mass violence.

The victimological implications of this observation are that these processes are deserving of much greater disciplinary acknowledgment and study. To do so, victimology must remain critical but also become more creative and ambitious in its research aims; it must also, ideally, become more interdisciplinary and more conceptually complex in order to capture the subtleties of responses to mass victimization. This is undoubtedly a very significant set of challenges but one that an outward-looking and reflexive critical victimology can be equipped to take forward.

NOTES

1. For definitions and methods see http://www.who.int/violence_injury_prevention/violence/status_report/2014/methodology/en/

2. Largely, inter- and intrastate armed conflict; for definitions and methods see http://www.pcr.uu.se/research/ucdp/definitions/

3. Multidimensional approaches to operationalizing "peace" exist—see for example Institute for Economics and Peace (2015) "positive peace index"—but are beyond the scope of this chapter.

4. Differences in the definition of lethal violence occur across jurisdictions and are a source of confound in comparisons.

5. See www.samm.org.uk

6. See http://www.corpsesofmassviolence.eu/

7. As it happens, the women were not safe; they were arrested, beaten, and harassed and early members themselves "disappeared" (Guzman-Bouvard 1994).

8. Indeed, the estimated figure of the disappeared was strongly contested, and is still claimed by the Madres to be in the order of thirty-thousand.

9. An acronym, translating as "Sons and Daughters for Identity and Justice Against Oblivion and Silence."

10. "Hijo" is the masculine form of "child," with "hija" the female equivalent. Forthwith, the gender neutral designation "Hijo/a" is used.

11. Ignacio Hurban recently changed his name to Ignacio Guido Montoya de Carlotto, reflecting his intended birth name and biological family names.

12. Later convicted for genocide.

Conclusion

Critical Victimology beyond Academe: Engaging Publics and Policy

Sandra Walklate and Dale C. Spencer

Tracing the victim "story" is fraught with difficulties: where to start geographically, where to start historically, whose story is to be listened to and so on. Nonetheless, it is without doubt that the twenty-first century is marked by a focus on victims and victimhood. The contemporary global condition and the communication systems associated with it bring to a wide range of publics the dilemmas faced by individuals and collectivities who find themselves in situations of suffering through no fault of their own. Whether as a result of climate change driven economically challenging circumstances, internal conflicts, externally imposed conflicts, religious extremism, or other factors, it is the case that the world could not walk away from the media image of a young child, lying on a beach, drowned trying to escape with his family to Europe. It is not the only image of victimhood to be headlined in the media. It is a moot point, however, how well equipped the academy, in the form of victimology, is to deal with these kinds of global events and the toll that they take on individuals and collectivities. This collection, while bringing together quite a disparate collection of particular concerns with victims and victimhood, is tied together by a common concern: to offer some insight into how the tools and concepts of a critical victimology might be better placed to make sense of victimhood and responses to it, in all its forms, in the twenty-first century.

In many respects, it goes without saying that a focal concern of victimology has been and still is suffering. While Young (2011, 181) castigates what might be called conventional criminology for patrolling its borders, shutting out the philosophical, the overtly theoretical as too reflective, and carefully excluding war, genocide, state crime, crimes against the environment and so on as outside its "scientific focus," victimology has never been so exclusionary. Indeed the emergence of victimology as a discipline came out of those very circumstances largely neglected by mainstream criminology. Fassin and Rechtman (2009) offer a detailed analysis of the emergence of what they call "psychiatric victimology" concomitant with an appreciation of the traumatic effects of the First World War and the work of Mendelsohn himself (considered to be one of the founding fathers of the discipline), writing post the Second World War posited the need for a discipline that could grasp and make sense of genocide. Thus, from its inception, victimology has offered a lens through which to think about both individual and collective suffering. However the way in which these connected forms of suffering have been addressed and understood is different depending upon which theoretical lens it is viewed through. As McGarry and Walklate (2015, chapter 1) suggest, whether a positivist, radical, or critical victimologist, all are concerned with understanding the interrelationship between choice, power, and suffering, though each of these perspectives emphasizes different elements of this relationship. Moreover, as the introduction to this volume has intimated the different strands within what is understood as critical victimology, add a nuanced appreciation of how suffering, from crime in particular, might be better understood and responded to. In this collection it is possible to trace some of the dynamics of that nuance.

THINKING CRITICALLY ABOUT VICTIMHOOD

In part 1 of this collection, the contributions by Lippens, Katz and Willis, Condry, Spencer and Patterson, and Chakraborti exhort us to think critically about who, how, and under what conditions individuals and collectivities are recognized and responded to as victims. In many respects this continues to be a very fruitful area of investigation becausee, as several of these contributions highlight, it is one that carries significant policy and practice implications. Yet, as these contributions imply, questions remain concerning the concepts available to make sense of this process, how it might be investigated, and what implications derived from such work sit comfortably with questions of justice.

In making sense of these questions Lippens foregrounds the changing nature of victim culture and the influences on that cultural form since the Second World War. Interestingly, his answer to the "how" questions is to draw upon literature and art as "data" for making sense of this culture and its articulation of the relationship between the self, the body, and the sovereign. He offers a provocative analysis of the ways in which changing understandings of the relationship between the self and the body in particular (drawing on work on the sociology of the body) gel with changing conceptions of victimhood on which the sovereign (the powerful) may differently elicit support for their various and varied projects of power. Here it is possible to discern that "victim culture" is not peculiarly a phenomenon of the late twentieth century (Furedi 1997) but one that is deeply embedded in the post–world war era. For Lippens it is present in the paintings of Rothko and Pollock, the writings of Camus, and the policies and practices of different sovereigns from articulations of dependency culture to the emergence of human rights. "Victim cultures" have been translated into policies and practices and have become embedded in interpersonal communications. Such practices are sometimes reflected in the nonverbal (bodily) communication as well as the verbal, as the work of Spencer and Patterson suggests.

As the introduction to this volume has intimated, one strand of critical victimological thought has focused on the importance of interpersonal interaction (Miller and Holstein 1990), and the foundation of that interaction in shared meanings and understandings around who has legitimate access to the status of victim and the conditions under which that status is both ascribed and achieved (Miers 1990). Much work on this dynamic has been informed by Christie's (1986) seminal essay on the "ideal victim" and for some of the contributions in this collection, his intervention constitutes a significant conceptual influence. Embedded in the concept of the ideal victim are assumptions concerning both vulnerability and the body (Spencer 2015). These have purchase in everyday interaction and this is nowhere more telling than in the interactive processes that take place between victims, police officers, and victim service workers. This chapter draws on qualitative empirical work with victim service workers and deploys Bourdieu's concepts of field and habitus. From this data, Spencer and Patterson offer remarkable insights into how the perceived bodily interactions between police officers and victims in the presence of victim service workers convey the message that the world of policing and that of victim support remain "worlds apart" (Jordan 2001). This leads them to reflect upon how the demands of a "stoic masculinity" required as a routine response in the field of policing mitigates against the possibilities of a more "caring" response that might bridge the gap between victim expectations emanating from their experience of victimhood and service delivery. Positing the implications of a more "paternalistic masculinity," Spencer and Patterson suggest that further work needs to be done on the efficacy of such an approach for the delivery of justice more generally, not only for female victims of sexual assault (an arena in which criticisms of policing are most acute) but also for male victims of sexual assault as well as victims more generally. So through qualitative research, and drawing on conceptual agendas outside victimology, this work carries with it some interesting and provocative implications for the practice of justice in terms of service delivery. In so doing, this chapter foregrounds the concept of masculinity. This conceptual starting point is developed by Katz and Willis.

Also emanating from qualitative research, Katz and Willis adopt a life narrative approach for understanding the multilayered and multidimensional victim experiences of twenty-five incarcerated men of different ages and ethnic backgrounds. There are two constant features underpinning these men's life narratives. They were all physically and/or sexually abused as children (offering a different appreciation of the corporeal dimensions of victimhood) and their responses to these experiences are all mediated by their expression and expectations of them as men: masculinity. This intervention adds to that increasingly important research demonstrating the significant links between victimhood and offending behavior for women (see inter alia, Chesney-Lind and Pasko 2013, 3) by pointing to similar links between victimhood and offending behavior for men. In this latter respect, such offending behavior, more often than not directed toward women, reminds us of the self-evident gendered feature of victimhood while simultaneously affording a deeper understanding of what might lie behind that statistical pattern. The narratives of these men's lives are permeated in complex ways by the presence of alcohol and drugs (in their own and their parents' lives) alongside structural deprivations characterized by poverty, parental neglect, and racism. The multifaceted and intersectional nature of their "victimhood" render any simple or straightforward understanding of their lives problematic. What is evident from these stories is that, despite their victimizing experiences the likelihood for them of achieving victim status and thus eliciting different responses from the justice system seem remote indeed. Their victimization and consequent route into criminality remains largely hidden. Moreover, to recognize such experiences in terms of policy would be challenging indeed, particularly to the "sovereign" spoken about by Lippens: a sovereign who, in order to remain in control, would rather invoke other images of victimhood and demand a disciplined body as a response. Nonetheless, the patterns of the men's lives and their hidden nature, as delineated in the chapter by Katz and Willis, are difficult to deny. The hidden nature of the "victimality" (Rafter and Walklate 2012) of these men's lives is taken along a different path in the chapter by Condry.

Condry's work explores the hidden nature and status of parents who are victims of their own children's violences. This work sensitizes us to the consequences for the victim of the absence of being assigned victim status. In documenting the experiences of the victimization of parents, Condry suggests that they become "paradoxical victims": considered responsible for their children's behavior but simultaneously victims of it. They thus experience the pain of suffering both in real terms, from their children, from their own capacity for self-blame, and from the ambiguous response they receive. A response which oscillates from understanding to blame, from family, friends, and any support services they might encounter. Not all of this suffering is driven by their victim experience. It does not exist in a vacuum. The nature and extent of their hidden status as victims is clearly connected to wider public discourse (in the UK and elsewhere) designed to render parents more accountable for their children's behavior from school attendance to their criminality. At this juncture, Condry connects the interactional difficulties experienced by this hidden victim group in gaining victim recognition to the wider mechanisms of the state in creating the victims seen alongside those not seen (qua McGarry and Walklate 2015). Parents as victims of adolescent violence are hidden from the policy gaze. The visible or invisible nature of some forms of victimization is pursued further by Chakraborti.

The focus of Chakraborti's chapter is hate crime. In many ways the nature and impact of hate crime has risen up the policy and practice agenda so much so that, contemporarily, it would be easy to conclude that victims of hate crime have achieved victim recognition. Indeed, as Chakraborti documents, there has been an exponential growth in new knowledge, understanding, and policies around hate crime and its consequences. Much of this is associated with the wider cultural appreciation of the importance of identity and the politics associated with recognition. However, Chakraborti points out that this focus on identity in the singular can serve to emphasize the invisibility of some groups whose sense of identity may not be fixed and simultaneously fails to acknowledge the multiple nature of identity itself. Consequently within hate crime, some groups are more visible and are the focus of policy, and some are less visible because they fall outside the hate crime rubric. This lack of connection between people's real lives and policy creates the conditions under which what policy responses there are stand to be accused of tokenism or, as in Chakraborti's title, a "tick box" approach. In order to be better heard, the suggestion here is for the academic agenda to embrace the intersectionality of people's real lives (qua Katz and Willis above) so that policies can be better formulated and produce better results.

Taken together, these chapters afford some interesting insights and conceptual development of a critical victimological stance that pose important questions about the process of victim recognition, the changing cultural context in which that emerges, the dynamics of who is made visible and who remains invisible in that process, and the implicit interconnection between those dynamics and the nature of policy intervention. The chapters that follow develop this stance toward policy and policy developments in and of themselves.

VICTIMS AND VICTIM POLICY IN COMPARATIVE PERSPECTIVE

Victimology, like criminology, is a meeting place, not only for people of different intellectual persuasions joined together by their shared interest in the victim of crime, but also for practitioners from a wide range of criminal justice and service providers. Thus, the intellectual and the practical are intertwined, so much that in times past commentators like Ezzat Fattah (1989) became very perturbed by it. Nonetheless, it is the case that the growth and development of interest in victimhood has been paralleled by a growth and development in victim services, not always evenly or in a one-to-one relationship, but nevertheless interconnected. The chapters by Elias and Gallo, Miers, and McEvoy and McConnachie offer an appreciation of the development of victim-centered policy, sometimes informed by academic research, along three dimensions: victim services, national criminal justice policy, and internationally within transitional justice agendas.

In comparing and contrasting the emergence and development of victim services in the United States and Sweden, Elias and Gallo point to the importance of understanding the role of the specific cultural and policy context in contributing to the nature of services available. While Swedish support services emerged from a strong welfare tradition, those emanating from the United States have been much more influenced by a criminal justice orientation, focusing on improving the role of the victim in participation in that process particularly at the point of sentencing. While both of these routes to service delivery were initially also influenced by voices from the feminist movement (as they were in other parts of the world too) the different paths followed reflect the different political and ideological orientations of each society. The more individualistic orientation of the United States results in a greater emphasis on making the offender responsible for the harm caused to the individual victim, while the more collectivist orientation of Sweden results in a greater emphasis on support for victims from the state. As the authors point, out each of these paths have had different consequences for the victim; on the one hand victim voices have often been co-opted in support of stronger law-and-order policies and, on the other hand, the human rights orientation in Swedish policy has obscured as many victim issues as it has addressed. In the Swedish context this has largely meant that violence against women has been a comparative latecomer to the policy table. Perhaps more fundamentally, comparative studies such as these reveal much about the dangers of policy transfer, such as assuming that a policy will travel from one socio-economic context to another. Moreover, in particular, it points to the implicit problems associated with the belief that policy solutions formulated and underpinned by Westro-centric thinking will be viable elsewhere in the world. Each of these questions is differently developed in the next two chapters.

Miers explores the extent to which restorative justice has achieved the status of a "boundary object." By this he means whether or not it represents a community of interests and/or practices that result in the sharing of a common language and syntax. It is certainly the case that the presence of restorative justice, as a way of delivering justice that has the capacity to not only center the victim but also offer some healing to them, has grown apace since the early 1990s. It has without doubt traveled the Anglo-speaking world. Yet, as Miers's analysis reveals, despite its omnipresence in certain parts of the globe, there is still much work to be done before it shares in a common enough language to achieve the status of a boundary object. This, of course, does not mean that those committed to and engaged with this vision of delivering justice have not succeeded in persuading politicians and policy-makers otherwise. Despite its limitations it has been, without doubt, a popular response in the face of the rising tide of victims' voices claiming a space to be heard within different criminal justice settings. To offer a critique of such orientations can be seen in itself to be problematic. Yet, as the chapter by Miers implies and as Tavuchi (1990) has articulated very clearly, the giving and the receiving of an apology (of which restorative justice is a particular form) can only be genuinely and authentically given and received under very particular social conditions, those in which, when a third party is included (in this case a criminal justice system), are militated against. So restorative justice in failing to achieve the status of a boundary object also runs the risk of failing victims by offering what cannot be delivered in this particular form. It becomes a tick-box response rather like the responses to hate crime documented by Chakraborti. Nonetheless, engagement with restorative justice has proceeded apace, as have initiatives designed to engage the victim in the processes associated with transitional justice initiatives.

McEvoy and McConnachie, in a deep and thought-provoking analysis of the victim turn in the development of transitional justice initiatives, point to the symbolic importance of the victim language in this arena in a way not too dissimilar to Miers's analysis of the victim in restorative justice. In overviewing a wide range of different processes of reconciliation put in place to "make amends" in societies torn apart by different types of conflicts, McEvoy and McConnachie make some provocative observations about some common features endemic to them all. Indeed, in the examples on which they draw—all from different international settings—the construction and reconstruction of a hierarchy of victimization (Carrabine et al. 2004) is marked. Moreover, in the deployment of this hierarchy, what they call the "urge to blame," alongside the drive to make someone (an individual) responsible, is more than evident. Of course, in conflict-ridden societies, history matters. Consequently who qualifies for victim status and who does not, and when, is built on the shifting sands of who the defining powers might be at any particular point in time. However, what is also interesting and implied by this overview is the apparent strain to make the policy response fit the circumstances rather than the reverse. It is here that it is possible to discern the way in which transitional justice, rather like restorative justice, has the capacity to fail the victim in the overriding drive to meet the needs of the entrepreneurs charged with the delivery of the process. It is within these spaces that the problems of policy transfer can emerge, as can the difficulties associated with Western-centric thinking dominant in victimology.

BRINGING THE STATE BACK IN

The dynamics of victim recognition—who is and who is not recognized as a victim—as several of the contributions in this collection intimate, does not happen in a vacuum. Different socioeconomic, cultural, and political circumstances are important drivers underpinning such dynamics, leading to some of the fundamental difficulties associated with policy transfer and the constraining effects of Western-centric thinking alluded to above. Developing the imperative to appreciate the specificity of history and context, and the way in which these factors produce different contestations of victimhood, is taken further by Ballinger, McGarry, and Shute.

One of the key features of the development of critical victimology, as expressed in the work of Mawby and Walklate (1994) was not only to recognize those processes of victimization that went on "behind people's backs" but were nonetheless real in their consequences, but also to embrace the recognition, already put squarely on the criminological agenda by feminist-informed work, that such processes were gendered. This feature of the patterns of victimization has long been recognized from interventions on the fear of crime (Stanko 1985) to those relating to patterns of violence by men against women (see inter alia Dobash and Dobash 1979). As contributions in this volume have illustrated, in embracing this feature of victimization, it has taken a while longer to also recognize men's victimization as a hidden dimension in this patterning. However, even more invisible has been the role of gendered practices of the state, as articulated in the law, in reproducing hetero-patriarchal power relations. This is powerfully illustrated in the ways in which particular cases are responded to in law. Ballinger, in a thought-provoking comparative analysis of case studies of the state's response to women faced with the law, illustrates how these power relations are produced and reproduced in different cases spanning over a hundred years. Embedded in these case studies is the role of expert knowledge and its comparative deployment in the court to support these power relationships whether such knowledge is relevant to the case at hand or not. This is ultimately the crux of miscarriages of justice. The harm done to the participants of these processes in the name of the state goes largely unrecognized and unacknowledged, the potential payment of compensation notwithstanding (see also Shute's chapter in this volume). Ballinger's work renders these processes and their gendered presumptions visible for all to see.

McGarry also faces head-on the thorny question of the victims seen and unseen in the work of the state. In his chapter, this question is explored through the lens of terrorism and war. Using case studies as a methodological tool, this chapter offers a challenging critique of how different victims and victim groups are "imagined" in the context of war and explores the sociocultural dynamics that underpin such imaginings.

Here we are not only faced with the sovereign who calls upon different imaginings for their own purposes (qua Lippens in this volume) we are also faced with situating such self-interest in its global context. Thus the victims seen "out there" more often than not equate with Western assumptions surrounding victimhood (that is closer to "us," victims seen "in here") mediated by (again) notions of ideal victimhood. Thus the victims of attacks in Paris are more easily "seen" than those in Baghdad. At the same time victims "in here," like soldiers sent to fight in a legally suspect war with inadequate equipment and subsequently charged with "war crimes" and/or murder, fall short for victim recognition. In developing a detailed hierarchy of victimization, the role of the state is placed front and center in these processes. As McGarry alludes to, the "penal couple" commented on by von Hentig (1948), another founding father of the discipline of victimology, is married by the role of the state. This is nowhere more the case than in the context of mass violence.

Shute marries McGarry's concern with the state's involvement in creating a hierarchy of victimization in and around state violence with Mendelsohn's early concern with a victimology of genocide. However Shute takes as his starting point what it is that we know and do not know about the individual and collective responses to state perpetration of lethal violence and the capacity for victim activism under these circumstances. His approach to this is historical, comparative and longitudinal. Taking the post-Junta period in Argentina (1976–1983) and postwar Bosnia (1991–1995) as his case studies, he is concerned with the capacity of bereaved families to engage in activism in the face of profound absences, from the absence of a corpse to the absence of state acknowledgment that anything happened. Such material absences add further weight in a real, rather than an ironic, sense to visible and invisible victims. They usefully remind us of the importance of the corporeality of victimization not only for the victim but to the process of bereavement. For Shute the contested questions of searching for the dead and speaking for them are significant features of the process of victim recognition. Without these elements the kinds of closure sought by initiatives associated with transitional justice (as discussed by McEvoy and McConnachie) become elusive indeed, the vested interests of the state in such justice initiatives notwithstanding.

CONCLUDING THOUGHTS: ENGAGING PUBLICS AND POLICY

When Walklate (1990) made her first intervention adding to the emergent call for a critical victimology, part of that agenda included a call for research that was longitudinal and qualitative in nature and comparative in form. This collection is characterized by research of this kind. True, not all of it is comparative and not all of it is necessarily longitudinal, but all of it is qualitative and all of it is sensitive to the political, economic, social, and cultural context in which it has been produced. Thus this book demonstrates the value of work informed in this way and the nuanced but critical understanding it affords in making sense of people's routine and not-so-routine experiences of victimization. In taking this methodological direction, this work also demonstrates significant conceptual developments afforded by it. Noting, as it does, the ongoing power of older conceptual frameworks (like ideal, deserving, blameless, and innocent victimhood) and the value of thinking about how these concepts are framed and delivered by "newer" conceptual interventions (like, for example, boundary objects and intersectionality). This methodological starting place, as suggested in the early 1990s, also has the potential to feed into the policy domain, as several of the chapters in this volume intimate. However, it is at this juncture that the issue of engagement becomes a little more difficult. The question remains, why might it be important to engage, who with, and for what purpose?

This is not the place to rehearse (again) the debates about public social science set in train by Buroway (2005) some time ago. Suffice it to say that it many ways this debate has largely been sidestepped by victimology and victimologists. There are a number of reasons for this; however, one returns us to the issue posed earlier in this conclusion. That reason lies in understanding the power of the domain assumptions and practices embedded within victimology and the intimate connection between the "science" and the "activism" commented on by Fattah (1989). Many prominent voices within victimology occupy the same space as those engaged in policy development. This is particularly evident in Europe in the use and deployment of the international criminal victimization survey as the basis for policy alongside the policy and funding network associated with it. This survey method, despite its evidenced weaknesses (see inter alia Hope 2007), is of course intimately connected with a different kind of victimology: positivism. The influence of that version of victimology, alongside the current propensity of politicians in a wide range of jurisdictions to listen and promote one victim's voice as though they spoke for all victims (see also Lippens in this volume) is profound indeed. The challenge for critical victimology is to engender a greater interest in the kind of work that might flow from a different conceptual agenda (as exemplified in this collection) within the wider victimological community. This agenda does, after all, carry with it policy implications. It may be, of course, that the grasp of positivism is too deep. However, if we are to make sense of the power of different voices emanating from different parts of the world (see for example Carrington et al. 2015) and to truly grasp the political and economic victims that we see (as in the case of the drowned child with which this conclusion began) alongside those that we do not see, casting aside the mantle of positivism would be one place to start. In this sense, it is the wider victimological community public that needs to be engaged with the kind of methodologically nuanced and conceptually sensitive but critical work as represented by the contributions to this book. There is much to be done in this respect and much to be learned, all of which at the end of the day will benefit victims of all shapes, sizes, color, and geographical locations.

Bibliography

Ackers, P. 2001. "Paternalism, Participation and Partnership: rethinking the employment relationship." *Human Relations* 54: 373–384.

Acorn, A. 2005. *Compulsory Compassion: A Critique Of Restorative Justice.* Vancouver: University of British Columbia Press.

ACPO (Association of Chief Police Officers). 2000. *ACPO Guide to Identifying and Combating Hate Crime.* London: ACPO.

———. 2005. *Hate Crime: Delivering a Quality Service: Good Practice and Tactical Guidance.* London: ACPO.

Adams, S. 2012. "Malala Yousafzai: Pakistani Schoolgirl to Be Treated Alongside Injured Soldiers." *Telegraph.* http://www.telegraph.co.uk/news/worldnews/asia/pakistan/9609909/Malala-Yousafzai-Pakistani-schoolgirl-to-be-treated-alongside-injured-soldiers.html.

Adlam, R. 2002. "Governmental Rationalities in Police Leadership: An Essay Exploring Some of the 'Deep Structure' in Police Leadership Praxis." *Policing and Society: An International Journal of Research and Policy* 12: 15–36.

Aertsen, I., T. Daems, and L. Robert. 2006. *The Institutionalisation of Restorative Justice in a Changing Society.* Cullompton: Willan.

af Sandeberg, A., and C. Ljungwald. 2012. "Brottsofferjourens Självbild, Målgrupper, och Oberoende" [Swedish victim support, self-image, target groups, and independence]. In *Viktimologisk forskning: Brottsoffer i teori och metod* [Victimology: Crime victims in theory and method], edited by A. Heber, E. Tiby, and S. Wikman, 317–336. Lund: Studentlitteratur.

Agamben, G. 1999. *Remnants of Auschwitz: The Witness and the Archive.* New York: Zone Books.

———. 2005. *State of Exception.* Chicago: Chicago University Press.

Alcoff, L. 1991. "The Problem of Speaking for Others." *Cultural Critique* 20: 5–32.

Allen, D. 2009. "From Boundary Concept to Boundary Object: The Practice and Politics of Care Pathway Development." *Social Science and Medicine* 69: 354–361.

Allen, H. 1987. *Justice Unbalanced.* Milton Keynes: Open University Press.

Amir, M. 1971. *Patterns of Forcible Rape.* Chicago: Chicago University Press.

Anderson, E. 2009. *Inclusive Masculinity: The Changing Nature of Masculinities.* New York: Routledge.

Andersson, R. 2002. "Kriminalpolitikens väsen [The nature of crime policy]." Unpublished PhD diss., Stockholm University.

Aradau, C. 2004. "The Perverse Politics of Four-Letter Words: Risk and Pity in the Securitization of Human Trafficking." *Millennium: Journal of International Studies* 33: 251–277.

Arendt, H., and K. Jaspers. 1992. *Correspondence, 1926–1969.* New York: Harcourt Brace.

Argentina's National Commission on Disappeared People. 1986. Nunca Mas (Never Again). London: Faber and Faber.

Arriaza, L., and N. Roht-Arriaza. 2008. "Social Repair at the Local Level: The Case of Guatemala." In *Transitional Justice from Below: Grassroots Activism and the Struggle for Change,* edited by K. McEvoy and L. Mcgregor, 143–166. London: Hart Publishing.

Arthur, R. 2005. "Punishing Parents for the Crimes of Their Children." *The Howard Journal* 44: 233–253.

Ashworth, A. 1993. "Victim Impact Statements And Sentencing." *Criminal Law Review*: 498–509.

———. 2002. "Responsibilities, Rights and Restorative Justice." *British Journal of Criminology* 42: 578–595.

———. 2003. Some Doubts about Restorative Justice. *Criminal Law Forum* 4: 277–299.

Asquith, N. 2014. "A Governance of Denial: Hate Crime in Australia and New Zealand." In *The Routledge International Handbook on Hate Crime*, edited by N. Hall, A. Corb, P. Giannasi, and John Grieve, 174–189. London: Routledge.

Ballinger, A. 2000. *Dead Woman Walking: Executed Women in England & Wales 1900–1955*. Dartmouth: Ashgate.

———. 2003. "Researching and Redefining State Crime: Feminism and the Capital Punishment of Women." In *Researching the Crimes of the Powerful: Scrutinising States and Corporations*, edited by S. Tombs and D. Whyte, 219–238. New York: Peter Lang Publishing.

———. 2005. "Reasonable Women Who Kill." *Outlines* 2: 65–82.

———. 2007. "Masculinity in the Dock: Legal Responses to Male Violence and Female Retaliation in England and Wales 1900–1965." *Social & Legal Studies* 16: 459–481.

———. 2011. "Feminist Research, State Power and Executed Women: The Case of Louie Calvert." In *Escape Routes: Contemporary Perspectives on Life after Punishment*, edited by S. Farrall, M. Hough, S. Maruna, and R. Sparks, 107–133. London: Routledge.

———. 2012. "A Muted Voice from the Past: The 'Silent Silencing' of Ruth Ellis." *Social & Legal Studies* 21:445–467.

———. 2016. *Gender, Truth and State Power: Capitalising on Punishment*. Dartmouth: Ashgate.

Balvig, F., H. Gunnlaugsson, K. Jerre, A. Kinnunen, and H. Tham. 2015. "The Public Sense of Justice in Scandinavia: A Study of Attitudes towards Punishments." *European Journal of Criminology* 12: 1–20.

Baraković, D., E. Avdibegović, and O. Sinanović. 2013. "Depression, Anxiety and Somatization in Women with War Missing Family Members." *Materia socio-medica* 25: 199.

Barker, R. 2001. *Legitimating Identities: The Self-Presentations of Rulers and Subjects*. Cambridge, UK: Cambridge University Press.

Barker, V. 2007. "The Politics of Pain: A Political Institutionalist Analysis of Crime Victims' Moral Protests." *Law and Society Review* 41: 619–664.

Bartkowiak-Théron, I. and N. Asquith. 2012. "Vulnerability and Diversity in Policing." In *Policing Vulnerability*, edited by I. Bartkowiak-Théron and N. Asquith, 3–19. Sydney: The Federation Press.

Bartov, O. 1998. "Defining Enemies, Making Victims: Germans, Jews, and the Holocaust." *The American Historical Review* 103: 771–816.

Bataille, G. 2001. *Eroticism*. London: Penguin.

———. 2012. *La Souveraineté*. Paris: Ligne.

Batt, J. 2004. *Stolen Innocence*. London: Ebury Press.

Baxi, U. 2002. *The Future of Human Rights*. Oxford: Oxford University Press.

Bazemore, G. and Schiff, M. 2004. "Paradigm Muddle or Paradigm Paralysis? The Wide and Narrow Roads to Restorative Justice Reform (or, a Little Confusion May Be a Good Thing)." *Contemporary Justice Review* 7: 37–57.

BBC Education. 2015. "School Truancies Lead to Rise in Prosecution of Parents." http://www.bbc.co.uk/news/education-33861985.

BBC News. 2012. "Malala Yousafzai: Taliban Shooting Victim Flown to UK." http://www.bbc.co.uk/news/world-asia-19944078.

———. 2015. "Eight out of 10 Malala Suspects 'Secretly Acquitted.'" http://www.bbc.co.uk/news/world-asia-33018334.

———. 2007. "UK." 22 November 2007.

Becker, H. S. 1967. "Whose Side Are We On?" *Social Problems* 14: 239–247.

Behr, E. 1985. *Anyone Here Been Raped and Speaks English?* London: New English Library.

Beirne, P. 2011. "A Note on the Facticity of Animal Trials in Early Modern Britain; Or, the Curious Prosecution of Farmer Carter's Dog for Murder." *Crime, Law and Social Change* 55: 359–374.

Bell, C. 2009. "Transitional Justice, Interdisciplinarity and the State of the 'Field' or 'Non-Field.'" *International Journal of Transitional Justice* 3: 5–27.

Belur, J. 2008. "Is Policing Domestic Violence Institutionally Racist? A Case Study of South Asian Women." *Policing and Society: An International Journal of Research and Policy* 18: 426–444.

Ben Mair, A. 2013. "Perpetuating Historic Victimhood Breeds New Victims." http://www.alonben-meir.com.

Blackett, J. 2013. "Regina v Sergeant Alexander Wayne Blackman ('Marine A')." http://www.judiciary.gov.uk/wp-content/uploads/JCO/Documents/Judgments/r-v-blackman-marine-a-sentencing+remarks.pdf.

Blair Woods, J., and J. Herman. 2014. "Anti-Transgender Hate Crime." In *The Routledge International Handbook on Hate Crime*, edited by N. Hall, A. Corb, P. Giannasi, and J. Grieve, 278–288. London: Routledge.

Blazak, R. 2009. "The Prison Hate Machine." *Criminology and Public Policy* 8: 633–640.

Boraine, A. 2000. *A Country Unmasked*. Oxford: Oxford University Press.

Bottoms, A. 2003. "Some Sociological Reflections on Restorative Justice." In *Restorative Justice and Criminal Justice*, edited by A. von Hirsch, J. Roberts, and A. Bottoms, 79–114. Oxford: Hart Publishing.

Bottoms, A., and J.V. Roberts, trans. 2010. *Hearing the Victim: Adversarial Justice, Crime Victims and the State*. Cullompton: Willan.

Bourdieu, P. 1977. *Outline of a Theory of Practice*. Cambridge, UK: Cambridge University Press.

———. 1990. *The Logic of Practice*. Stanford: Stanford University Press.

———. 1992. *An Invitation to Reflexive Sociology*. Chicago: University of Chicago Press.

———. 1993. *Language and Symbolic Power*. Cambridge, Mass.: Harvard University Press.

———. 2001. *Masculine Domination*. Stanford: Stanford University Press.

———. 2010. *Sociology Is a Martial Art: Political Writings by Pierre Bourdieu*. New York and London: The New Press.

Bouris, E. 2007. *Complex Political Victims*. Bloomfield: Kumarian Press.

Bowker, G., and S. Star. 2000. Sorting Things Out: Classification and Its Consequences. Cambridge, Mass.: MIT Press.

Bowling, B. 1993. "Racial Harassment and the Process of Victimisation." *British Journal of Criminology* 33: 231–250.

———. 1999. *Violent Racism: Victimisation, Policing and Social Context*. Oxford: Oxford University Press.

Bradford, B., J. Jackson, and E. A. Stanko. 2009. "Contact and Confidence: Revisiting the Impact of Public Encounters with the Police." *Policing and Society: An International Journal of Research and Policy* 19: 20–46.

Braithwaite, J. 1989. *Crime, Shame and Reintegration*. Cambridge, UK: Cambridge University Press.

———. 2002. *Restorative Justice and Responsive Regulation*. Oxford: Oxford University Press.

———. 2003. "Principles of Restorative Justice." In *Restorative Justice and Criminal Justice*, edited by A. von Hirsch, A. Roberts, and A. Bottoms, 1–20. Oxford: Hart Publishing.

Braithwaite, J., and P. Pettit. 1990. *Not Just Deserts: A Republican Theory of Criminal Justice*. Oxford: The Clarendon Press.

Broad, L. 1952. *The Innocence of Edith Thompson* London: Hutchinson.

Brown, B., P. Nolan, P. Crawford, and A. Lewis. 1996. "Interaction, Language and the "Narrative Turn" in Psychotherapy and Psychiatry." *Social Science & Medicine* 43: 1569–1578.

Brown, J. 2007. "From Cult of Masculinity to Smart Macho: Gender Perspectives on Police Occupational Culture." In *Police Occupational Cultures: New Debates and Directions*, edited by M. O'Neill, M. Marks, and A-M. Singh, 205–226. United Kingdom: Elsevier JAI Press.

———. 2010. *Peace Processes: A Sociological Approach*. Cambridge, UK: Polity Press.

Brown, J., and P. Duguid. 2002. *The Social Life of Information*. Cambridge, Mass.: Harvard Business Press.

Brown, J., and S. Woolfenden. 2011. "Implications of the Changing Gender Ratio amongst Warranted Police Officers." *Policing: A Journal of Policy and Practice* 5: 356–364.

Bullimer, K. 2008. *In an Abusive State: How Neo-Liberalism Appropriated the Feminist Movement against Sexual Violence*. Durham: Duke University Press.

Burgess, A. 2004. "Research and Practice in Victim Services: Perspective from Education and Research." In *American Society of Victimology Symposium Proceedings*, edited by A. Burgess and T. Underwood. Topeka: Washburn University

Burnett, J. 2012. "After Lawrence: Racial Violence and Policing in the UK." *Race and Class* 54: 91–98.

———. 2013. "Britain: Racial Violence and the Politics of Hate." *Race and Class* 54: 5–21.

Burowoy, M. 2005. "For Public Sociology." *American Sociological Review* 70:4–28.

Burton, F., and P. Carlen. 1979. *Official Discourse: On Discourse, Analysis, Government Publications, Ideology and the State*. London: Routledge & Kegan Paul.

California Department of Corrections and Rehabilitation (CDPR). 2010. "Sex offender supervision and gps monitoring task force." http://www.cdcr.ca.gov/News/docs/Sex_Offender_and_GPSTask_Force_Report.pdf.

California State Bill. 2015. "SB. 519 Victims of crime." http://leginfo.legislature.ca.gov/faces/billNavClient.xhtml?bill_id=201520160SB519.

Calvert, L. 1926. *My Life Story* in HO144/6012.

Campbell, K., and C. Walker. (Undated.) "Medical Mistakes and Miscarriages of Justice: Perspectives on the Experiences in England and Wales." www.atterneygeneral.jus.gov.on.ca/.../Campbell_Walker

Campbell, R. 2014. "Not Getting Away with It: Linking Sex Work and Hate Crime in Merseyside." In *Responding to Hate Crime: The Case for Connecting Policy and Research*, edited by Neil Chakraborti and Jon Garland, 55–70. Bristol: The Policy Press.

Camus, A. 1942. *L'Etranger*. Paris: Gallimard.

———. 1942. *Le Mythe de Sisyphe*. Paris: Gallimard.

———. 1947. *Caligula*. Paris: Gallimard.

———. 1947. *La Peste*. Paris: Gallimard.

———. 1950. *Les Justes*. Paris: Gallimard.

Carlen, P. 1983. *Women's Imprisonment*. London: Routledge & Kegan Paul.

———. 1985. *Criminal Women*. Cambridge, UK: Polity Press.

Carlile, P. 2002. "A Pragmatic View of Knowledge and Boundaries: Boundary Objects in New Product Development." *Organization Science* 13: 442–455.

Carrabine, E., P. Cox, M. Lee, K. Plummer, and N. South. 2004. *Criminology: A Sociological Introduction*. Oxon: Routledge.

Carrington, K., R. Hogg, and M. Sozzo. (2015) "Southern Criminology." *British Journal of Criminology*, advance access 20/8/15 doi: 10.1093/bjc/azv083.

Cavanagh, C., R. Dobash, and R. Dobash. 2007. "The Murder of Children by Fathers in the Context of Child Abuse." *Child Abuse Neglect* 31: 731–734.

Celermajer, D., and J. Kidman. 2012. "Embedding the Apology in the Nation's Identity." *Journal of the Polynesian Society* 121: 219–242.

Cernuschi, C., and A. Herczynski. 2008. "The Subversion of Gravity in Jackson Pollock's Abstractions." *The Art Bulletin* 4: 616–639.

Chakraborti, N. 2010. "Crimes against the 'Other': Conceptual, Operational and Empirical Challenges for Hate Studies." *Journal of Hate Studies* 8: 9–28.

Chakraborti, N., and J. Garland. 2012. "Reconceptualising Hate Crime Victimization through the Lens of Vulnerability and 'Difference.'" *Theoretical Criminology* 16: 499–514.

———. 2015. *Hate Crime: Impact, Causes and Responses* (2nd edition). London: Sage.

Chakraborti, N., and J. Garland, trans. 2014. *Responding to Hate Crime: The Case for Connecting Policy and Research*. Bristol: The Policy Press.

Chakraborti, N., J. Garland, and S. Hardy. 2014. *The Leicester Hate Crime Project: Findings and Conclusions*. Leicester: University of Leicester.

Chakraborti, Neil, and Irene Zempi. 2012. "The Veil under Attack: Gendered Dimensions of Islamophobic Victimization." *International Review of Victimology* 18: 269–284.

Chambers, C. 2005. "Masculine Domination, Radical Feminism and Change." *Feminist Theory* 6: 325–346.

Chan, J. 1996. "Changing Police Culture." *British Journal of Criminology* 36: 109–134.

Chapman, J., and P. Broster. 2003. "Six Killer Mums to be Freed." *Daily Express* 31 January pp. 1–7.

Cherif Bassiouni, M. 2006. "International Recognition of Victims' Rights." *Human Rights Law Review* 6: 203–279.

Chesney-Lind, M., and L. Pasko. (2013) *The Female Offender*. London: Sage.

Christie, N. 1977. "Conflicts as Property." *British Journal of Criminology* 17: 1–14.

———. 1986. "The Ideal Victim." In *From Crime Policy to Victim Policy: Reinventing the Justice System*, edited by E. Fattah, 17–30. London: Macmillan Press.

Clamp, K. 2013. *Restorative Justice in Transition*. London: Routledge.

Clark, L., and D. Lewis. 1977. *Rape: The Price of Coercive Sexuality*. Toronto: Canadian Women's Educational Press.

Clark, P. 2010. *The Gacaca Courts, Post-Genocide Justice and Reconciliation in Rwanda: Justice without Lawyers*. Cambridge, UK: Cambridge University Press.

Clarke, K. M. 2009. *Fictions of Justice: The International Criminal Court and the Challenges of Legal Pluralism in Sub-Saharan Africa*. Cambridge, UK: Cambridge University Press.

Clinton, W. 1996. "Text of President Clinton's Announcement on Welfare Legislation." *New York Times*. http://www.nytimes.com/1996/08/01/us/text-of-president-clinton-s-announcement-on-welfare-legislation.html.

Cohen, J., and P. Harvey 2006. "Misconceptions of Gender: Sex, Masculinity and the Measurement of Crime." *The Journal of Men's Studies*, 14: 223–233.

Cohen, S. 2001. *State of Denial: Knowing about Atrocities and Suffering*. Cambridge, UK: Polity.

Cole, C. 2010. *Performing South Africa's Truth Commission: Stages of Transition*. Bloomington: Indiana University Press.

Coleman, K., P. Kaiza, J. Hoare, and K. Jansson. 2008. *Homicides, Firearm Offences and Intimate Violence 2007/07*. London: Home Office Research Development and Statistics Directorate.

College of Policing. 2014. *Hate Crime Operational Guidance*. Coventry: College of Policing.

Collins, P. H. 1998. "It's All in the Family: Intersections of Gender, Race, and Nation." *Hypatia* 13: 62–82.

Collinson, D. L., and J. Hearn. 1994. "Naming Men as Men: Implications for Work, Organization and Management." *Gender, Work and Organization* 1:2—22.

Colquhoun, K. 2014. *Did She Kill Him?* London: Little, Brown.

Comack, E., and G. Balfour. 2004. *The Power to Criminalize: Violence, Inequality and the Law*. Halifax: Fernwood.

Condry, R. 2007. *Families Shamed: The Consequences of Crime for Relatives of Serious Offenders*. Cullompton: Willan.

———. 2010. "Secondary Victims and Secondary Victimisation". In *International Handbook of Victimology*, edited by S. G. Shoham, P. Knepper, and M. Kett, 219–247. Boca Raton: CRC Press.

Condry, R., and C. Miles. 2012. "Adolescent to Parent Violence and Youth Justice in England and Wales." *Social Policy & Society* 11: 241–250.

———. 2014. "Adolescent to Parent Violence: Framing and Mapping a Hidden Problem." *Criminology and Criminal Justice*. 14: 257–275.

Connell, R. W. 1995 [2005]. *Masculinities*. 2nd edition. Berkeley and Los Angeles: University of California Press.

———. 2002. *Gender*. Cambridge, UK: Polity.

———. 2008. "A Thousand Miles from Kind: Men, Masculinities and Modern Institutions." *The Journal of Men's Studies* 16: 237–252.

Connolly, J., and R. Gordon. 2014. "Co-Victims of Homicide: A Systematic Review of the Literature." *Trauma, Violence and Abuse* 16: 495–505.

Corb, A. 2014. "Hate and Hate Crime in Canada." In *The Routledge International Handbook on Hate Crime*, edited by N. Hall, A. Corb, P. Giannasi, and J. Grieve, 163–173. London: Routledge.

Corsianos, M. 2009. *Policing and Gendered Justice: Examining the Possibilities*. Toronto: University of Toronto Press.

Council of Europe. 1999. *Mediation in Penal Matters:* Recommendation No. R(99)19 adopted by the Council of Ministers of the Council of Europe on 15 September 1999.

Courtenay, W. H. 2000. "Constructions of Masculinity and Their Influence on Well-Being: A Theory of Gender and Health." *Social Science and Medicine* 50: 1385–1401.

Crawford, A., and T. Newburn. 2013. *Youth Offending and Restorative Justice*. London: Routledge.

Crenshaw, K. 1991. "Mapping the Margins: Intersectionality, Identity Politics, and Violence against Women of Color." *Stanford Law Review* 43: 1241–1299.

Criminal Injuries Compensation Authority. 2008. "Criminal Injuries Compensation Scheme." http://www.Justice.Gov.Uk/Downloads/Victims-And-Witnesses/Cic-A/Cica/Am-I-Eligible/Criminal-Injuries-Compensation-Scheme-2008.Pdf.

Criminal Justice System. 2001. "Justice for All." https://www.cps.gov.uk/publications/docs/jfawhitepaper.pdf.

Crosby, A., and M. B. Lykes. 2011. "Mayan Women Survivors Speak: The Gendered Relations of Truth Telling in Postwar Guatemala." *International Journal of Transitional Justice* 5: 44.

Crown Prosecution Service. 2013. *The Director's Guidance on Adult Conditional Cautions.* https://www.cps.gov.uk/publications/directors_guidance/adult_conditional_cautions.html.

Cuneen, C., and C. Hoyle. 2010. *Debating Restorative Justice*. Oxford: Hart Publishing.

Czarniawska, B. 2004. *Narratives in Social Science Research*. London: Sage.

Dalley-Trim, L. 2007. "The boys' present . . . Hegemonic Masculinity: A Performance of Multiple Acts." *Gender and Education* 19: 199–217.

Daly, K. 2000. "Revisiting the Relationship between Retributive and Restorative Justice." In *Restorative Justice: Philosophy to Practice*, edited by H. Strang and J. Braithwaite, 33–54. Aldershot: Ashgate.

———. 2003. "Making Variation a Virtue." In *Restorative Justice in Context*, edited by E. Weitekamp and H-J. Kerner, 23–50. Cullompton: Willan.

Davies, P. 2011. *Gender, Crime and Victimisation*. London: Sage.

Davies P., P. Francis, and V. Jupp. 2004. *Victimisation: Theory, Research and Practice*. Basingstoke: Palgrave Macmillan.

Death Penalty Information Center (DPIC). 2015. "Introduction to the Death Penalty: History of the Death Penalty." http://www.deathpenaltyinfo.org/part-i-history-death-penalty.

Debord, G. 1967. *La Société du Spectacle*. Paris: Buchet-Chastel.

Deleuze, G. 1995 [1990]. "Postscript on Control Societies." In *Negotiations*, edited by G. Deleuze, 177–182. New York: Columbia University Press.

Dembour, M., and E. Haslam. 2004. "Silencing Hearings? Victim-Witnesses at War Crimes Trials." *European Journal of International Law* 15: 151–177.

Demker, M., and G. Duus-Otterstrom. 2009. "Realigning criminal policy: Offender and victim in the Swedish party system over time." *International Review of Sociology* 9: 273–296.

Denzin, N. 1989. *Interpretive Biography*. Beverly Hills: Sage.

Derrida, J. 2009. *The Beast and Sovereign*. Vol. 1. Chicago: University of Chicago Press.

Deukmedjian, J. 2006. "From Community to Intelligence: Executive Realignment of RCMP Mission." *Canadian Journal of Criminology and Criminal Justice* 48: 523–542.

Dignan, J. 2003. "Towards a Systemic Model of Restorative Justice." In *Restorative Justice and Criminal Justice*, edited by A. von Hirsch, J. Roberts, and A. Bottoms 135–156. Oxford: Hart Publishing.

———. 2007. "The Victim in Restorative Justice." In *Handbook of Victims and Victimology*, edited by S. Walklate, 309–331. Cullompton: Willan.

Dixon, B., and D. Gadd. 2006. "Getting the Message? 'New' Labour and the Criminalisation of 'Hate.'" *Criminology and Criminal Justice* 6: 309–328.

Doak, J. 2008. *Victims' Rights, Human Rights and Criminal Justice*. Oxford: Hart.

———. 2011. "Therapeutic Dimension of Transitional Justice: Emotional Repair and Victim Satisfaction in International Trials and Truth Commissions." *International Criminal Law Review* 11: 263–298.

Doak, J., and D. O'Mahony. 2011. "In Search of Legitimacy: Restorative Youth Conferencing in Northern Ireland." *Legal Studies* 31: 305–325.

Dobash, R. E., and R. Dobash. 1979. *Violence against Wives*. New York: Free Press.

Douglas, L. 2001. *The Memory of Judgment: Making Law and History in the Trials of the Holocaust*. New Haven: Yale University Press.

Douglas, M. 1992. *Risk and Blame: Essays in Cultural Theory*. London: Routledge.

Drake, D. 2012. *Prison, Punishment and the Pursuit of Security*. London: Palgrave.

Drews, K. 2011. "Robert Pickton Inquiry: Victim's Missing Report Sat in Drawer for Years, According to a Relative." *The Canadian Press Online*. http://www.huffingtonpost.ca/2011/10/25/pickton-inquiry-missing-report_n_1030959.html.

Drumbl, M. 2007. *Atrocity, Punishment, And International Law*. Cambridge, UK: Cambridge University Press.

———. 2012. *Reimagining Child Soldiers in International Law and Policy*. Oxford: Oxford University Press.

Du Bois-Pedain, A. 2007. *Transitional Amnesty in South Africa*. Cambridge, UK: Cambridge University Press.

Dubber, M. 2006. *Victims in the War on Crime: The Use and Abuse of Victims' Rights*. New York: NYU Press.

Dudai, R., and K. McEvoy. 2012. "Thinking Critically about Armed Groups and Human Rights Praxis." *Journal of Human Rights Practice* 4: 1–29.

Duff, A. 2003. "Restoration and Retribution." In *Restorative Justice and Criminal Justice*, edited by A. von Hirsch, A. Roberts, and A. Bottoms, 43–60. Oxford: Hart Publishing.

Duff, A., L. Farmer, S. Marshall, and V. Tadros, trans. 2004. *The Trial on Trial: Truth and Due Process*. Oxford And Portland: Hart Publishing.

Duggan, M., and V. Heap. 2014. *Administrating Victimisation: The Social Politics of Anti-Social Behaviour and Hate Crime Policy*. Basingstoke: Palgrave Macmillan.

Dunn, J. L. 2001. "Innocence Lost: Accomplishing Victimization in Intimate Stalking Cases." *Symbolic Interaction* 24: 285–313.

Durkheim, E. 1933. *The Division of Labor*. New York: Macmillan.

———. 1995. *Elementary Forms of Religious Life*. New York: Free Press.

Duthie, R., and I. Specht. 2010. *DDR, Transitional Justice, and the Reintegration of Former Child Combatants*. New York: International Center For Transitional Justice.

Edling, S. 2004. "Fängelsestrejkerna blev nyhetsstoff över hela världen [Prison strikes became worldwide news]." In *När botten stack upp: om de utslagnas kamp för frihet och människovärde* [When the bottom surfaced: About the outcasts' struggle for freedom and dignity], edited by M. Adamson, C. Modig, L. Grip, and H. Nestius. Södertälje: Gidlunds.

Elander, M. 2013. "The Victim's Address: Expressivism and the Victim at the Extraordinary Chambers in the Courts of Cambodia." *International Journal of Transitional Justice* 7: 91–115.

Elias, R. 1986. *The Politics of Victimization: Victims, Victimology and Human Rights.* New York: Oxford University Press.

———. *Victims Still: The Political Manipulation of Crime Victims.* Newbury Park: Sage.

———. 1996. "Paradigms and Paradoxes of Victimology." In *International Victimology: Selected Papers from the 8th International Symposium: Proceedings of a Symposium, held 21–26 August 1994,* edited by C. Summer, M. Israel, M. O'Connell, and R. Sarre, 9–34. Canberra: Australian Institute of Criminology.

Elman, A. 2001. "Unprotected by the Swedish Welfare State Revisited: Assessing a Decade of Reforms for Battered Women." *Women's Studies International Forum* 24: 39–52.

Elman, A., and M. Eduards. 1991. "Unprotected by the Swedish Welfare State: A Survey of Battered Women and the Assistance They Received." *Women's Studies International Forum* 14: 314–421.

Enander, V., C. Holmberg, and A. Lindgren. 2013. *Att följa med samtiden: Kvinnojourrörelse i förändring* [To accompany our time: Women's movement in transition]. Stockholm: Atlas.

Equality and Human Rights Commission (EHRC). 2011. *Hidden in Plain Sight: Inquiry into Disability-Related Harassment.* London: Equality and Human Rights Commission.

Esping-Andersen, G. 1990. *The three worlds of welfare capitalism.* Cambridge, UK: Polity Press.

Esping-Andersen, G., D. Gallie, A. Hemerijk, and J. Myers. 2002. *Why We Need a New Welfare State.* Oxford: Oxford University Press.

Estrada, F., and A. Nilsson. 2004. "Exposure to Threatening and Violent Behaviour among Single Mothers: The Significance of Lifestyle, Neighbourhood and Welfare Situation." *The British Journal of Criminology* 44: 168–187.

European Commission. 2013. "Directive 2012/29/EU of the European Parliament and of the Council of 25 October 2012 establishing minimum standards on the rights, support and protection of victims of crime, and replacing Council Framework Decision 2001/220/JHA." http://ec.europa.eu/justice/criminal/files/victims/guidance_victims_rights_directive_en.pdf .

European Union. 2012. Directive 2012/29/EU of the European Parliament and of the Council of 25 October 2012 establishing minimum standards on the rights, support and protection of victims of crime, and replacing Council Framework Decision 2001/220/JHA.

European Union Agency for Fundamental Rights (FRA). 2013a. *Discrimination and Hate Crime against Jews in EU Member States: Experiences and Perceptions of Antisemitism.* Luxembourg: Publications Office of the European Union.

———. 2013b. *European Union Lesbian, Gay, Bisexual and Transgender Survey.* Luxembourg: Publications Office of the European Union.

Ewald, F. 2002. "The Return of Descartes's Malicious Demon: An Outline of a Philosophy of Precaution." In *Embracing Risk,* edited by T. Baker and J. Simon. Chicago: University of Chicago Press.

Falk, R. 2008. *Achieving Human Rights.* London: Routledge.

Fassin, D., and R. Rechtman. 2009. *Empire of Trauma.* Princeton: Princeton University Press.

Fattah, E. 1989. Victims and Victimology: The Facts and the Rhetoric. *International Review of Victimology* 1: 1–21.

———. 1991. *Understanding Criminal Victimization: An Introduction To Theoretical Victimology.* Scarborough: Prentice-Hall Canada.

———. 1992. *Towards a Critical Victimology*. London: Palgrave.

———. 1997. *Criminology: Past, Present, and Future: A Critical Overview*. St. Martin's Press.

———. 2000. "Victimology: Past, Present and Future." *Criminologie* 33: 17–46.

———. 2010. "The Evolution of a Young, Promising Discipline: Sixty Years of Victimology, a Retrospective and Prospective Look." In *International Handbook of Victimology*, edited by S. G. Shoham, P. Knepper, and M. Kett, 43–94. Boca Raton, FL: CRC Press.

Fattah, E., and Parmentier, S. 2001. *Victim Policies and Criminal Justice on the Road to Restorative Justice*. Belgium: Leuven University Press.

Faust, K. L., and D. Kauzlarich. 2008. "Hurricane Katrina Victimization as a State Crime of Omission." *Critical Criminology* 16: 85–103.

Federal Bureau of Investigation. 2001. "Uniform Crime Reports. Section V - Special Report - The Terrorist Attacks of September 11, 2001." *US Department of Justice*. https://www.fbi.gov/about-us/cjis/ucr/crime-in-the-u.s/2001/01sec5.pdf.

———. 2004. "Uniform Crime Reporting Handbook." US Department of Justice. https://www2.fbi.gov/ucr/handbook/ucrhandbook04.pdf.

Fekete, L., and F. Webber. 2010. "Foreign Nationals, Enemy Penology and the Criminal Justice System." *Race and Class*. 51: 1–25.

Ferstman, C. 2010. "International Criminal Law and Victims' Rights." In *Routledge Handbook of International Criminal Law*, edited by W. Schabas. London: Routledge.

Findlay, M. 2009. "Activating a Victim Constituency in International Criminal Justice." *International Journal of Transitional Justice* 3: 183–206.

Findlay, M., and R. Henman. 2009. *Beyond Punishment: Achieving International Criminal Justice*. London: Macmillan.

———. 2012. *Transforming International Criminal Justice*. London: Routledge.

Foucault, M. 1977. *Discipline and Punish*. Harmondsworth: Penguin.

Fox, N. (2011). Boundary objects, social meanings and the success of new technologies. *Sociology 45*: 70–85.

Frank, A. W. 1991. "For a Sociology of the Body: an Analytical Review" In *The Body: Social Process and Cultural Theory*, edited by M. Featherstone, M. Hepworth, and B. Turner, 36–102. London: Sage.

Franke, K. 2006. "Gendered Subject of Transitional Justice." *Columbia Journal of Gender & Law* 15: 813–828.

Fraser, N. (2013) *Fortunes of Feminism: From State-Managed Capitalism to Neoliberal Crisis* London: Verso.

Friedrichs, D. O. 1981. "Violence and the Politics of Crime." *Social Research,* 48: 135–156.

Fullard, M. 2004. *Displacing Race: The South African Truth and Reconciliation Commission and Interpretations of Violence*. Braamfontein: Centre for the Study of Violence and Reconciliation.

Furedi, F. 1997. *Culture of Fear: Risk Taking and the Morality of Low Expectation*. London: Cassell.

———. 2004. *Therapy Culture: Cultivating Vulnerability in an Uncertain Age*. New York: Psychology Press.

———. 2008. *Paranoid Parenting: Why Ignoring the Experts Might be Best for Your Child*. New York: Continuum.

Gadd, D. 2009. "Aggravating Racism and Elusive Motivation." *British Journal of Criminology* 49: 755–771.

Galaway, B., and J. Hudson. 1996. *Restorative Justice: International Perspectives*. Monsey, NY: Criminal Justice Press.

Garbett, C. 2013. "The Truth and the Trial: Victim Participation, Restorative Justice, and the International Criminal Court." *Contemporary Justice Review* 16: 193–213.

Garland, D. 2001. *The Culture of Control: Crime and Social Order in Contemporary Society*. New York: Oxford University Press.

———. 2011. *Peculiar Institution: America's Death Penalty in an Age of Abolition*. Oxford: Oxford University Press.

Garland, J. 2012. "Difficulties in Defining Hate Crime Victimisation." *International Review of Victimology* 18: 25–37.

Garland, J., and N. Chakraborti. 2012. "Divided By a Common Concept? Assessing the Implications of Different Conceptualisations of Hate Crime in the European Union." *European Journal of Criminology* 9: 38–52.

Garland, J., and P. Hodkinson. 2014. "'F**king Freak! What the hell do you think you look like?' Experiences of Targeted Victimisation Among Goths and Developing Notions of Hate Crime." *British Journal of Criminology* 54(4): 613–631.

Gavrielides, T. 2007. *Restorative Justice Theory and Practice: Addressing the Discrepancy*. European Institute for Crime Prevention and Control, affiliated with the United Nations (HEUNI).

Geis, G. 1990. "Crime Victims: Practices and Prospects." In *Victims of Crime: Problems, Policies, and Programs*, edited by A. Lurigio, W. Skogan, and R. Davis, 251–268. Newbury Park: Sage.

Gibson, J. 2009. "Group-Conflict Resolution, Sources of Resistance to Reconciliation: On Legitimacy Theory and the Effectiveness of Truth." *Law & Contemporary Problems* 72: 123–141.

Gilligan, G. 2004. "Official Inquiry, Truth and Criminal Justice." In *Crime, Truth and Justice: Official Inquiry, Discourse, Knowledge*, edited by G. Gilligan and J. Pratt, 11–25. Cullompton: Willan.

Girard, R. 1977. *Violence and the Sacred*. Baltimore: Johns Hopkins University Press.

———. 1989. *The Scapegoat* (repr). Baltimore: John Hopkins Press.

Glasius, M. 2009. "What Is Global Justice and Who Decides?: Civil Society and Victim Responses to the International Criminal Court's First Investigations." *Human Rights Quarterly* 31: 496–520.

Goldson, B. 2013. "Unsafe, Unjust and Harmful to Wider Society: Grounds for Raising the Minimum Age of Criminal Responsibility in England and Wales." *Youth Justice: An International Journal* 13:111–130.

Goodey, J. 2005. *Victims and Victimology: Research, Policy and Practice*. Harlow: Pearson Longman.

Government bill (2000/01:79. *Stöd till brottsoffer* [Support to crime victims]. Ministry of Justice: Stockholm.

Government Communication (2007/08:39). *Handlingsplan för att bekämpa mäns våld mot kvinnor, hedersrelaterat våld och förtryck samt våld i samkönade relationer*. Minister of Justice, Stockholm.

Gready, P. 2011. *The Era of Transitional Justice: The Aftermath of the Truth And Reconciliation Commission in South Africa and Beyond*. Abingdon and New York: Routledge.

Green, P., and Ward, T. 2004. *State Crime: Government Violence & Corruption*. London: Pluto Press.

Green, S. 2007. "The Victims' Movement and Restorative Justice." In *Restorative Justice Handbook*, edited by G. Johnstone and D. Van ness, 171–191. Cullompton: Willan.

Greer, C. 2007. "News Media, Victims and Crime." In *Victims, Crime and Society*, edited by P. Davies, P. Francis, and C. Greer. London: SAGE.

Greer, D. 1994. "A Transatlantic Perspective on the Compensation of Crime Victims in the United States." *Criminal Law And Criminology* 85: 333–401.

Goni, U. 2015. "A Grandmother's 36-Year Hunt for the Child Stolen by the Argentinian Junta." *Guardian*, 7 June 2015.

Guardian 17 February 1997, 15 March 2011, 20 June 2006, 9 September 2011.

Guston, D. 1999. "Stabilizing the Boundary between US Politics and Science: The Role of the Office of Technology Transfer as a Boundary Organization." *Social Studies of Science* 29: 87–111.

Guzman Bouvard, M. 1994. *Revolutionizing Motherhood. The Mothers of the Plaza de Mayo*. Lanham, MD: Rowman & Littlefield.

Hagan, J. 2003. *Justice in the Balkans: Prosecuting War Crimes in the Hague Tribunal*. London. University of Chicago Press.

Hagan, J., and W. Rymond-Richmond. 2009. *Darfur and the Crime of Genocide*. Cambridge, UK: Cambridge University Press.

Hagan, J., and Kaiser, J. 2011. "The Displaced and Dispossessed of Darfur: Explaining the Sources of a Continuing State-Led Genocide." The British Journal of Sociology 62: 1–25.

Hagan, J., W. Rymond-Richmond, and P. Parker. 2012. "Criminology of Genocide: The Death and Rape of Darfur." *Criminology* 43: 525–562.

Hagan, P., B. McCarthy, and H. Foster. 2002. "A Gendered Theory of Delinquency and Despair in the Life Course." *Acta Sociologica* 45: 37–46.

Hall, M. 2010. *Victims and Policy Making: A Comparative Perspective*. Cullompton: Willan.

———. 2013a. *Victims of Environmental Harm: Rights, Recognition and Redress Under National and International Law*. London: Routledge.

———. 2013b. "Environmental Harm and Environmental Victims: Scoping Out a 'Green Victimology.'" *International Review of Victimology* 20: 129–143.

Hall, N. 2013. *Hate Crime* (2nd edition). London: Routledge.

Halberstam, J. 1998. *Female Masculinity*. Durham: Duke University Press.

Hamber, B. 2009. *Transforming Societies after Political Violence*. Heidelberg: Springer.

Haslam, E. 2011. "Subjects and Objects: International Criminal Law and the Institutionalization of Civil Society." *International Journal of Transitional Justice* 5: 221–240.

Hayner, P. 2011. *Unspeakable Truths: Transitional Justice and the Challenge of Truth Commissions*. Abingdon And New York: Routledge.

Hays, S. 1996. *The Cultural Conditions of Motherhood*. New Haven and London: Yale University Press.

Hayslip, Bert Jr., and Kyle Page. 2013. "Family Characteristics and Dynamics: A Systems Approach to Grief." *Family Science* 4: 50–58.

Heber, A. 2014. "Good versus Evil? Victims, Offenders and Victim-Offenders in Swedish Crime Policy Bills." *The European Journal of Criminology* 11(4): 410–428.

Heidensohn, F. 1986. *Women & Crime*. Basingstoke: Macmillan.

Helman, C. 1991. *Body Myths*. London: Chatto & Windus.

Helms, E. 2013. *Innocence and Victimhood. Gender, Nation, and Women's Activism in Postwar Bosnia-Herzegovina*. Madison: University of Wisconsin Press.

Henderson, L. 1985. "The Wrongs Of Victim's Rights." *Stanford Law Review* 37: 937–1021.

Henman, R. 2004. "Conceptualizing Access to Justice And Victims' Rights in International Sentencing." *Social And Legal Studies* 13: 27–55.

Henricson, C., and A. Bainham. 2005. "The Child and Family Policy Divide: Tensions, Convergence and Rights." London: Family and Parenting Institute.

Hentig, H. 1948. *The Criminal And His Victim: Studies in the Sociobiology of Crime*. Yale: Yale University Press.

Hillyard, P., C. Pantazis, S. Tombs, and D. Gordon. 2004. *Beyond Criminology: Taking Harm Seriously*. London: Pluto Press.

Hirsch, S. 2010. "The Victim Deserving of Global Justice: Power, Caution, and Recovering Individuals." In *Mirrors of Justice: Law and Power in the Post–Cold War Era*, edited by M. Goodale and K. Clarke. Cambridge, UK: Cambridge University Press.

HM Government. 2012. *Challenge It, Report It, Stop It: The Government's Plan to Tackle Hate Crime*. London: HM Government.

HMIC. 2014. "Everyone's business: improving the police response to domestic abuse." http://www.hmic.gov.uk/wp-content/uploads/2014/04/improving-the-police-response-to-domestic-abuse.pdf.

HMSO. 2004. "Domestic Violence, Crime and Victims Act 2004." London: The Stationery Office. http://www.legislation.gov.uk/ukpga/2004/28/pdfs/ukpga_20040028_en.pdf.

Holstein, J. A., and G. Miller. 1990. "Rethinking Victimization: An Interactional Approach to Victimology." *Symbolic Interaction* 13: 103–122.

Home Affairs Select Committee. 2007. *Young Black People and the Criminal Justice System. Second Report of Session 2006–7, Vol.* 1. London: House of Commons.

Home Office. 2003. *Restorative Justice: The Government's Strategy* (London: Home Office Communication Directorate). Available at: http://www.homeoffice.gov.uk/justice/victims/restorative/index.html.

———. 2005. *Restorative Justice: Helping to Meet Local Needs: A Guide for Local Criminal Justice Boards and Agencies* (London: Home Office Communications Directorate).

———. 2005. *Rebuilding Lives: Supporting Victims of Crime.* London: HMSO.

———. 2005. *The Code of Practice for Victims of Crime.* London: The Stationery Office.

———. 2006. *A Five Year Strategy for Protecting the Public and Reducing Re-Offending.* London: The Stationery Office, Cm. 717.

———. 2013. "New government domestic violence and abuse definition." *Home Office Circular 003/2013.* https://www.gov.uk/government/publications/new-government-domestic-violence-and-abuse-definition.

———. 2014. "A Call to End Violence against Women and Girls: Action Plan." *HM Government.* https://www.gov.uk/government/uploads/system/uploads/attachment_data/file/287758/VAWG_Action_Plan.pdf.

———. 2015. "Information Guide on Responding to Adolescent to Parent Violence and Abuse." *London: Home Office.* https://www.gov.uk/domestic-violence-and-abuse#adolescent-to-parent-violence-and-abuse.

Home Office, with Office for National Statistics and Ministry of Justice. 2013. *An Overview of Hate Crime in England and Wales.* London: Home Office, Office for National Statistics and Ministry of Justice.

hooks, bell. 1990. *Yearning: Race, Gender, and Cultural Politics.* Cambridge, Mass.: South End Press.

Hope, T. 2007. "Theory and Method: The Social Epidemiology of Crime Victims." In *Handbook of Victims and Victimology*, edited by S. Walklate. Cullompton: Willan.

Houellebecq, M. 2010. *Les Particules Elémentaires.* Paris: J'ai Lu.

Hough, M., and P. Mayhew. 1983. *The British Crime Survey.* London: Home Office Research Study No. 76.

Hoyle, C. 2002. "Restorative Justice and the Non-Participating Victim." In *New Visions of Crime Victims*, edited by C. Hoyle and R. Young, 97–131. Oxford: Hart Publishing.

———. 2009. *Restorative Justice.* London: Routledge.

Hoyle, C., and L. Ullrich. 2014. "New Court, New Justice? The Evolution of 'Justice for Victims' at Domestic Courts and at the International Criminal Court." *Journal of International Criminal Justice* 12: 681–703.

Hoyle, C., and L. Zedner. 2007. "Victims, Victimization, and Criminal Justice." In *The Oxford Handbook Of Criminology*, edited by M. Maguire, R. Morgan, and R. Reiner, 461–494. Oxford: Oxford University Press.

Hunt, A. 1993. *Explorations in Law and Society: Towards a Constitutive Theory of Law.* New York: Routledge.

Hunter, C., J. Nixon, and S. Parr. 2010. "Mother Abuse: A Matter of Youth Justice, Child Welfare or Domestic Violence?" *Journal of Law and Society* 37: 264–284.

Husain, M. 2013. "Malala: The Girl Who Was Shot for Going to School." *BBC News Magazine.* http://www.bbc.co.uk/news/magazine-24379018.

Iganski, P. 2001. "Hate Crimes Hurt More." *American Behavioural Scientist* 45(4): 626–638.

———. 2008. "*'Hate Crime' and the City.* Bristol: The Policy Press.

Iganski, P., with K. Ainsworth, L. Geraght, S. Lagou, and N. Patel. 2014. "Understanding How 'Hate' Hurts: A Case Study of Working with Offenders and Potential

Offenders." In *Responding to Hate Crime: The Case for Connecting Policy and Research,* edited by N. Chakraborti and J. Garland, 231–242. Bristol: The Policy Press.

Inglis, T. 2003. *Truth, Power and Lies.* Dublin: University College Dublin Press.

International Centre for Prison Studies (ICPS). 2015a. *World Prison Brief–United States of America.* http://www.prisonstudies.org/country/united-states-america.

———. 2015b. *World Prison Brief —Sweden.* http://www.prisonstudies.org/country/sweden.

International Criminal Court (Undated) Booklet. *Victims before the International Criminal Court: A Guide for the Participation of Victims in the Proceedings of the Court.* Hague: International Criminal Court.

International Commission for Missing Persons. 2014. *Bosnia-Herzegovina. Missing Persons from the Armed Conflicts of the 1990s: A Stocktaking.* Sarajevo: ICMP.

Iraq Body Count. 2015. *Documented Civilian Deaths from Violence.* https://www.iraqbodycount.org/database.

Jacobs, J., and K. Potter. 1998. *Hate Crimes: Criminal Law and Identity Politics.* Oxford: Oxford University Press.

Jackson A., and L. Mazzei. 2008. *Voice in Qualitative Inquiry: Challenging Conventional, Interpretive, and Critical Conceptions in Qualitative Research.* Abingdon and New York: Routledge.

James, Z. 2014. "Hate Crimes against Gypsies, Travellers and Roma in Europe." In *The Routledge International Handbook on Hate Crime,* edited by N. Hall, A. Corb, P. Giannasi, and J. Grieve, 237–248. London: Routledge.

Jamieson, R., and K. McEvoy. 2005. "State Crime by Proxy and Juridical Othering." *British Journal of Criminology* 45: 504–527.

Jiwani, Y., and M. L. Young. 2006. "Missing and Murdered Women: Reproducing Marginality in News Discourse." *Canadian Journal of Communication* 31(4). http://www.cjc-online.ca/index.php/journal/article/view/1825.

Johnstone, G. 2011. *Restorative Justice: Ideas, Values, Debates.* London: Routledge.

Johnstone, G. and D. Van Ness. 2007. *Handbook of Restorative Justice.* Cullompton: Willan.

Jones, T., B. Maclean, and J. Young. 1986. *The Islington Crime Survey: Crime, Victimization and Policing in Inner-City London.* Brookfield: Gower.

Jordan, J. 2001. "Worlds Apart? Women, Rape and the Police Reporting Process." *British Journal of Criminology,* 41: 679–706.

The Justice Gap: http://thejusticegap.com/2015/03/ccrc-suffers-deepest-cut-entire-criminal-justice-system/.

Karmen, A. 1983. "Introduction: Deviance and Victimology." In *Deviants; Victims or Victimizers?* edited by D. MacNamara and A. Karmen. Beverly Hills: Sage.

Karstedt, S. 2002. "Emotions and Criminal Justice." *Theoretical Criminology* 6(3): 299–317.

———. 2010. "From Absence to Presence, from Silence to Voice: Victims in International and Transitional Justice since the Nuremberg Trials." *International Review Of Victimology* 17: 9–30.

Katz, J. 1988. *Seductions of Crime: Moral and Sensual Attractions in Doing Evil.* New York: Basic Books.

Katz, R. 2000. "Explaining Violence, Substance Abuse, and Persistence Violence Among Men: Elaborating a Side-by-Side Integrative Model of Four Theoretical Perspectives." *Sociology of Crime, Law and Deviance* 2: 325–342.

Kauzlarich, D., R. Matthews, and W. J. Miller. 2001. "Toward a Victimology of State Crime." *Critical Criminology* 10: 173–94.

Kearon, T., and R. Leach. 2000. "The Invasion of the 'Body Snatchers': Burglary Reconsidered." *Theoretical Criminology* 4: 451–472

Kelly, L. 1987. "The Continuum of Sexual Violence." In *Women, Violence and Social Control,* edited by Jalna Hanmer and Mary Maynard, 46–60. London: Macmillan.

Kennedy, D. 2002. "The International Human Rights Movement: Part of the Problem?" *Harvard Human Rights Journal* 15: 101–126.

Kennedy, H. 2005. *Eve Was Framed*. London: Vintage Books.

Kent, L. 2011. "Local Memory Practices in East Timor: Disrupting Transitional Justice Narratives." *International Journal of Transitional Justice* 5: 434–455.

Killean, R. 2015. "An Incomplete Narrative: Prosecuting Sexual Violence Crimes at the Extraordinary Chambers in the Courts of Cambodia." *Journal of International Criminal Justice* 13: 331–52.

———. "Procedural Justice in International Criminal Courts: Assessing Civil Parties' Perceptions of Justice at the Extraordinary Chambers in the Courts of Cambodia." *International Criminal Law Review* 16, in press.

Kilty, J., and S. C. Fabian. 2010. "Deconstructing an Invisible Identity: The Reena Virk Case." In *Reena Virk: Critical Perspectives on a Canadian Murder*, edited by M. Rajiva and S. Batacharya, 122–155. Toronto: Canadian Scholar's Press.

Kitchen, T., and R. H. Schneider. 2005. "Crime and the Design of the Built Environment: Anglo-American Comparisons of Policy and Practice." In *Habitus: A Sense of Place*, edited by J. Hillier and E. Rooksby, 258–282. Surrey: Ashgate.

Klette, H. 2001. "Mänskliga rättigheter [Human Rights]." In *Brottsoffer: Från teori till praktik* [Crime victims- From theory to practice], edited by M. Lindgren, K. Pettersson, and B. Hagglund, 39–54. Stockholm: Jure CLN AB.

———. 2004. "Mänskliga rättigheter [Human rights]." In *Utsatta och sårbara: Brottsoffer* [Exposed and vulnerable crime victims], edited by M. Lindgren, K. Pettersson, and B. Hägglund, 45–62. Stockholm: Jure Forlag AB.

Koomen, J. 2013. "'Without These Women, the Tribunal Cannot Do Anything': The Politics of Witness Testimony on Sexual Violence at the International Criminal Tribunal for Rwanda." *Signs* 38: 253–277.

Kramer, R. C., and R. J. Michalowski. 2005. "War, Aggression and State Crime: A Criminological Analysis of the Invasion and Occupation of Iraq." *British Journal of Criminology* 45: 446–469.

Krane, V., P. Choi, S. M. Baird, C. Aimar, and K. Kauer. 2004. "Living the Paradox: Female Athletes Negotiate Femininity and Muscularity." *Sex Roles: A Journal of Research* 50: 315–329.

Kristensen, P., L. Weisæth, L., and T. Heir. 2012. "Bereavement and Mental Health after Sudden and Violent Losses: A Review." *Psychiatry* 75: 76–97.

Krog, A. 2000. *Country of My Skull: Guilt, Sorrow, and the Limits of Forgiveness in the New South Africa*. London: Jonathan Cape.

Kuokkanen, R. 2008. "Globalization as Racialized, Sexualized Violence." *International Feminist Journal of Politics* 10: 216–233.

Lacey, N., C. Wells, and D. Meure. 1990. *Reconstructing Criminal Law*. London: Weidenfeld Paperbacks.

Lamb, S. 1999. *The Trouble With Blame: Victims, Perpetrators, And Responsibility*. Cambridge, Mass.: Harvard University Press.

Landau, T. C. 2006. *Challenging Notions: Critical Victimology in Canada*. Toronto: Canadian Scholars' Press Inc.

Larsson, S. 2005. *Luftslottet som sprängdes* [The air castle that was blown up]. Stockholm: Nordstedt.

———. 2006. *Flickan som lekte med elden* [The girl who played with fire]. Stockholm: Nordstedt.

———. 2007. *Män som hatar kvinnor* [Men who hate women]. Stockholm: Nordstedt.

Laster, K., and P. O'Malley. 1992. "Sensitive New-Age Laws: The Reassertion of Emotionality in Law." *International Journal of the Sociology of Law* 24: 21–40.

Lea, J., and J. Young. 1984. *What Is to Be Done about Law and Order?* London: Pluto Press.

Leighton, P. 2002. "Decision on 9/11 Victims Is a Crime." *Long Island Newsday*. http://www.newsday.com/decision-on-9-11-victims-is-a-crime-1.399909.

Letschert, R., and K. Ammerlaan. 2010. "Compensation and Reparation for Victims of Terrorism." In *A ssisting Victims of Terrorism: Towards a European Standard of Justice*, edited by R. Letschert, S. Ines, and A. Pemberton. London: Springer.

Letschert, R., R. Haveman, A. de Brouwer, and A. Pemberton, eds. 2011. *Victimological Approaches to International Crimes: Africa.* Intersentia. http://intersentia.com/en/victimological-approaches-to-international-crimes-africa.html.

Levi, P. 1986. *The Drowned and the Saved.* London: Abacus.

Leydesdorff, S. 2011. *Surviving the Bosnian Genocide. The Women of Srebrenica Speak.* Bloomington: Indiana University Press.

Liebmann, M. 2007. *Restorative Justice: How It Works.* London: Jessica Kingsley Publishers.

Light, J., J. Rusby, C. Niles, M. Kimberley, and T. Snijders. 2013. "Antisocial Behaviorial Trajectories and Social Victimization within and between School Years in Early Adolescence." *Journal of Research on Adolescence* 24: 332–336.

Lippens, R. 2010. "Law, Code and Late Modern Governance in Prophetic Painting: Notes on Jackson Pollock, Mark Rothko and Gilles Deleuze" In *Prospects of Legal Semiotics,* edited by A. Wagner and J. Broekman, 171–192. Dordrecht: Springer.

———. 2011a. "Jackson Pollock's Flight from Law and Code: Theses on Responsive Choice and the Dawn of Control Society." *International Journal for the Semiotics of Law* 1: 117–138.

———. 2011b. "Mystical Sovereignty and the Emergence of Control Society" In *Crime, Governance, and Existential Predicaments,* edited by R. Lippens and J. Hardie-Bick, 175–193. Basingstoke: Palgrave Macmillan.

———. 2012. "Control over Emergence: Images of Radical Sovereignty in Pollock, Rothko and Rebeyrolle." *Human Studies: International Journal for Philosophy and Social Sciences* 3: 351–364.

———. 2015a. "Ambivalent Sovereigns and Restorative Justice. Exploring Conditions of Possibility and Impossibility for Restorative Justice in a Post-Communicative Age." *Critical Criminology* 1: 125–139.

———. 2015b. "Absolutely Sovereign Victims: Rethinking the Victim Movement." *Social Justice* 3: forthcoming.

Ljungwald, C. 2011. *The Emergence of the Crime Victim in the Swedish Social Services Act.* Unpublished Doctoral Dissertation. Stockholm University: Stockholm.

Loftus, B. 2007. "Policing the Irrelevant: Class, Diversity and Contemporary Police Culture." In *Police Occupational Cultures: New Debates and Directions,* edited by M. O'Neill, M. Marks, A-M. Singh, 181–204. UK: Elsevier JAI Press.

Longman, T. 2006. "Justice At The Grassroots? Gacaca Trials In Rwanda." In *Transitional Justice in the Twenty-First Century: Beyond Truth versus Justice,* edited by N. Roht-Arriaza and J. Mariezcurrena. Cambridge, UK: Cambridge University Press.

Loseke, D., R. Gelles, and M. Cavanaugh, trans. *Current Controversies on Family Violence.* Thousand Oaks: Sage.

Lovell, T. 2000. "Thinking Feminism with and against Bourdieu." *Feminist Theory* 1: 11–32.

Lundgren, E., G. Heimer, J. Westerstrand, and A-M. Kalliokoski. 2001. *Captured Queen: Men's Violence against Women in 'Equal' Sweden: A Prevalence Study.* Stockholm: Fritzes.

Lundy, P. 2010. "Commissioning the Past." *Review of International Affairs* 61: 1138–1139. 101–113.

Lundy, P., and M. McGovern. 2008. "Whose Justice? Rethinking Transitional Justice from the Bottom Up." *Journal of Law and Society* 35: 265–292.

Lustgarten, E. 1960. *The Murder and the Trial.* London: Oldhams Press.

Mackay, R. 1998. "Restorative Justice and the Scottish Children's Justice System." In *Restorative Justice for Juveniles: Potentialities, Risks and Problems for Research,* edited by L. Walgrave, 19–53. Belgium: Leuven University Press.

MacManus, D., K. Dean, M. Jones, R. J. Rona, N. Greenberg, L. Hull, T. Fahy, S. Wessley, and N. T. Fear. 2013. "Violent Offending by UK Military Personnel Deployed to Iraq and Afghanistan: A Data Linkage Cohort Study." *The Lancet* 381: 907–917.

Madlingozi, T. 2010. "On Transitional Justice Entrepreneurs and the Production of Victims." *Journal of Human Rights Practice* 2: 208–228.

Maffesoli, M. 1996. *The Times of the Tribes*. London: Sage.

Maier, S. L. 2008. "'I Have Heard Horrible Stories . . .': Rape Victim Advocates' Perceptions of the Revictimization of Rape Victims by the Police and Medical System." *Violence Against Women* 14: 786–808.

Mallinder, L., and K. McEvoy. 2011. "Rethinking Amnesties: Atrocity, Accountability And Impunity In Post-Conflict Societies." *Contemporary Social Science* 6: 107–128.

Manning, P. 2007. "A Dialectic of Organisational and Occupational Culture." In *Police Occupational Cultures: New Debates and Directions*, edited by M. O'Neill, M. Marks, and A-M. Singh, 47–84. UK: Elsevier JAI Press.

Mardorossian, C. 2002. "Toward A New Feminist Theory Of Rape." *Signs: Journal of Women in Culture and Society* 27: 743–775.

Marshall, T. 1999. *Restorative Justice: An Overview*. London: Home Office Research Development and Statistics Directorate.

Maruna, S. 2001. *Making Good: How Ex-Convicts Reform and Rebuild Their Lives*. Washington: American Psychological Association.

Mason-Bish, H. 2010. "Future Challenges for Hate Crime Policy: Lessons from the Past." In *Hate Crime: Concepts, Policy, Future Directions*, edited by N. Chakraborti, 58–77. London: Routledge.

Matthews, R. 2006. "Reintegrative Shaming and Restorative Justice: Reconciliation or Divorce?" In *The Institutionalisation of Restorative Justice in a Changing Society*, edited by I. Aertsen, T. Daems, and L. Robert, 237–260. Cullompton: Willan.

Mauss, M. 1973. "Techniques of the Body." *Economy and Society* 2: 70-88.

Mawby, R. 2007. "Public Sector Services And The Victim Of Crime." In *Handbook Of Victims And Victimology*, edited by S. Walklate. Cullompten: Willan.

Mawby, R., and M. Gill. 1987. *Crime Victims: Needs, Services and the Voluntary Sector*. London: Tavistock Publications.

Mawby, R., and S. Walklate. 1994. *Critical Victimology*. London: Sage.

McAlinden, A. M. 2007. *The Shaming of Sexual Offenders: Risk, Retribution and Rehabilitation*. Oxford: Hart Publishing.

———. 2012. "An Inconvenient Truth: Barriers to Truth Recovery in the Aftermath of Institutional Child Abuse in Ireland." *Legal Studies* 33: 189–214.

———. 2014. "Deconstructing Victim and Offender Identities in Discourses on Child Sexual Abuse." *British Journal of Criminology* 54: 180–198.

McCarthy, C. 2012. *Reparations and Victim Support in the International Criminal Court*. Cambridge, UK: Cambridge University Press.

McCold, P., and T. Wachtel. 2003. "Restorative Justice Theory Validation." In *Restorative Justice: Theoretical Foundations*, edited by E. Weitekamp and H-J. Kerner, 110–142. Cullompton: Willan.

McDevitt, J., J. Levin, J. Nolan, and S. Bennett. 2010. "Hate Crime Offenders." In *Hate Crime: Concepts, Policy, Future Directions*, edited by N. Chakraborti, 124–148. London: Routledge.

McEvoy, K. 2000. "Law, Struggle and Political Transformation In Northern Ireland." *Journal of Law and Society* 27: 542–571.

———. 2007. "Beyond Legalism: Towards a Thicker Understanding of Transitional Justice." *Journal of Law and Society* 34: 411–440.

McEvoy, K., and K. McConnachie. 2012. "Victimology in Transitional Justice: Victimhood, Innocence and Hierarchy." *European Journal of Criminology* 9: 527–538.

McEvoy, K., and L. McGregor. 2008. "Transitional Justice from Below: An Agenda for Research, Policy and Praxis." In *Transitional Justice from Below: Grassroots Activism and the Struggle for Change*, edited by K. McEvoy and L. McGregor. London: Hart Publishing.

McEvoy, K., and A. Eriksson. 2006. "Restorative Justice in Transition: Ownership, Leadership and 'Bottom-Up' Human Rights." In *Handbook of Restorative Justice: A Global Perspective*, D. Sullivan and L. Tifft, eds., 321–335. London: Routledge.

McGarry, R. 2012. "The Workplace of War: Unlimited Liability or Safety Crimes?" *Criminal Justice Matters* 89: 6–7.

———. "Soldiers of 'Choice'?" In *Work and Society: Places, Spaces and Identities*, edited by P. Taylor and P. Wagg. Chester: Chester University Press.

———. 2015. "War, Crime and Military Victimhood." *Critical Criminology : An International Journal* 23: 255–275.

McGarry, R., and S. Walklate. 2011. "The Soldier as Victim: Peering through the Looking Glass." *British Journal of Criminology* 51: 900–917.

———. 2015. *Victims: Trauma, Testimony and Justice*. Abingdon: Routledge.

McGarry, R., G. Mythen, and S. Walklate. 2012. "The Soldier, Human Rights and the Military Covenant: A Permissible State of Exception?" *International Journal of Human Rights. Special Issue: New Directions in the Sociology of Human Rights* 16: 1183–1195.

McGhee, D. 2007. "The Challenge of Working with Racially Motivated Offenders: An Exercise in Ambivalence?" *Probation Journal* 54: 213–226.

McGonigle Leyh, B. 2011. *Procedural Justice?: Victim Participation in International Criminal Proceedings*. Cambridge, UK: Intersentia.

———. 2011. "Victim-Oriented Measures at International Criminal Institutions: Participation and its Pitfalls." *International Criminal Law Review* 12: 375–408.

McLaughlin, E. 1996. "Political Violence, Terrorism and States of Fear." In *The Problem of Crime*, edited by J. Muncie and E. McLaughlin, 283–330. London: Sage/Open University Press.

McNay, L. 1999. "Gender, Habitus and the Field." *Theory, Culture & Society* 16: 95–117.

———. 2004. "Situated Intersubjectivity." In *Engendering the Social: Feminist Encounters with Sociological Theory*, B. Marshall and A. Witz, 171–186. Maidenhead: Open University Press.

McSherry, J. P. 2005. *Predatory States: Operation Condor and Covert War in Latin America*. Plymouth, UK: Rowman & Littlefield.

Mehrabian, A. 1997. "Relations Among Personality Scales of Aggression, Violence and Empathy: Validational Evidence Bearing on the Risk of Eruptive Violence Scale." *Aggressive Behavior*, 23: 443–445.

Melander, Erik. 2015. Organized Violence in the World 2015. An Assessment by the Uppsala Conflict Data Program. UCDP Paper 9.Uppsala: Uppsala Conflict Data Programme.

Mendelsohn, B. 1956. "A New Branch Of Bio-Psychological Science: La Victimology." *Revue Internationale De Criminologie Et De Police Technique* 10: 782–789.

———. 1963. "The Origins of the Doctrine of Victimology." *Excerpta Criminologica* 3: 239–245.

———. 1974. "Victimology and the Technical and Social Sciences: A Call for the Establishment of Victimology Clinics." In *Victimology: A New Focus*, edited by I. Drapkin and E. Viano. Lexington: D. C. Heath.

Merleau-Ponty, M. 1968 [1964]. *The Visible and the Invisible*. Evanston: Northwestern University Press.

Merriam, S. 2009. *Qualitative Research: A Guide to Design and Implementation*. San Francisco: Jossey-Bass.

Merry, S. E. 2006. *Human Rights and Gender Violence: Translating International Law into Local Justice*. Chicago: Chicago University Press.

Merton, R. 1968. *Social Theory and Social Structure* (1968 enlarged ed.). New York: Free Press.

Mertus, J. 2009. "Shouting from the Bottom of the Well: The Impact of International Trials for Wartime Rape on Women's Agency." *International Feminist Journal of Politics* 6: 110–128.

Messerschmidt, J. 1993. *Masculinities and Crime: Critique and Reconceptualization of Theory*. Lanham: Rowman & Littlefield.

———. 2000. *Nine Lives. Adolescent Masculinities, the Body and Violence*. Westview Press.

———. 2004. *Flesh and Blood: Adolescent Gender Diversity and Violence*. Lanham, MD: Rowman & Littlefield.

———. 2005. "Masculinities and Crime: Beyond Dualist Criminology." In *Rethinking Gender, Crime and Criminal Justice: Feminist Readings*, edited by C. Renzetti and L. Goodstein, 29–43. Oxford: Oxford University Press.

———. 2010. *Hegemonic Masculinities and Camouflaged Politics. Unmasking the Bush Dynasty and Its War against Iraq.* New York: Routledge.

Mestitz, A., and S. Ghetti. 2005. *Victim-Offender Mediation with Youth Offenders in Europe.* The Netherlands: Springer.

Meyers, D. 2011. "Two Victim Paradigms and the Problem of 'Impure' Victims." *Humanity: An International Journal of Human Rights, Humanitarianism and Development* 2: 255–275.

Michael, C., and Cooper, M. 2013. "Post-traumatic growth following bereavement: A systematic review of the literature." *Counselling Psychology Review* 28: 18–33.

Miers, D. 1990. "Positivist Victimology: A Critique, Part 2." *International Review of Victimology* 1: 219–230.

———. 2001. *An International Review of Restorative Justice.* London: Home Office, Crime Reduction Research Series, paper 10.

———. 2006. "Rebuilding Lives: Operational and Policy Issues in the Compensation of Victims of Violent and Terrorist Crimes." *Criminal Law Review*: 695–721.

———. 2006. "Book review: *Handbook of Restorative Justice: A Global Perspective.*" *Australian and New Zealand Journal of Criminology* 39(3): 422–428.

———. 2007. "Looking Beyond Great Britain: The Development of Criminal Injuries Compensation." In *Handbook of Victims and Victimology*, edited by S. Walklate. London: Routledge.

Miers, D. 2014a. State Compensation for Victims of Violent Crime. In *Justice for Victims: Perspectives on Rights, Transition and Reconciliation*, edited by I. Vanfraechem, A. Pemberton, and F. Ndahinda, 105–139. London, Routledge.

Miers, D. 2014b. Offender and State Compensation for Victims of Crime: Two Decades of Development and Change. *International Review of Victimology* 20: 145–168.

Miers, D., and I. Aertsen. 2012. "Restorative Justice: A Comparative Analysis of Legislative Provision in Europe." In *Regulating Restorative Justice: A Comparative Study of Legislative Provision in European Countries*, edited by D. Miers and I. Aertsen, 511–548. Frankfurt am Main, Verlag für Polizeiwissenschaft.

Miers, D., M. Maguire, S. Goldie, K. Sharpe, C. Hale, A. Netten, K. Doolin, S. Uglow, J. Enterkin, = and T. Newburn. 2001. *An Exploratory Evaluation of Restorative Justice Schemes.* London: Home Office; Crime Reduction Research Series, paper 9.

Miers, D., and J. Willemsens, eds. 2004. *Mapping Restorative Justice: Developments in 25 European Countries.* Belgium: The European Forum for Victim-Offender Mediation and Restorative Justice.

Miles, C., and R. Condry. 2015a. "Adolescent to Parent Violence: The Police Response to Parents Reporting Violence from their Children." *Policing and Society* (forthcoming).

———. 2015b. "Responding to Adolescent to Parent Violence: Challenges for Policy and Practice." *British Journal of Criminology* 55: 1076–1095.

Miller, S., L. Kay, B. Forest, and N. C. Jurik. 2003. "Diversity in Blue: Lesbian and Gay Police Officers in a Masculine Occupation." *Men and Masculinities* 5: 355–385.

Ministry of Defence. 2000. *Army Doctrine Publication Vol. 5: Soldiering—The Military Covenant.* London: Directorate General of Development & Doctrine.

———. 2008. "The Government's Response to the Report of Inquiry into National Recognition of our Armed Forces." https://www.gov.uk/government/uploads/system/uploads/attachment_data/file/28287/govt_response_recognition_armed_forces.pdf.

———. 2015. *Armed Forces Compensation: A Guide.* https://www.gov.uk/government/publications/armed-forces-compensation.

Ministry of Justice. 2003. "The Criminal Injuries Compensation (Overseas) Scheme 2003— Guidance on the exclusion of compensation payments when the injury or death is the result of war operations or military activity by warring factions." https:/

/www.gov.uk/government/uploads/system/uploads/attachment_data/file/28036/ci-cowarfaction.pdf.

———. 2010. *Breaking the Cycle: Effective Punishment, Rehabilitation and Sentencing of Offenders*. London: The Stationery Office, Cm. 7972.

———. 2012a. "Getting it Right for Victims and Witnesses." London: The Stationery Office. https://www.gov.uk/government/uploads/system/uploads/attach-ment_data/file/228691/8288.pdf.

———. 2012b. "The Victims of Overseas Terrorism Compensation Scheme." London: The Stationery Office. https://www.gov.uk/government/uploads/system/uploads/attachment_data/file/243508/9780108512124.pdf.

———. 2012c. *Restorative Justice Action Plan for the Criminal Justice System.*

———. 2013. "The Code of Practice for Victims of Crime." London: The Stationery Office. https://www.gov.uk/government/uploads/system/uploads/attach-ment_data/file/254459/code-of-practice-victims-of-crime.pdf.

———. 2013a. *Code of Practice for Victims of Crime* (October 2013).

———. 2013b. *Code of Practice for Adult Conditional Cautions* (January 2013).

———. 2013c. *Code of Practice for Youth Conditional Cautions* (18 March 2013).

———. 2014. *Restorative Justice Action Plan for the Criminal Justice Period to March 2018.*

———. 2015. *Referral Order Guidance* (revised April 2015) http://www.yjlc.uk/legal-materials/referral-orders.

Moffett, L. 2013. "Reparative Complementarity: Ensuring an Effective Remedy for Victims in the Reparation Regime of the International Criminal Court." *International Journal of Human Rights* 17: 368–390.

Moody, S. R. 1995. "Images of Women: Sentencing in Sexual Assault Cases in Scot-land." In *Law and Body Politics*, edited by J. Bridgeman and S. Millins, 213–239. Aldershot: Dartmouth.

Moon, C. 2009. *Narrating Political Reconciliation: South Africa's Truth and Reconciliation Commission*. Lanham: Lexington Books.

———. 2013. "Interpreters of the Dead Forensic Knowledge, Human Remains and the Politics of the Past." Social and Legal Studies 22: 149–169.

Mooney, J. and J. Young. 2005. "Imagining Terrorism: Terrorism and Anti-Terrorism Terrorism, Two Ways of Doing Evil." *Social Justice* 32: 113–125.

Moore, M. 2015. "Neo-Nazi Attack on Asian Dentist Was a 'Terrorist Act', Say Fami-ly." *The Independent*. Accessed November 10. http://www.independent.co.uk/news/uk/crime/neo-nazi-attack-on-asian-dentist-was-a-terrorist-act-say-family-10346416.html.

Moran, L., and A. Sharpe. 2004. "Violence, Identity and Policing: The Case of Violence against Transgender People." *Criminal Justice* 4: 395–417.

Morash, M., and R. Haar. 2012. "Doing, Redoing, and Undoing Gender Variation in Gender Identities of Women Working as Police Officers." *Feminist Criminology* 7: 3–23.

Morina, N., V. Rudari, G. Bleichhardt, and H. G. Prigerson. 2010. "Prolonged Grief Disorder, Depression, and Posttraumatic Stress Disorder among Bereaved Kosovar Civilian War Survivors: A Preliminary Investigation." *International Journal of Social Psychiatry* 56: 288–297.

Morris, A. 1987. *Women, Crime and Criminal Justice*. Oxford: Basil Blackwell.

Morris, A., and G. Maxwell. 2001. *Restorative Justice for Juveniles: Conferencing, Media-tion and Circles*. London: Bloomsbury Publishing.

Morris, A., and W. Young. 2000. "Reforming Criminal Justice: The Potential of Resto-rative Justice. In *Restorative Justice: Philosophy to Practice*, edited by H. Strang and J. Braithwaite, 11–32. Aldershot: Ashgate.

Moser, C., and C. Mcilwaine. 2001. "Gender and Social Capital in Contexts of Political Violence: Community Perceptions from Colombia and Guatemala" In *Victims, Per-petrators or Actors? Gender, Armed Conflict and Political Violence*, edited by C. Moser and F. Clark. London: Zed Books.

Muncie, J. 1999. "Institutionalised Intolerance: Youth Justice and the 1998 Crime and Disorder Act." *Critical Social Policy* 19: 147–175.

Munck, R., and D. O'Hearn, trans. 1999. *Critical Development Theory: Contributions to a New Paradigm.* London: Zed Books.

Myers, B., and E. Greene. 2004. "The Prejudicial Nature of Victim Impact Statements: Implications for Capital Sentencing Policy." *Psychology, Public Policy, and Law* 10: 492–515

Mythen, G. 2007. "Cultural Victimology: Are We All Victims Now?" in *Handbook of Victims and Victimology*, edited by S. Walklate. Cullompton: Willan.

Naffine, N. 1990. *Law & The Sexes.* London: Allen & Unwin.

Nagy, R. 2013. "The Scope and Bounds of Transitional Justice and the Canadian Truth and Reconciliation Commission." *International Journal of Transitional Justice* 7: 52–73.

The National Organization of Murdered Children (POMC). 2015. Parole Block Program. http://www.pomc.org/pbp.html.

Naughton, M. 2004. "Re-orientating miscarriages of justice." In *Beyond Criminology: Taking Harm Seriously*, edited by P. Hillyard, C. Pantazis, S. Tombs, and D. Gordon, 101–112. London: Pluto Press.

———. 2007. *Rethinking Miscarriages of Justice.* London: Palgrave.

———. 2010. *The Criminal Review Commission: Hope for the Innocent?* Basingstoke: Palgrave Macmillan.

Nelken, D. 2003. "Beyond Compare? Criticising the American Way of Law." *Law and Social Inquiry* 28: 181–213.

———. 2009. "Comparative Criminal Justice: Beyond Ethnocentricism and Relativism." *European Journal of Criminology* 6: 291–311.

Newburn, T. 2008. *Handbook of Policing.* Cullompton: Willan.

Newburn, T., and Stanko, E. 1995. "When Men Are Victims: The Failure of Victimology." In *Just Boys Doing Business?: Men, Masculinities and Crime*, edited by Tim Newburn and Elizabeth Stanko. New York and London: Routledge.

Ni Aolain, F. 2012. "Advancing Feminist Positioning in the Field of Transitional Justice." *International Journal of Transitional Justice* 6: 205–228.

Ni Aolain, F., and C. Turner. 2007. "Gender, Truth and Transition." *UCLA Women's Law Journal* 16: 229–279.

Nicol, M. 2005. *Last Round: The Redcaps, the Paras and the Battle for Majar.* London: Cassell Military Paperbacks.

Nietzsche, F. 1996. *On the Genealogy of Morality.* Cambridge, UK: Cambridge University Press.

Nixon, R. 2011. *Slow Violence and the Environmentalism of the Poor.* Cambridge, Mass: Harvard University Press.

Nobles, R. and Schiff, D. 2004. "A Story of Miscarriage: Law in the Media." *Journal of Law and Society* 31, 221–244.

Nolan, T. 2009. "Behind the Blue Wall of Silence." *Men and Masculinities* 12: 250–257.

Nolin Hanlon, C., and F. Shankar. 2000. "Gendered Spaces of Terror and Assault: The Testimonio of REMHI and the Commission for Historical Clarification in Guatemala." *Gender, Place and Culture* 7: 265–286.

The Norwegian Criminal Injuries Compensation Authority. 2015. *Kontorets historie* [The agency's history]. http://www.voldsoffererstatning.no/kontorets-historie.292710.no.html.

Nussbaum, M. C. 2004. *Hiding from Humanity: Disgust, Shame and the Law.* Princeton: Princeton University Press.

O'Brien, R., K. Hunt, and G. Hart. 2005. "It's Caveman Stuff, but That Is to a Certain Extent How Guys Still Operate: Men's Accounts of Masculinity and Help Seeking." *Social Science and Medicine* 61: 503–516.

O'Connell, M. 2008. "Victimology: A Social Science in Waiting?" *International Review of Victimology* 15: 91–104.

ODIHR (The Office for Democratic Institutions and Human Rights). 2009. *Hate Crime Laws: A Practical Guide*. Warsaw: The OSCE Office for Democratic Institutions and Human Rights.

————. 2014. *Hate Crimes in the OSCE Region: Incidents and Responses—Annual Report for 2013*. Warsaw: The OSCE Office for Democratic Institutions and Human Rights.

O'Donnell, B. 1956. *Should Women Hang?* London: W. H. Allen.

Office for National Statistics. 2015. "Violent Crime and Sexual Offences – Homicide." In *Crime Statistics: Focus on Violent and Sexual Offences*. London: TSO.

Office for Victims of Crime. 2015. "OVC Fact Sheet. The Crime Victim Fund." http://ojp.gov/ovc/pubs/crimevictimsfundfs/intro.html.

O'Malley, P. 2004. "The Uncertain Promise of Risk." *Australian and New Zealand Journal of Criminology* 37: 323–343.

————. 2004a. *Risk, Uncertainty and Government*. New York and London: Routledge-Cavendish.

Onfray, M. 2012. *Abrégé Hédoniste*. Paris: Editions 84.

Orentlicher, D. 2007. "Settling Accounts' Revisited: Reconciling Global Norms with Local Agency." *International Journal of Transitional Justice*: 10–22.

Ortega, L. 2009. "Transitional Justice And Female Ex-Combatants: Lessons Learned From The International Experience." In *Disarming the Past: Transitional Justice and Ex-Combatants*, edited by A. Patel, P. De Greif, and L. Waldorf. New York: Social Science Research Council.

Osborne, G. 2004. in *Parliamentary Debate on Family Court Cases* 24 February. Transcript available on http://sallyclark.org.uk/Parliament0204.html.

Osiel, M. 2007. *Atrocity, Punishment and International Law*. Cambridge, UK: Cambridge University Press.

Österberg, E. 2002. "Upptäckten av den oskyldiga människan [The discovery of the innocent human]." In *Offer för brott. Våldtäkt, incest och barnamord I Sveriges historia från reformationen till nutid* [Rape, incest, and infanticide in Swedish history from the Reformation to the present], edited by E. Bergenlöv and M. Lindstedt Cronberg, 9–24. Lund: Nordic Academic Press.

Paechter, C. 2003. "Masculinities and Femininities as Communities of Practice." *Women's Studies International Forum* 26: 69–77.

————. 2006. "Power, Knowledge and Embodiment in Communities of Sex/Gender Practice." *Women's Studies International Forum* 29: 13–26.

Pakes, F. 2004. *Comparative Criminal Justice*. Cullompton: Willan.

Paternoster, R., and Deise, J. 2011. "A Heavy Thumb on the Scale: The Effect of Victim Impact Evidence on Capital Decision Making." *Criminology* 49: 129–161.

Paterson A, P. Dunn, K. Chaston, and L. Malone. 2006. *In the Aftermath: The Support Needs of People Bereaved by Homicide: A Research Report*. London: Victim Support.

Pavlich, G. 2005. *Governing Paradoxes of Restorative Justice*. London: Glasshouse Press.

Pelikan, C. 2004. "The Impact of Council of Europe Recommendation No. R(99)19 on Mediation in Penal Matters." In *Crime Policy in Europe*, edited by Council of Europe, 49–74. Strasbourg, Council of Europe Publishing.

Peluffo, A. 2007. "The Boundaries of Sisterhood: Gender and Class in the Mothers and Grandmothers of the Plaza de Mayo." A contracorriente 4: 77–102.

Pemberton, A., F. Winkel, and M. Groehhuijsen. 2007. "Taking Victims Seriously in Restorative Justice." *International Perspectives in Victimology* 3: 4–14.

Perry, B. 2001. *In the Name of Hate: Understanding Hate Crimes*. London: Routledge.

Perry, B., and R. Dyck. 2014. "Courage in the Face of Hate: a Curricular Resource for Confronting Anti-LGBTQ Violence." In *Responding to Hate Crime: The Case for Connecting Policy and Research*, edited by N. Chakraborti and J. Garland, 185–197. Bristol: The Policy Press.

Persson, Å. 2004. *De politiska partiernas rättspolitik* [Political Parties, Law, and Politics]. Unpublished doctoral dissertation. Umeå University: Uppsala.

Peter, T. 2005. "Domestic Violence in United States and Sweden: A Welfare State Typology Comparison within a Power Rsources Framework." *Women's Studies International Forum* 29: 96–107.

Peters, T. 2000. "Victim-Offender Mediation: Reality and Challenges." In *Victim-Offender Mediation in Europe,* edited by The European Forum for Victim-Offender Mediation and Restorative Justice, 9–15. Belgium: Leuven University Press.

Pini, B. 2004. "Managerial masculinities in the Australian sugar industry." *Rural Society* 14: 22–35.

Pion-Berlin, D., and G. Lopez, G. 1991. "Of Victims and Executioners: Argentine State Terror, 1975–1979." *International Studies Quarterly* 35: 63–86.

Posel, D. 2002. "What Kind of History, What Kind of Truth." In *Commissioning the Past: Understanding South Africa's Truth and Reconciliation Commission,* edited by D. Posel and G. Simpson. Johannesburg: Witwatersrand University Press.

Posner, E., and A. Vermeule. 2004. "Transitional Justice as Ordinary Justice." *Harvard Law Review* 117: 761–825.

Powell, S., Butollo, W., and Hagl, M. 2010. "Missing or Killed." European Psychologist 15: 185–192.

Pranis, K. 2007. "Restorative Values." In *Restorative Justice Handbook,* edited by G. Johnstone, and D. Van nessl, 59–74. Cullompton: Willan.

Pratt, J. 2008. "Scandinavian Exceptionalism in an Era of Penal Excess. Part I: The Nature and Roots of Scandinavian Exceptionalism." *British Journal of Criminology* 48: 119–137.

Pratt, J. and Gilligan, G. 2004. "Introduction: Crime, Truth and Justice—Official Inquiry and the Production of Knowledge." In *Crime, Truth and Justice: Official Inquiry, Discourse, Knowledge,* edited by G. Gilligan and J. Pratt, 1–10. Collumpton: Willan.

Presser, L. 2015. *Narrative Criminology: Understanding Stories of Crime.* New York: NYU Press.

Prokos, A., and I. Padavic. 2002. "'There Oughtta Be A Law Against Bitches': Masculinity Lessons in Police Academy Training." *Gender, Work and Organization* 9: 439–459.

Punch, M. 2003. "Rotten Orchards: 'Pestilence', Police Misconduct and System Failure." *Policing and Society: An International Journal of Research and Policy* 13: 171–196.

Quarmby, K. 2011. *Scapegoat: Why We Are Failing Disabled People.* London: Portobello Books.

Quinney, R. 1972. "Who is the Victim?" *Criminology* 10: 314–323.

Rabe-Hemp, C. 2009. "POLICEwomen or policeWOMEN? Doing Gender and Police Work." *Feminist Criminology* 4: 114–129.

Rafter, N., And S. Walklate. 2012. " Genocide and the Dynamics of Victimization: Some Observations on Armenia." *European Journal of Criminology* 9: 514 – 526 .

Ramirez-Barrat, C. 2011. *Making an Impact : Guidelines on Designing and Implementing Outreach Programs for Transitional Justice.* New York: International Centre for Transitional Justice.

Ray, L., D. Smith, and L. Wastell. 2004. "Shame, Rage and Racist Violence." *British Journal of Criminology.* 44: 350–368.

Rayment, S. 2006. "Wounded Get Millions in Compensation." *The Telegraph.* http://www.telegraph.co.uk/news/uknews/1536459/Wounded-to-get-millions-in-compensation.html.

Razack, S. 2000. "Gendered Racial Violence and Spatialized Justice: The Murder of Pamela George." *Canadian Journal of Law and Society* 15: 91–130.

———. 2007. "Stealing the Pain of Others: Reflections on Canadian Humanitarian Responses." *Review of Education, Pedagogy, and Cultural Studies* 29: 375–394.

Regehr, C., R. Alaggia, L. Lambert, and M. Saini. 2008. "Victims of Sexual Violence in Canadian Criminal Courts." *Victims and Offenders* 3: 99–113.

Renzetti, C. 2009. "Violence Against Women." *Violence Against Women* 15: 511–523.

Richardson-Foster, H., N. Stanley, P. Miller, and G. Thomson. 2012. "Police Intervention in Domestic Violence Incidents Where Children Are Present: Police and Children's Perspectives." *Policing and Society: An International Journal of Research and Policy* 22: 220–234.

Roach, K. 1999. *Due Process And Victims' Rights: The New Law and Politics of Criminal Justice*. Toronto: University of Toronto Press.

Robins, S. 2011. "Towards Victim-Centred Transitional Justice: Understanding the Needs of Families of the Disappeared in Postconflict Nepal." *International Journal of Transitional Justice* 5: 75–98.

Roche, D. 2001. "The Evolving Definition of Restorative Justice." *Contemporary Justice Review* 43: 341–353.

———. 2003. *Accountability in Restorative Justice*. Oxford: Clarendon Studies in Criminology.

———. 2007. "Retribution and Restorative Justice." In *Restorative Justice Handbook*, edited by G. Johnstone and D. Van ness, 75–90. Cullompton: Willan.

Rock, P. 1994. *Victimology*. Dartmouth.

———. 1998a. "Murderers, Victims And 'Survivors.'" *British Journal of Criminology* 38:185–200.

———. 1998b. *After Homicide. Practical Responses to Bereavement*. Oxford Press: Clarendon.

———. 2002. "On Becoming a Victim." In *New Visions of Crime Victims*, edited by C. Hoyle and R. Young, 1–22. Hart Publishing.

———. 2004. *Constructing Victims' Rights: The Home Office, New Labour and Victims Of Crime*. Oxford: Oxford University Press.

———. 2007. "Theoretical Perspectives on Victimization." In *Handbook of Victims and Victimology*, edited by Sandra Walklate, 37–61. Cullompton: Willan.

Roeder, O., L-B Eisen, and J. Bowling. 2015. *What Caused the Crime Decline?* New York: Brennan Center for Justice.

Ross, F. 2003. *Bearing Witness: Women and the Truth and Reconciliation Commission in South Africa*. London: Pluto.

Rothaupt, J. W., and K. Becker. 2007. "A Literature Review of Western Bereavement Theory: From Decathecting to Continuing Bonds." *The Family Journal: Counselling Therapy for Couples and Families* 15: 6–15.

Rothbart, D., K. Korostelina, and M. Cherkaoui. 2012. *Civilians and Modern War: Armed Conflict and the Ideology of Violence*. London: Routledge.

Rothe, D. L., and K. F. Steinmetz. 2013. "The Case of Bradley Manning: State Victimization, Realpolitik and WikiLeaks." *Contemporary Justice Review* 16: 280–292.

Rothko, M. 2006. *Writings on Art*. New Haven: Yale University Press.

Roulstone, A., and H. Mason-Bish, trans. 2013. *Disability, Hate Crime and Violence*. London: Routledge.

Royal Statistical Society 23 October 2001 (News Release).

Ruggiero, V., and N. South. 2010. "Critical Criminology and Crimes Against the Environment." *Critical Criminology* 18: 245–250.

Ryan, B., with the Rt Hon The Lord Havers 1977. *The Poisoned Life of Mrs Maybrick*. Harmondsworth: Penguin.

Scheingold, S. 2004. *The Politics of Rights: Lawyers, Public Policy and Political Change,* 2nd edition. Ann Arbor: University Of Michigan Press.

Schiff, M. 2003. "Models, Challenges and the Promise of Restorative Justice Conferencing Strategies." In *Restorative Justice and Criminal Justice*, edited by A. von Hirsch, J. Roberts, and A. Bottoms, 315–338. Oxford: Hart Publishing.

Scott, J. C. 1988. *Seeing Like a State*. New Haven: Yale University Press.

Scraton, P. 1999. *Hillsborough: The Truth*. Edinburgh: Mainstream Publishing.

Scraton, P. 2013. "The Legacy of Hillsborough: Liberating Truth, Challenging Power." *Race and Class* 55: 1–27.

Shute, Jon. 2015. "Moral Discourse and Action in Relation to the Corpse: Integrative Concepts for a Criminology of Mass Violence." In Human Remains and Mass Violence: Methodological Approaches , edited by E. Anstett and F. M. Dreyfus. Manchester: Manchester University Press.

Silvestri, M. 2007. "'Doing' Police Leadership: Enter the 'New Smart Macho.'" *Policing and Society: An International Journal of Research and Policy* 17: 38–58.

Simon, J. 2003. "Wechsler's Century and Ours: Reforming Criminal Law in a Time of Shifting Rationalities of Government." Paper presented at the Center for the Study of Law and Society CSLS Series, University of California, Berkeley, September 8, 2003. http://repositories.cdlib.org/cgi/viewcontent.cgi?article=1032&context=csls.

Shapland, J. 2003. "Restorative Justice and Criminal Justice: Just Responses to Crime?" In *Restorative Justice and Criminal Justice*, edited by A. von Hirsch, J. Roberts, and A. Bottoms, 195–218. Oxford: Hart Publishing.

Shapland, J. 2014. "Implications of Growth: Challenges for Restorative Justice." *International Review of Victimology* 20: 111–127.

Shapland, J., G. Robinson, and A. Sorsby. 2011. *Restorative Justice in Practice: Evaluating What Works for Victims and Offenders*. London: Routledge.

Shaw, R., L. Waldorf, and P. Hazan. 2010. *Localizing Transitional Justice: Interventions and Priorities after Mass Violence*. Stanford: Stanford University Press.

Shirlow, P., and K. McEvoy. 2008. *Beyond the Wire: Ex-Prisoners and Conflict Transformation in Northern Ireland*. London: Pluto.

Simon, J. 2007. *Governing through Crime: How the War on Crime Transformed American Democracy and Created a Culture of Fear*. Oxford: Oxford University Press.

Slim, H. 2010. *Killing Civilians: Method, Madness, and Morality in War*. Princeton: Princeton University Press.

Smart, B., and C. Smart. 1978. *Women, Sexuality and Social Control*. London: Routledge and Kegan Paul.

Smart, C. 1977. *Women, Crime and Criminology: A Feminist Critique*. London: Routledge.

———. 1989. *Feminism and the Power of Law*. London: Routledge.

SOU. 1976:9. *Sexuellla ö vergrepp: förslag till ny lydelse av brottsbalkens bestämmelser om sedlighetsbrott* [Sexual abuse: Proposals for a new wording of the regulations of the penal code of sexual offenses]. Stockholm.

———. 1998:40. *Brottsoffer. Vad har gjorts? Vad bor goras?* [Crime victims- What has been done? What should be done?] Stockholm.

Spalek, B. 2006. *Crime Victims: Theory Policy and Practice*. London: Palgrave.

Spencer, D. C. 2009. "Habit(us), Body Techniques and Body Callusing: An Ethnography of Mixed Martial Arts." *Body & Society* 15: 119–143.

———. 2011. *Ultimate Fighting and Embodiment: Violence, Gender and Mixed Martial Arts*. New York and London: Routledge.

———. 2011a. "Event and Victimization." *Criminal Law and Philosophy* 5: 39–52.

———. 2014. "Exposing the Conditions of Precarity: Compounding Victimization and Marginalized Young People." *Contemporary Justice Review* 17: 87–103.

———. 2015. "Corporeal Realism and Victimology." *International Review of Victimology* 21: 31–44.

Spencer, D. C., and Fitzgerald, A. 2013. "Three Ecologies, Transversality and Victimization: The Case of the British Petroleum Oil Spill." *Crime, Law and Social Change* 59: 209–223.

———. 2015. "Criminology and Animality: Stupidity and the Anthropological Machine." *Contemporary Justice Review* 18 (4): 1–14.

Spinoza, B. 1996 [1677]. *Ethics*. London: Penguin

Spivak, G. 1988. "Can the Subaltern Speak?" In *Marxism and the Interpretation of Culture*, edited by C. Nelson and L. Grossberg, 271–313. Basingstoke: Macmillan.

Sriram, C., J. Garcia-Godos, J. Herman, and O. Martin-Ortega, trans. 2013. *Transitional Justice and Peacebuilding on the Ground: Victims and Ex-combatants*. London: Routledge.

Staggs Kelsall, M., and S. Stepakoff. 2009. "When We Wanted to Talk About Rape: Silencing Sexual Violence at the Special Court for Sierra Leone." *International Journal of Transitional Justice* 3: 355-374.

Stanko, E. 1985. *Everyday Violence: How Women and Men Experience Sexual and Physical Danger*. New York: Harper Collins.

Star, S. 2010. "This Is Not a Boundary Object: Reflections on the Origin of a Concept." *Science, Technology & Human Values* 35: 601–607.

Star, S., and J. Griesemer. 1989. "Institutional Ecology, Translations and Boundary Objects: Amateurs and Professionals in Berkeley's Museum of Vertebrate Zoology 1907–1939." *Social Studies of Science* 19: 387–420.

Steinhert, H. 1997. "Fin de Siècle Criminology." *Theoretical Criminology* 1: 111–119.

Stephens, S., and D. Day. 2013. "Distinguishing among Weapons Offenders, Drug Offenders, and Weapons and Drug Offenders Based on Childhood Predictors and Adolescent Correlates." *Criminal Behaviour and Mental Health*, 23:177–190.

Stockwell, J. 2014. "'The Country that Doesn't Want to Heal Itself': The Burden of History, Affect and Women's Memories in Post-Dictatorial Argentina." *International Journal of Conflict and Violence* 8: 30–44.

Stover, E. 2007. *The Witnesses: War Crimes and the Promise of Justice in The Hague*. Philadelphia: University Of Pennsylvania Press.

Strang, H. 2002. *Repair or Revenge: Victims and Restorative Justice*. Oxford: Clarendon Studies in Criminology.

Strang, H., and J. Braithwaite. 2000. *Restorative Justice: Philosophy to Practice*. Aldershot: Ashgate.

Strang, H., and J. Braithwaite. 2001. *Restorative Justice and Civil Society*. Cambridge, UK: Cambridge University Press.

Strobl, R. 2010. "Becoming a Victim." In *International Handbook of Victimology*, edited by S. G. Shoham, P. Knepper, and M. Kett, 3–26. Boca Raton: CRC Press.

Stroebe, M., H. Schut, and W. Stroebe. 2007. "Health Outcomes of Bereavement." *Lancet* 370: 160–173.

Sullivan, D., and L. Tifft. 2006. *Handbook of Restorative Justice*. London: Routledge.

Svensson, B. 1997. "The Power of Biography: Criminal Policy, Prison Life, and the Formation of Criminal Identities in the Swedish Welfare State". In *Auto/Ethnography: Rewriting the Self and Social,* edited by D. Reed-Danahay, 71–106. Oxford: Berg.

The Swedish Crime Victim Compensation and Support Authority. 2013. "Brottsoffer och mänskliga rättigheter [Crime victims and human rights]." http://www.brottsoffermyndigheten.se/default.aspx?id=1593.

———. 2014. *Brottsofferfondens stöd till brottsofferforskning å ren 1994-2013*. [The Crime victim fund's support to crime victim research 1994-2013]. Umeå: The Swedish Crime Victim Compensation and Support Authority.

Sweeney, J. 2002. File on Four broadcast 2 July 2002, Reporter: John Sweeney. Transcript available at http://www.sallyclark.org.uk/FileonFour.html.

Sweeting A., R. Owen, C. Turley, and P. Rock. 2008. *Evaluation of the Victims' Advocate Scheme Pilots*. London: Ministry of Justice.

Tavuchis, N. 1990. *Mea Culpa: A Sociology of Apology and Reconciliation*. Stanford: Stanford University Press.

Telegraph. 2012. "Malala Yousafzai: UK Hospital is Centre for Treating Soldiers Injured in Battlefield." http://www.telegraph.co.uk/news/worldnews/asia/pakistan/9608975/Malala-Yousafzai-UK-hospital-is-centre-for-treating-soldiers-injured-in-battlefield.html.

Temkin, J., and J. Krahe. 2007. *Sexual Assault and the Justice Gap: A Question of Attitude*. Oxford: Hart.

Tham, H. 2001a. "Law and order as a leftist project?: The case of Sweden." *Punishment and Society* 3: 409-426.

———. 2001b. "Brottsoffrets uppkomst och framtid. [The Rise and Future of the Crime Victim]." In *Det motspänstiga offret* [The Obstinate Victim], edited by M. Åkerström and I. Sahlin, 27–45. Lund: Studentlitteratur.

Tham, H., A. Rönneling, and L-L Rytterbo. 2011. "The Emergence of the Crime Victim: Sweden in a Scandinavian Context." *Crime and Justice* 40: 555–611.

Theidon, K. 2007. "Gender in Transition: Common Sense, Women, and War." *Journal of Human Rights* 6: 453–478.

Thumala, A., B. Gold, and I. Loader. 2011. "A Tainted Trade? Moral Ambivalence and Legitimation Work in the Private Security Industry." *British Journal of Sociology* 62: 283–303.

Tilly, C. 2008. *Credit and Blame*. Princeton: Princeton University Press.

Toews, B., and H. Zehr. 2003. "Ways of knowing for a restorative worldview." In *Restorative Justice in Context: International Practice and Directions*, edited by E. Weitekamp and H. Kerner, 257–271. Cullompton: Willan.

Tonry, M. 2004. *Thinking About Crime: Sense and Sensibility in American Penal Culture*. Oxford: Oxford University Press.

———. 2010. "Rebalancing the Criminal Justice System in Favour of the Victim: The Costly Consequences of Populist Rhetoric." In *Hearing the Victim: Adversarial Justice, Crime Victims and the State*, edited by A. Bottoms and J. Roberts, 72–103. Cullompton: Willan.

Tonry, M., and M. Melewski. 2008. "The Malign Effects of Drug and Crime Control Policies on Black Americans." *Crime and Justice: A Review of Research* 37: 1–44.

Tsianos, V., and D. Papadopoulos. 2015. "DIWY! Precarity in Embodied Capitalism." In *Economy: Art, Production and the Subject in the 21st Century*, edited by A. Dimitrakaki and K. Lloyd, 123–139. Liverpool: Liverpool University Press.

Twinning, W. 1990. *Rethinking Evidence*. Oxford: Basil Blackwell.

Tyler, K., and M. Beal. 2010. "The High-Risk Environment of Homeless Young Adults: Consequences for Physical and Sexual Victimization." *Violence and Victims* 25: 101–115.

United Nations. 2005. *The Rule of Law and Transitional Justice*. New York: United Nations.

United Nations Assistance Mission in Afghanistan. 2007. "Civilian Casualties During 2007." http://www.unama.unmissions.org/Portals/UNAMA/human%20rights/PoC-Civilian-Casualties-report-2007.pdf.

———. 2008. "Afghanistan: Annual Report on Protection of Civilians in Armed Conflict, 2008." http://www.unama.unmissions.org/Portals/UNAMA/human%20rights/UNAMA_09february-Annual%20Report_PoC%202008_FINAL_11Feb09.pdf.

———. 2014. "Civilians Casualties rise by 24 per cent in first half of 2014. Ground engagements and crossfire now killing and injuring more Afghan civilians than IEDs." http://www.unama.unmissions.org/LinkClick.aspx?fileticket=OhsZ29Dgeyw%3d&tabid=12254&mid=15756&language=en-US.

United Nations Secretary General. 2011. "The Rule of Law and Transitional Justice in Conflict and Post-Conflict Societies: Report of the Secretary-General to the Security Council (S/2011/634)." http://www.unrol.org/doc.aspx?d=3096.

University of Akron. 2002. "An Oral History of the Crime Victim Assistance Field." Video and Audio Archive: Marlene A. Young JD, PhD Interview Transcript. http://vroh.uakron.edu/transcripts/Young.php.

van Denderen, M., J. de Keijser, M. Kleen, and P. Boelan. 2015. "Psychopathology among Homicidally Bereaved Individuals: A Systematic Review." Trauma, Violence and Abuse 16: 71–80.

Van Dijk, J. 1988. "A New Society of Victimology? A Letter from the President." *The Victimologist*, 1: 2–3.

Van Dijk, J., P. Mayhew, and M. Killias. 1990. *Experiences of Crime across the World: Key Findings from the 1989 International Crime Survey*. Deventer: Kluwer Law And Taxation.

Van Dijk, J., J. Van Kesteren, and P. Smit. 2008. *Criminal Victimisation in International Perspective, Key Findings from the 2004-2005 ICVS And EU ICS*. The Hague: Boom Legal Publishers.

Vanfraechem, I., I. Aertsen, and J. Willemnsens. 2010. *Restorative Justice Realities: Empirical Research in a European Context*. The Hague: Eleven International Publishing.

Vanfraechem, I., and D. Bolivar. 2015. "Restorative Justice and Victims of Crime." In *Victims and Restorative Justice*, edited by I. Vanfraechem, D. Bolivar, and I. Aertsen, 48–75. London: Routledge.

Van Ness, D. 2003a. "The Shape of Things to Come: A Framework for Thinking about a Restorative Justice System." In *Restorative Justice: Theoretical Foundations*, edited by E. Weitekamp and H-J Kerner: 1–20. Cullompton: Willan.

Van Ness, D. 2003b. Proposed Basic Principles on the Use of Restorative Justice: Recognising the Aims and Limits of Restorative Justice." In *Restorative Justice and Criminal Justice*, edited by A. von Hirsch, J. Roberts, and A. Bottoms, 157–176. Oxford: Hart Publishing.

Veltmeyer, H. 2011. *The Critical Development Studies Handbook: Tools For Change*. London: Pluto Press.

Victim Support Sweden. 2008. "Tema mänskliga rättigheter [Theme: Human rights]." *Tidningen Brottsoffer* [The Crime Victim Magazine] 3: 11–15.

———. 2015. Mänskliga rättigheter [Human rights]. http://www.brottsofferjouren.se/fakta-om-brottsoffer/manskliga-rattigheter/.

Von Hentig, H. 1948. *The Criminal and His Victim*. New Haven: Yale University Press.

———. 2009. "The Criminal and His Victim: Studies in the Sociobiology of Crime." In *Victims and Victimization: A Reader*, edited by Brian Williams and Hannah Chong-Goodman, 5–25. Berkshire and New York: Open University Press.

von Hirsch, A., J. Roberts, and A. Bottoms. 2003. "Specifying Aims and Limits for Restorative Justice: A 'Making Amends' Model?" In *Restorative Justice and Criminal Justice*, edited by A. von Hirsch, J. Roberts, and A. Bottoms, 21–42. Oxford: Hart Publishing.

Wachholz, S. 2009. "Pathways through Hate: Exploring the Victimization of the Homeless." In *Hate Crimes: The Victims of Hate Crime*, edited by B. Perry, 199–222. Westport: Praeger.

Wacquant, L. 2009. *Prisons of Poverty*. Minneapolis: University of Minnesota Press.

———. 2011. "Habitus as Topic and Tool: Reflections on Becoming a Prizefighter." *Qualitative Research in Psychology* 8: 81–92.

Wagner, S. 2008. *To Know Where He Lies: DNA Technology and the Search for Srebrenica's Missing*. London: University of California Press.

Walgrave, L. 2003. "Imposing Restoration Instead of Inflicting Pain: Reflections on the Judicial Reaction to Crime." In *Restorative Justice and Criminal Justice*, edited by A. von Hirsch, J. Roberts, and A. Bottoms, 61–78. Oxford: Hart Publishing.

———. 2008. *Restorative Justice, Self-Interest and Responsible Citizenship*. London: Routledge.

Walker, A., C. Kershaw, and S. Nicholas. 2006. "Crime in England and Wales 2005/06." London: Home Office. http://tna.europarchive.org/20100413151441/http://homeoffice.gov.uk/rds/pdfs06/hosb1206.pdf.

Walklate, S. 1989. *Victimology: The Victim and the Criminal Justice Process*. London: Unwin Hyman.

———. 1990. "Researching Victims of Crime: Critical Victimology." *Social Justice* 17: 25–42.

———. 1991. "Victims, Crime Prevention And Social Control." In *Beyond Law And Order: Criminal Justice Policy And Politics Into The 1990s*, edited by R. Reiner and M. Cross. London: Macmillan.

———. 2003. "Can There Be a Feminist Victimology?" In *Victimisation: Theory, Research and Policy*, edited by P. Davies, P. Francis, and V. Jupp. Basingstoke: Palgrave Macmillan.

———. 2007. *Imagining the Victim of Crime*. Maidenhead: Open University Press.

———. 2011. "Reframing Criminal Victimization: Finding a Place for Vulnerability and Resilience." *Theoretical Criminology* 15: 179–194.

———. 2012. "Courting Compassion: Victims, Policy and the Question of Justice." *Howard Journal of Criminal Justice* 51: 109–121.

————. 2012a. "Who Is the Victim of Crime? Paying Homage to the Work of Richard Quinney." *Crime, Media, Culture* 8: 173–184.

Walklate, S., and R. McGarry. 2015. *Victims: Trauma, Testimony and Justice*. London: Routledge.

Walklate, S., G. Mythen, and R. McGarry. 2015. "'When you see the lipstick kisses…' Military Repatriation, Public Mourning and the Politics of Respect." Palgrave Communications. http://www.palgrave-journals.com/articles/palcomms20159.

Waller, I. 2010. *Rights for Victims of Crime: Rebalancing Justice*. Plymouth: Rowman & Littlefield.

Walters, M. 2014a. "Conceptualizing 'Hostility' for Hate Crime Law: Minding 'the Minutiae' when Interpreting Section 28(1)(a) of the Crime and Disorder Act 1998." *Oxford Journal of Legal Studies* 34: 47–74.

————. 2014b. *Hate Crime and Restorative Justice: Exploring Causes, Repairing Harms.* Oxford: Oxford University Press.

Walters, M. 2011. "A General *Theories* of Hate Crime? Strain, Doing Difference and Self Control." *Critical Criminology* 19: 313–330.

Walters, M., and C. Hoyle. 2012. "Exploring the Everyday World of Hate Victimisation through Community Mediation." *International Review of Victimology*. 18: 7–24.

Waterhouse, C. 2009. "The Good, the Bad, and the Ugly: Moral Agency and the Role of Victims in Reparations Programs." *University of Pennsylvania Journal of International Law* 31: 257–294.

Webb, J., T. Schirato, and G. Danaher. 2002. *Understanding Bourdieu*. Sydney: Allen & Unwin.

Websdale, N. 2010. *Familicidal Hearts: The Emotional Styles of 211 Killers*. Oxford: Oxford University Press.

Weinstein, H. 2014. "Victims, Transitional Justice and Social Reconstruction: Who Is Setting the Agenda?" In *Justice for Victims*, edited by I. Vanfraechem, A. Pemberton, and F. Ndahinda, 161–182. London: Routledge.

Weis, R. 1990. *Criminal Justice*. Harmondsworth: Penguin.

Weitekamp, E. 2002. "Restorative Justice: Present Prospects and Future Direction." In *Restorative Justice: Theoretical Foundations*, edited by E. Weitekamp, and H-J. Kerner, 322–338. Cullompton: Willan.

Weitekamp, E., and H. Kerner. 2002. *Restorative Justice: Theoretical Foundations*. Cullompton: Willan.

Weitekamp, E., and H. Kerner. 2003. *Restorative Justice in Context: International Practice and Directions*. Cullompton: Willan.

Wemmers, J. M. 1996. *Victims in the Criminal Justice System*. Amsterdam: Kugler.

————. 2010. "The Meaning of Justice for Victims. In *International Handbook of Victimology*, edited by S. Shoham, P. Knepper, and M. Kett. Boca Raton: CRC Press.

Wenger, E. 1998. *Communities of Practice: Learning, Meaning and Identity*. Cambridge, UK: Cambridge University Press.

Wergens, A. 2014. *Human Rights for Victims of Non-State Crime: Taking Victims Seriously*. Oisterwijk: Wolf Legal Publishers (WLP).

Wexler, D. 2008. *Rehabilitating Lawyers: Principles of Therapeutic Jurisprudence for Criminal Law Practice*. Charlotte: Carolina Academic Press.

White, R. 2003. "Environmental Issues and the Criminological Imagination." *Theoretical Criminology* 7: 483–506.

————. 2011. *Transnational Environmental Crime: Toward an Eco-Global Criminology*. New York: Routledge.

————. 2013. *Global Environmental Harm: Criminological Perspectives*. New York: Routledge.

Whitehead, S. M. 2002. *Men and Masculinities*. Cambridge, UK: Polity.

Whyte, D. 2007. "Crimes of the Neo-Liberal State in occupied Iraq." *British Journal of Criminology* 47: 177–195.

Williams, M., and J. Tregidga. 2013. *All Wales Hate Crime Research Project: Research Overview and Executive Summary*. Cardiff: Race Equality First.

Wilson, R. 2001. *The Politics of Truth and Reconciliation in South Africa: Legitimizing the Post-Apartheid State*. Cambridge, UK: Cambridge University Press.

Wilson, R., and R. Brown. 2009. "Introduction." In *Humanitarianism and Suffering: The Mobilization of Empathy*, edited by R. Wilson and R. Brown. New York: Cambridge University Press.

Wolfgang, M. 1958. "Victim Precipitated Criminal Homicide." *The Journal of Criminal Law, Criminology, and Police Science* 48: 1–11.

———. 1958. *Patterns in Criminal Homicide*. Philadelphia: University of Pennsylvania Press

Wolhuter, L., N. Olley, and D. Denham. 2008. *Victimology: Victimisation and Victims' Rights*. London: Routledge Cavendish.

World Health Organisation. 2014. *Global Status Report on Violence Prevention 2014*. Luxembourg: World Health Organisation.

Young, F. 1923. *The Trial of Frederick Bywaters and Edith Thompson*. Edinburgh and London: William Hodge & Co Ltd.

Young, J. 2003. *The Vertigo of Late Modernity*. London: SAGE.

———. 2011. *The Criminological Imagination*. Cambridge, UK: Polity.

Young, M., and J. Stein. 2004. "The History of the Crime Victims' Movement in the United States." *National Organization for Victim Assistance, U.S. Department of Justice Grant Number 2002-VF-GX-0009*. https://www.ncjrs.gov/ovc_archives/ncvrw/2005/pg4c.html.

———. 2013. *I am Malala: The Girl Who Stood Up for Education and Was Shot by the Taliban*. London: Weidenfeld & Nicolson.

Yousafzai, M. 2014. "Nobel Lecture by Malala Yousafzai." http://www.nobelprize.org/nobel_prizes/peace/laureates/2014/yousafzai-lecture_en.html.

Youth Justice Board. 2008. *Key Elements of Restorative Practice* https://www.gov.uk/government/uploads/system/uploads/attachment_data/file/356273/KEEP_Restorative_Justice__1_.pdf.

———. 2010. *The Youth Rehabilitation Order and other Youth Justice Provisions of the Criminal Justice and Immigration Act 2008*. Youth_Rehabilitation_Order_and_the_Criminal_Justice_and_Immigration_Act_200 8%20(2).pdf

Zartman, I. 2005. "Comparative Case Studies." *International Negotiation* 10: 3–16.

Zedner, L. 2002. "Victims." In *The Oxford Handbook of Criminology*, edited by M. Maguire, R. Morgan, and R. Reiner, 443–444. Oxford: Oxford University Press.

———. 2004. *Criminal Justice*. Oxford: Oxford University Press.

Zehr. H. 1990. *Changing Lenses*. Scottdale, Pa: Herald Press.

———. *Retributive Justice, Restorative Justice*. Mennonite Central Committee.

———. 2015. *The Little Book of Restorative Justice: Revised and Updated*. New York: Skyhorse Publishing, Inc.

Zimmermann, P., C. Mohr, and G. Spangler. 2009. "Genetic and Attachment Influences on Adolescents' Regulation of Autonomy and Aggressiveness." *The Journal of Child Psychiatry* 50: 1339–1347.

Cases:

Criminal Appeals Reports Vol XV II July to December 1922.

Judgement R v Sally Clark (2000) Case No: 1999/07495/Y3.

Judgement R V Sally Clark (2003) *EWCA Crim 1020*, Case No:200203824 Y3.

The Queen v Sally Clark, Skeleton Argument (Clare Montgomery QC) 2002/3824/Y3

HO45/2685

HO144/6012

PCOM 9/1983 XC2662.

Index

7/7, 158, 159, 160, 164, 166
9/11, 157, 158, 159, 160, 161, 164
9/11 Victim Compensation Fund, 159

absolute control 1.6 1.10 1.17. *See also* sovereignty, absolute
Abuelas, 132n10, 182, 183, 184, 185
ACPO. *See* Association of Chief Police Officers
adolescent to parent violence, 45, 46, 47, 48, 49, 52, 53, 54, 55, 57, 60; as a gendered problem 4.55 4.62; Holes in the Wall, 50; lack of recognition of, 51, 52; parent experiences of adolescent violence, 49–51. *See also* parent as paradoxical victim
Alcoff, Linda, 122
Amir, Menachem, 156
Anti-Social Behaviour Act of 2003, 56
APV. *See* adolescent to parent violence
Arendt, Hanna, 128
Ashworth, Andrew, 105, 107
aspiring sovereign. *See* sovereign aspirations
Asquith, Nicole and Isabelle Bartkowiak-Théron, 75
Association of Chief Police Officers, 67
Atrocities Documentation Survey, 177

Barker, Rodney, 111, 130n1
Barker, Vanessa, 122
Barnes de Carlotto, Estela, 183
Bataille, Georges, 2, 5, 8, 11
Becker, Howard, 167
Behr, Edward, 120
bell hooks, 121
bereaved families. *See* family bereavement
bereaved family activism, 173, 182
Bhambra, Sarandev, xi

Birmingham Six, 148
Blackman, Alexander, 166
blame: politics of, 45; zero-sum notions of, 58–60. *See also* ideal victim; transitional justice
body myths, 1
Boraine, Alex, 119, 120
Bosnia-Herzegovina's 2004 Law on Missing Persons, 186, 187
Bosnian War, 185
boundary object,7.38 D01.13: definitions of, 96–97; in relation to communities of interest, 96, 97; in relation to communities of practice, 96, 97, 98; restorative justice as, 96, 99–103, 104, 105, 106, 107, 108, 109n8
Bourdieu, Pierre, 16, 17, 18, 193
Bouvard, Guzman, 181
Brewer, John, 130, 132n13
Bullimer, Kristin, 114
Burton, Frank and Pat Carlen, 149
Bywaters, Freddy. *See* Thompson, Edith case

CACD. *See* Court of Criminal Appeal
Calata, Nomonde, 119
Calvert, Louie case, 140–144, 151
Camus, Albert, 2, 3, 5, 6, 7, 12, 192
Captured Queen study, 87
care ideology. *See* van Dijk
Carlen, Pat, 138
Carrabine, Eamonn, 168
CCRC. *See* Criminal Cases Review Commission
CDCs. *See* clandestine detention centers
Chakraborti, Neil, 73
Child offenders, 56
Christie, Nils,. *See also* ideal victim 21, 117, 165, 193

Criminal Injuries Compensation Authority CIC(O)S. *See* Criminal Injury Compensation (Overseas) Scheme
CICS. *See* Criminal Injury Compensation Scheme
clandestine detention centers, 180
Clarke, Kamari Maxine, 129
climate change, 191
Clinton, Bill, 83, 186
Coalition Government Action Plan, 67
Code of Practice for Victims of Crime, 105, 155
Cohen, Stanley, 128
Cole, Catherine, 120
College of Policing, 67
Commission for Historical Clarification, 119
Commission on Violence Against Women, 87
CONADEP, 180, 181
Connell, Raewyn, 33, 34
consumer culture, 8, 9
Corpses of Mass Violence and Genocide program, 179
Council of Europe, 89, 100
Court of Appeal. *See* Court of Criminal Appeal
Court of Criminal Appeal, 134, 135, 136, 137, 144, 146, 148, 150
Crime and Disorder Act of 1998, 56, 109n13, 109n23
Crime Survey for England and Wales, 65, 76
Crime Victim Commission, 87, 90
Crime Victim Fund, 87, 88
crime victim movement: of the United States, 80–85; of Sweden, 85–91
Criminal Cases Review Commission, 146, 148, 150, 152
Criminal Injuries Compensation Authority, 159, 160, 166
Criminal Injuries Compensation Scheme, 160, 161, 163
Criminal Injury Compensation (Overseas) Scheme, 162, 163
Criminal Injury Compensation Scheme, 163

Criminal Procedures and Investigations Act, 148
criminal victimization, 22, 157
criminology, xii, xiii, 113, 114, 126, 171, 174, 182, 191, 195; feminist, 156; Left Realist, 156; positivist, xiii

Davies, Zackery, xi
Debord, Guy, 8, 10, 12
Deepwater Horizon rig, xi
Demker, Marie and Duus-Otterström, Göran, 88
disciplined body, 1, 8, 194
doer-sufferer relationship, xii
Domestic Trafficking Victims' Fund, 85
domestic violence, 16, 26, 87, 115; police intervention, 22, 24, 26, 28; relating to APV, 46, 52, 59; victims of, 20, 24, 29, 30
dominating bodies, 1, 10, 12
Douglas, Lawrence, 127
Douglas, Mary, 126
drip-painting. *See* drip-technique
drip-technique, 3–5
Dubber, Markus, 84
Duggan, Marian and Heap, Vicky, 167, 169
Durkheim, Émile, 126

ECCC. *See* Extra-ordinary Chamber of the Courts of Cambodia
economy of precarity, 8
Edith Thompson case, 135–137, 138, 139
Elder abuse, 57
Ellis, Cara, 15, 30
Ellis, Lori-Ann, 15
ethic of care, 28
Extra-ordinary Chamber of the Courts of Cambodia, 117, 118, 123

familial shame, 54
Familicidal Hearts, 43
family bereavement, 159, 173, 176, 178, 181, 186, 199
family group conferencing, 99, 100, 101
family survivor scripts: quest/ yearning, 183, 184; redemption/ resolution, 183, 189; rejection, 184

family violence, 45, 47, 48, 52
Fassin, Didier and Richard Rechtman,.
    See also psychiatric victimology 191
Fattah, Ezzat, xiv, 195, 200
faux sovereignty. *See* sovereign
    consumer
female masculinity, 24
femininity: hegemonic, 19, 22, 138, 140,
    143, 144, 148; less-than-ideal, 21, 22,
    27
femininity, acceptable. See femininity,
    hegemonic
femininity, discourses relating to. *See*
    femininity, hegemonic
femininity, normative. *See* femininity,
    hegemonic
feminist movement. *See* women's
    movement
feminist victimology, xiii
Ferstman, Carla, 116
field, 16, 17–18, 193; bridging fields, 27,
    28; policing fields, 18, 23, 26;
    policing and victims fields, 28, 30;
    victim fields, 22, 24. *See also*
    Bourdieu, Pierre; habitus
flesh: of bodies,1.0 1.4 1.15: of the
    world, 4, 5, 7, 8
Florence Maybrick case, 135, 138, 148,
    151, 153n1
forms of life, 2, 6, 7, 10, 12
Frank, Arthur, 1, 2, 7, 8, 9, 11
Fraser, Nancy, 152
Friedrichs, David, 162
Furedi, Frank, xv, 54

Garbett, Claire, 118
Garland, David, 86, 114, 126, 155, 157,
    161, 167, 171
Geijer, Lennart, 86
gender, 18–19, 21, 35, 70, 87, 119, 137,
    152, 166, 189, 198
genocide, xii, xv, 117, 119, 164, 177, 179,
    191
Girard, René, 128

habitus, 16, 17, 17–18, 25, 193; policing
    habitus, 18, 19, 23, 24, 26, 27, 29, 31.
    See also Bourdieu, Pierre; field
Hagan, John, xv, 186

Hamber, Brandon, 120
Harper, Stephen, xi
hate crime, 63–65, 168, 195, 197;
    conventional frameworks, 66–68,
    68, 70, 76; needs of victims, 72–75,
    76; policy, 66, 68, 68–69, 72;
    victimization, 63, 65, 67, 70, 72, 76
Helman, Cecil,. *See also* body myths 1
Helms, Elissa, 186, 189
Hijo/as, 182, 184, 190n10
Hillsborough Family Support Group,
    176, 189
Holstein, James and Gale Miller, 46, 47,
    60
Home Office, 53, 102, 105, 114, 115, 140,
    141, 144, 145, 152, 158
Houellebecq, Michel, 5, 10
human rights, 10, 58, 70, 130, 168, 182,
    190; activists, 111, 112, 114, 122, 127,
    181; movement, 81, 190, 193; in
    Sweden, 90–91, 93, 196; violations,
    xi, 119, 120, 129, 168
Hunt, Alan, 129
Hurban. Ignacio, 183, 184, 190n11

ICC. *See* International Criminal Court
ICMP. *See* International Commission
    for Missing Persons
ICTR. *See* International Criminal
    Tribunal for Rwanda
ICTY. *See* International Criminal
    Tribunal for the former Yugoslavia
ideal victim, xvi, 21–22, 115, 157, 164,
    165, 167, 169, 170, 193; less-than-
    ideal victims, 22. *See also* Christie,
    Nils
Iganski, Paul, 64
imagined victim, 112, 157, 198; group
    affiliation, 168
imagining victimhood. *See* imagined
    victim
indifference: of Camus' character
    Meursault's, 2–3; of Nietzsche's
    Zarathustra, 5; of the economy, 8
indigenous women, murdered and
    missing, xi
Inglis, Tom, 149
International Commission for Missing
    Persons, 186, 187, 189

International Crime Victim Day, 89
International Criminal Court, 111, 116, 118, 122, 123, 131n7
International Criminal Tribunal for Rwanda, 111, 116, 117
International Criminal Tribunal for the Former Yugoslavia, 111, 116, 117, 186

Jaspers, Karl, 128
Jordan, Jan, 16, 30
judicial misogyny, 138, 143, 149
Justice for Victims of Trafficking Act, 85

Katz, Jack, 175
Kilty, Jennifer and Sheryl Fabian, xvii
kin contamination, 54
kin culpability, 54
Klette, Hans, 91
Krog, Antje, 119

Larsson, Stieg, 87
left realism, 133, 156
legitimation work, 112, 129
Leighton, Paul, 159, 160
lethal violence,. *See also* mass violence 173, 174, 176, 178, 182, 184, 188, 190n4, 199
Letschert, Rianne and Karin Ammerlaan, 159
Leydesdorff, Selma, 185
logic as life-code. *See* forms of life
Lundgren, Eva, 87

MacKinnon, Catharine, 152
Madlingozi, Tshepo, 121, 168
Maffesoli, Michel, 10
Marsy's law, 82
Maruna, Shadd, 182
Marxist criminology, xiii
masculinities: as haunting, 35, 43; hegemonic, 19, 33, 34, 37, 44; inclusive, 17, 20, 27, 28, 29, 30, 35; paternalistic, 27; policing, 16, 19; stoic, 23, 24, 25, 26, 30, 193
masculinities, normative. *See* masculinities, hegemonic

masculinities, traditional. *See* masculinities, hegemonic
Mason-Bish, Hannah, 69
mass lethal violence. *See* lethal violence
mass murder. *See* mass violence
mass violence,. *See also* lethal violence 158, 173, 177, 178, 179, 180, 188, 190, 199
Mawby, Rob, xv, 133, 134, 137, 139, 144, 149, 151, 152, 157, 198
Maybrick, James. *See* Florence Maybrick case
McAlindon, Anne-Marie, 59
McEvoy, Kieran, 125
McEvoy, Kieran and Kirsten McConnacchie 168, 169
McGarry, Ross, 60, 192
McSherry, Patrice, 178, 180
Megan and Jessica's laws, 82
Meir, Ben, 128
Mendelsohn, Benjamin, xii, xiii, xvi, 157, 192, 199
Merton, Robert, 112
Mertus, Julie, 116
Messerschmidt, James, 35
Meursault. *See* Camus, Albert. *See also* indifference
Meyers, Diana, 125
mid-range theorizing. *See* Merton, Robert
Miers, David, 160
mirroring body, 1, 9, 11, 13
miscarriages of justice, xvii, 134, 135, 138, 139, 144, 148, 150, 151, 152, 198
Missing Women Task Force, 15
Moody, Susan, 147
Moon, Claire, 120
Moran, Leslie and Andrew Sharpe, 70

National Organization for Victim Assistance, 83
National Organization of Parents of Murdered Children, 85
Naughton, Michael, 148, 150
Ni Aolain, Fionnuala, 119, 121
Nietzsche, Friedrich, 2, 5, 6, 126
Nixon, Richard, 80
Nolan, Thomas, 23

NOVA. *See* National Organization for Victim Assistance
Nuremberg trials, 116, 127
Nussbaum, Martha, 54

Obama, Barrack, xi
offender-centrism, xiii
offender shaming, 114
Onfray, Michael, 8
Orentlicher, Diane, 123
Organization for Security and Co-Operation in Europe, 65, 66, 76n1
OSCE. *See* Organization for Security and Co-Operation in Europe
Osiel, Mark, 127

Papadopoulos, Dimitris, 8
parent as paradoxical victim, 46, 54, 60, 194
The Parenting Order. *See* parental responsibility law
parental responsibility law, 45, 55, 56
penal couple, xii, 160, 161, 163, 166, 170, 199
penal exceptionalism, 85
penal welfarist state. *See* penal exceptionalism
Perry, Barbara, 67, 68
Personal Responsibility and Work Opportunity Responsibility Act, 83
Peters, Tony, 99, 101
Pickton, Robert, 15
Pilkington, Fiona, 70
Plan Condor, 180
police officer habitus. *See* policing habitus
policing culture, 16, 26, 31
policing masculinities, 16, 19, 23
politics of pity, 57
Pollock, Jackson, 2, 3–5, 6, 7, 192
POMC. *See* National Organization of Parents of Murdered Children
Pratt, John, 86
Presidential Task Force on the Victims of Crime, 81
primordial zone, 4, 11
Prison Realignment bill, 84
PRWORA. *See* Personal Responsibility and Work Opportunity

Responsibility Act
psychiatric victimology, 191

Quinney, Richard, xiv, 162

Reagan, Ronald, 81, 82, 84
reconciliation, 95, 98, 108n2, 120, 121, 124, 185, 197
Recovery of Historical Memory, 119
refugees, 178
rehabilitation, 84
REMHI. *See* Recovery of Historical Memory
restorative approaches to hate crime. *See* restorative justice
restorative justice, xvii, 74, 96, 98, 111, 196–197; Community Payback, 106. *See also* boundary object
Restorative Justice Council, 107
re-victimization. *See* secondary victimization
RJC. *See* Restorative Justice Council
Roche, Declan, 99, 107
Rock, Paul, xiii, xv, 59, 176
Rothko, Mark, 2, 3, 5, 6, 7, 192
Rymond-Richmond, Wenona, xv

Sally Clark case, 144–148
SAMM. *See* Support After Murder and Manslaughter
scientificity, claims to, 144, 145
Scraton, Phil, 176
secondary victimization, 23, 25, 26, 151
Second World War, xii, 1, 3, 6, 7, 128, 192
sexual assault, 16, 22, 23, 24, 25, 30, 193
sexual violence, 22, 29, 117, 119, 178
Snow, Clyde, 182, 186
sociological body, 1–2, 7
South African Truth and Reconciliation Commission, 119, 120, 127
sovereign aspirations, 5, 6, 7, 8, 10, 11–13
sovereignty, absolute, 4, 5, 7, 8. *See also* absolute control
sovereign-consumer, 8, 10, 12, 13
sovereign control, 4, 6, 7, 8, 10
sovereign life strategies. *See* forms of life

Spalek, Basia, 50
Spivak, Gayatri Chakravorty, 121, 123
Staggs, Michelle, 117
Star, Susan and James Griesemer, 96, 98, 99, 102
state as victim, xv
Sullivan, Dennis and Larry Tifft, 99
Support After Murder and Manslaughter group, 176
Svensson, Birgitta, 143
Sweden's Prison Worker Union, 86
Swedish Crime Victim and Support Authority, 87, 90

three strikes policy, 83
transitional justice, 104, 111, 112, 117, 119, 120–121, 121, 197, 199; as related to agecy, 113, 114, 115, 116, 121, 122, 123, 124, 129, 130; as related to blame, 113, 115, 116, 124, 125, 126, 127, 128, 129, 130; as related to voice, 113, 114, 115, 116, 117, 118–120, 121, 124, 129, 130
traumatic bereavement. *See* family bereavement
TRC. *See* South African Truth and Reconciliation Commission
truth-production, 143
Tsianos, Vassilis, 8

UCDP. *See* Uppsala Conflict Data Program
UCR. *See* Uniform Crime Reporting
Uniform Crime Reporting, 158
Uppsala Conflict Data Program, 177
US PATRIOT Act, 161

van Dijk, Jan, 91
van Ness, Daniel, 101, 105, 108n3
VAS. *See* Victim's Advocate Scheme
VAWA. *See* Violence Against Women Act
VAWG. *See* Violence Against Women and Girls
VCCLEA. *See* Violent Crime Control and Law Enforcement Act
Victim and Witness Protection Act, 82
victim blaming, xiv, xvi, 22, 54, 86, 132n11, 156

victim-centeredness. *See* victim-centered paradigm
victim-centered paradigm, xii, 104, 111, 118, 119
victim compensation programs, 79, 80, 85, 88, 90
Victim of Crime Act, 81
victim policy, 83, 156, 157, 159, 162, 167, 170
victim precipitation, xiii, 54, 156
victim restitution. *See* victim compensation programs
victim service organizations, 16, 17, 18, 20–21, 23, 24, 196
victim status, xii, xiv, xvii, 45, 46, 58, 161, 168, 170, 194
Victim Support Sweden, 89, 91
victim surveys, xiii, xiv, xvi, 87, 174
victimality, 193
victimhood, xi, xv, xvii, 34, 46, 60, 157, 168, 191, 193–195; military, 166, 169; transitional justice, 111, 112, 113, 114, 116, 122, 124, 125, 128, 129
victimhood, ideal. *See* ideal victim
victimological paradigm. *See* victim-centered paradigm
victimology literature, 16, 113, 115
victimology, positivist, xii, xiii, xiv, xvi, 133, 145, 156, 200
Victim's Advocate Scheme, 175
Victims Bill of Rights, 82, 83
Victims of Overseas Terrorism Compensation Scheme, 160
victims of terrorism, 157, 158, 160, 161, 164, 167, 168, 170
Violence Against Women Act, 83
Violence Against Women and Girls strategy, 53, 58
Violent Crime Control and Law Enforcement Act, 83
Virk, Reena, xvi
VOCA. *See* Victim of Crime Act
Von Hentig, Hans, xii, 199

Wachholz, Sandra, 69
Wagner, Sarah, 185
Walklate, Sandra, xv, 60, 112, 115, 133, 137, 139, 144, 149, 151, 157, 170
Waterhouse, Lily, 140

Websdale, Neil, 35, 44
Wemmers, Jo-Anne, 29
Wergens, Anna, 90, 93
Wilson, Richard, 120
Wolfgang, Martin, 156
Women of Srebrenica, 186
women's movement, 81, 86, 87, 88, 91, 134, 196

World War II. *See* Second World War

Young, Marlene, 83, 191
Yousafzai, Malala, 164–165, 171n1

Zempi, Irene, xv

About the Contributors

Anette Ballinger is a lecturer in the School of Social Science and Public Policy at Keele University. She is the author of the award-winning book *Dead Woman Walking: Executed Women in England & Wales 1900–1955* (Ashgate: 2000) (Hart Socio-Legal Prize 2001). She has written numerous book chapters and journal articles on the subject of gender and punishment in modern history, and her new book, titled *Capitalizing on Punishment: Gender, Truth and State Power*, will be published by Ashgate in 2016.

Neil Chakraborti is a professor of criminology at the University of Leicester and director of the Leicester Centre for Hate Studies. He has published extensively within the field of hate crime, and has been commissioned by the Economic and Social Research Council, the Equality and Human Rights Commission and a range of other funding bodies to conduct research on targeted hostility, victimization and policing diversity. In 2012 he was appointed as a Commissioner on the first ever nationwide review of sex inside prisons, and in 2015 he received a Lifetime Achievement Award from the University of Leicester for his work in the field of ethnic diversity. Neil is an adjunct professor at the University of Ontario, chair of research for the Board of Trustees of the Howard League for Penal Reform, series editor of Palgrave Hate Studies, and sits on the editorial boards of the *British Journal of Criminology* and *Palgrave Communications*.

Rachel Condry is associate professor of criminology at the University of Oxford and a Fellow of St. Hilda's College. Her work focuses on the intersection between crime and the family, which has included research on families of offenders, families of victims, and the family as a site of crime.

Robert Elias is a professor of politics and chair of the Legal Studies Program at the University of San Francisco. He is the editor of *Peace Review: A Social Justice Journal*, and the author/editor of nine books, including *Victims of the System* (Transaction Books), *The Politics of Victimization* (Oxford University Press), and *Victims Still* (Sage). He has been a researcher at the Vera Institute of Justice, and taught previously at Tufts University, Penn State University, the University of Maryland, and the University of California, Berkeley.

Carina Gallo is an assistant professor of criminology at Holy Names University in Oakland as well as a senior lecturer at the School of Social Work at Lund University in Sweden. Her research interest lies in the intersection between criminology and sociology of law, with particular attention to trends in criminal and welfare policies. She is especially interested in how countries develop policies and practices for victims of crime. Carina is currently working on the research project "Beyond Punishment: The origins and evolution of Swedish victim support." Carina is also a trained social worker, and has worked with many different actors involved in the criminal justice system. For instance, between 2001 and 2006 she was the director of a nongovernmental victim support center, which provides services to over five-hundred crime victims per year.

Rebecca S. Katz's research focuses on the intersection of race, class, and gender as well as both sociological and psychological precursors to criminal involvement. Some of her previous publications include articles in *Violence Against Women, Contemporary Justice Review* and *Critical Criminology*. Dr. Katz's career includes ten years as a mental health counselor and more than twenty years as a teacher at Morehead State University and the University of Central Oklahoma. Dr. Katz also served in the U.S. Army from 1978 through 1983.

Ronnie Lippens is professor of criminology at Keele University (UK). His research interests include critical criminology and organizational criminology, but latterly they have focused also on the imaginary of justice, law and order, as expressed in e.g. novels, paintings and public art. He has published numerous contributions (in Dutch as well as in English) on those topics in a wide variety of venues. He is currently working on a closer analysis of the emergence of forms of governance in what could be called prophetic art, painting and sculpture in particular.

Kirsten McConnachie is an assistant professor in law at the University of Warwick. She is a sociolegal researcher with interests in victimology, transitional justice, forced migration, and border criminologies. Her primary research project at present examines security and self-governance among urban refugees in India and Malaysia. Her book *Governing Refugees* (2014) was awarded the Socio-Legal Studies Association early career book prize of 2015.

Kieran McEvoy is professor of law and transitional justice in Queen's University Belfast. His areas of research interest include transitional justice, human rights, the legal profession, penology, comparative legal studies, victims, ex-combatants, conflict resolution, and restorative justice. He has written or edited six books and more than fifty journal articles and book chapters. His research has garnered significant national and international recognition including the British Society of Criminology book of the year award and the Socio-Legal Studies Association article of the year award three times. He has conducted research on transitional justice in more than a dozen countries in a number of projects funded by the AHRC, ESRC, Atlantic Philanthropies, Merck Foundation, and the Joseph Rowntree Charitable Trust.

Ross McGarry is lecturer in criminology within the Department of Sociology, Social Policy and Criminology at the University of Liverpool. He has written widely in international journals on criminology, victimology and critical military studies, including *The British Journal of Criminology* and *Armed Forces and Society*. He is the coeditor (with Sandra Walklate) of *Criminology and War: Transgressing the Borders* from Routledge, the forthcoming *Palgrave Handbook on Criminology and War*, and coauthor of *Victims: Trauma, Testimony and Justice*. He is currently writing a monograph for the New Directions in Critical Criminology series from Routledge entitled *Criminology and the Military*.

David Miers, Emeritus Professor, has a long-standing research interest in and is a leading authority on the role of restorative justice in the criminal justice system. He led the first major review of its use in England and Wales published in 2001 and also completed an international review for the Home Office. Between 2002 and 2006 he was one of the two UK national representatives on an EC COST Action researching restorative justice and victim offender mediation provision across Europe and participated as an expert in other EC funded research restorative justice, funded by the Grotius and AGIS programs. Throughout this time he contributed to international conferences and published widely both on restorative justice and the place of the victim in criminal justice.

Jillian Patterson received her Master of Arts in Sociology from the University of Manitoba in 2015. Her main interest is in violence against women and punishment reform. She volunteers at the John Howard Society.

Jon Shute is a criminologist working at the Centre for Criminology and Criminal Justice at the University of Manchester. He has enduring research interests in human development, family stress, and the criminology of mass violence. Jon is coinvestigator on the European Research Council-funded program "Corpses of Mass Violence & Genocide," and a co-Chair of the European Criminology Group on Atrocity Crime & Transitional Justice. He is also part of the "Eurogang" network of gang researchers.

Dale C. Spencer is a criminologist and sociolegal studies scholar and is an assistant professor in the Department of Law and Legal Studies at the Carleton University. His main interests are violence, victimization, and the criminalization of marginalized populations, with a specific focus on youth and homeless people. Dale is an ethnographic and qualitative researcher that has conducted research with/on youth involved in automotive theft, professional cage fighters, and street-involved and homeless males. In the last three years he has published two books, *Reimaging Intervention in Young Lives* (with Karen Foster, University of British Columbia Press) and *Ultimate Fighting and Embodiment* (Routledge), and two edited volumes, *Emotions Matter* (with Kevin Walby and Alan Hunt, University of Toronto Press) and *Fighting Scholars* (Raul Sanchez Garcia, Anthem Press) and his work can be found in a number of journals, including *Body and Society, Punishment and Society*, and *Ethnography*.

Sandra Walklate is Eleanor Rathbone chair of sociology at the University of Liverpool (United Kingdom) and adjunct professor at QUT in Brisbane. Internationally recognised for her work in victimology and research on criminal victimisation, her recent publications include: *Victims: Trauma, Testimony, Justice* (2015, Routledge with Ross McGarry), *The Contradictions of Terrorism* (2014, Routledge with Gabe Mythen), *Criminology and War: Transgressing the Borders* (edited collection, Routledge, 2015, with Ross McGarry). She is currently editor in chief of the *British Journal of Criminology*.

Hannah M. Willis graduated from Morehead State University in 2014 with a bachelor's degree in criminology and government. She worked in the University's Undergraduate Research Fellowship Program, under the guidance of Rebecca S. Katz. Ms. Willis has presented papers at the American Society of Criminology and has coauthored one other paper with Rebecca Katz.